MURDER UNDER TRUST

MURDER UNDER TRUST

The Crimes and Death of Sir Lachlan Mor Maclean of Duart, 1558–1598

NICHOLAS MACLEAN-BRISTOL

TUCKWELL PRESS

First published in Great Britain in 1999 by
Tuckwell Press Ltd
Phantassie
East Linton
East Lothian EH40 3DG
Scotland

ISBN 1 86232 016 0

British Library Cataloguing-in-Publication Data
A catalogue record for this book is available
from the British Library

Typeset in Monotype Bell by Carnegie Publishing, Lancaster
Printed and bound by Cromwell Press

Contents

Acknowledgements

It is once again a pleasure to acknowledge my gratitude to His Grace the Duke of Argyll for permission both to make use of his archives at Inveraray Castle and use the portrait of one of his ancestors in this book. I am also indebted to his former archivist Alastair Campbell of Airds, Unicorn Pursuivant, for his help in examining the archives at Inveraray Castle and for his permission to reproduce Fig. 10. It is also pleasing to be able to thank the staff of the Scottish Record Office, the National Library of Scotland, Edinburgh University Library, the School of Scottish Studies, the London Library, the Public Record Office and the British Library for their help and courtesy over many years.

This book was typed by my secretary Helen Ramage to whom I would also like to express my thanks. Thanks are also due to Sir Edward Peck and Alastair Stewart, formally of the University of Aberdeen, for information on the Battle of Glenlivet.

I have also to thank Kenneth Nicholls and Hiram Morgan, both of the Department of History, University College Cork, Ireland who read an earlier draft of this book and suggested improvements. The errors that remain are of course my own responsibility.

It is also a pleasure to thank the School of Scottish Studies for their permission to quote the traditional account of the battle of Tràigh Ghruinneart printed in *Tocher* in 1992.

Picture acknowledgements are as follows: Figs. 6 and 12: the Scottish National Portrait Gallery; Figs. 8 and 11: Historic Scotland; Figs. 9 and 13: The Royal Commission on the Ancient and Historical Monuments of Scotland.

Dedication

This book is dedicated to my two elder sons who have unwittingly followed the example of their ancestor Neil Mor Maclean of Quinish by being brought up on the Isle of Coll and having served in the army in Northern Ireland. They are:

Captain Charles Maclean-Bristol, 1st Battalion The King's Own Scottish Borderers, Armagh 1995–1996.

Lieutenant Alexander Maclean-Bristol, 1st Battalion The Argyll and Sutherland Highlanders (Princess Louise's), Armagh 1997.

Nomenclature

The spelling of Gaelic names in a book written in English is fraught with problems. In this book I have adopted the principle that patronymics should be distinguished from clan surnames. Thus John Macdonald (with a small 'd') is John who belonged to the clan Donald, but whose father was not necessarily called Donald, whilst John Mac-Donald (with a capital 'D') is John whose father's name was Donald who was not necessarily a member of the clan Donald. The surname Maclean is therefore spelt with a small 'l', the spelling that is preferred by almost all armigerous Macleans with proven descents and all the heads of the senior houses of Duart, Coll, Kingerloch and Ardgour. Even Lochbuie uses a small 'l' after Mac, though that family has consistently used the phonetic version 'Maclaine' since the early eighteenth century, when several other families who had previously used this spelling stopped doing so.

In an ideal world it would be wise to adopt the Anglo-Gaelic standard version for an individual suggested by G. F. Black in his work on Scottish surnames, rather than a mixture of English and Gaelic. Thus the seventeenth-century John Maclean of Ardgour would be styled *Iain Crúbach* or Lame John and not a mixture such as John Crubach Maclean. It is, I believe, too late to change this usage without muddling the non-scholarly reader. I have therefore referred to Sir Lachlan Maclean of Duart as Lachlan Mor throughout this book rather than as *Lachainn Mor* except when I am quoting verbatim from a Gaelic source.

Warning: In order to understand the society in which Lachlan Mor lived, it is necessary to appreciate how the different families of Macleans were related to each other. Highland genealogies, however, are not everyone's cup of tea. I suggest the faint-hearted skip Chapter 2 and perhaps read it later.

Illustrations

No contemporary portrait of Sir Lachlan Mor Maclean of Duart is known to exist. This is not surprising as the Gaeltachd relied on the spoken word, in the form of panegyrics in Gaelic, to portray its leaders. It was not until the eighteenth century that there is evidence that paintings were made of Maclean chiefs.

List of Maps and Tables

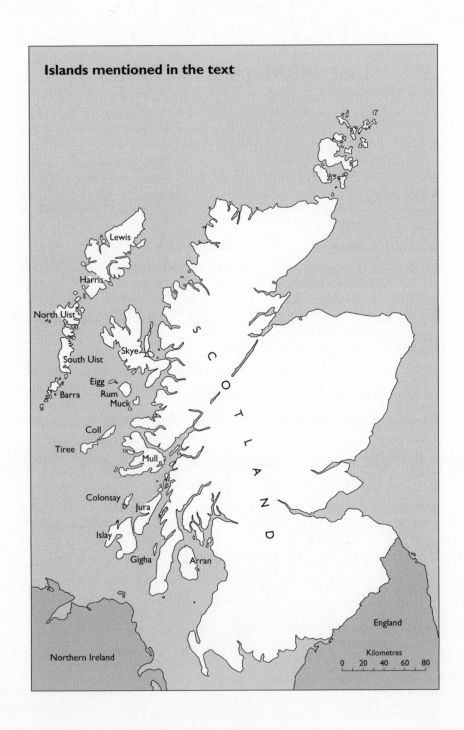

Islands mentioned in the text

Lewis

Harris

North Uist

South Uist

Skye

Eigg
Rum
Muck

Barra

Coll

Tiree

Mull

Colonsay

Jura

Islay

Gigha

Arran

SCOTLAND

England

Kilometres
0   20   40   60   80

Northern Ireland

Introduction

Murderer. Ay, my good lord: safe in a ditch he bides
With twenty trenched gashes on his head;
The least a death to nature.

Macbeth Act III, Scene iv

Some say she advised him to spend the night in his hiding place in the hills and he said that he had spent three years out of his own bed. He was going to sleep at home that night. Others say that he was proposing to sleep in his hiding place, but that she was furious. How dare he suggest that her brother, who had promised that all was now at peace between them, would break his word.

Whichever version is correct, he stayed at home.

Later that night twenty-four armed men surrounded the house. They broke down the door. Big Neil, however, was too quick for them. He escaped through the cordon and fled towards the hills. Then his luck ran out. Another party was coming up the track. They met at Clachan Dubh. Unable to escape, Neil stood and fought. He was greatly outnumbered and when the fight was over he lay on the ground half-dead.

The victorious party started to return home. It is said that they had not gone far when Red Dougall MacAlpin declared, 'I should not wonder if big Neil would come alive yet'. They all turned back to find out. When they came to the place where they had left him they found him crawling away on his hands and knees.

This time they made certain of him. They struck him again and again with their weapons. When his friends came later and found him, all that was left of him were pieces that were so small that they had to carry them home in a blanket.

Big Neil, otherwise Neil Maclean of Quinish, known in Gaelic as Niall Mor or in anglicised Gaelic as Neil Mor or by his patronymic 'Neil MacVcAne Abrych', was my ancestor. He founded our branch of the Macleans of Coll. It is said that he was murdered on the orders of Sir Lachlan Mor Maclean of Duart in 1596 or early in 1597.

This book began as an attempt to understand the society that condoned

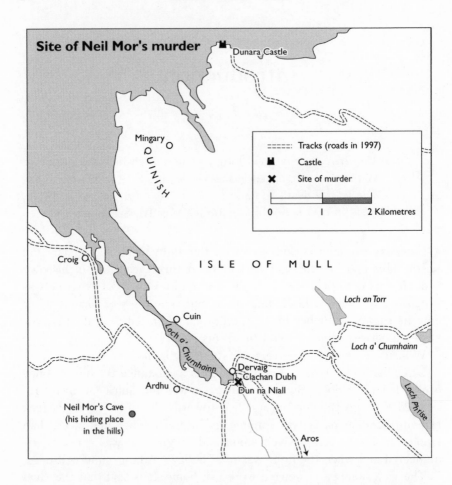

the murder of my ancestor. It quickly developed into a biography of the man behind the murder. Sir Lachlan Mor Maclean of Duart is a highly complex, many-faceted character: soldier, thug, conspirator, staunch Protestant, courtier, loyal husband and clan chief. He was a legend in his own time, and ever since in areas of Scotland as far apart as the Isle of Islay and Glenlivet. This is his story.

CHAPTER 1

Warfare in mid-sixteenth century Europe

Siward. Had I as many sons as I have hairs,
I would not wish them to a fairer death
Macbeth Act V, Scene viii

Sir Lachlan Mor Maclean of Duart was probably born in 1558. It was a momentous time to be alive. Mary of Guise, widow of King James V, was regent of Scotland. Mary Tudor, 'bloody Mary', was queen of England. France was at war with Spain and both Scotland and England had taken up their traditional alliances: Scotland as the ally of France and England as the ally of Spain. On 10th August 1557 the constable of France suffered a crushing defeat at Saint-Quentin and for a time it seemed that Paris itself must fall. The duke of Guise came to the rescue of France. In January 1558 he captured Calais, which had been an English possession for 220 years. The prestige of the family of Guise was at its height and in April 1558 the regent's daughter, Mary Queen of Scots, married the dauphin of France.

Mary Tudor died in November 1558. She was succeeded as queen by her half-sister Elizabeth, who was to undo all Mary's efforts to bring Roman Catholicism back to England. In April 1559 the peace treaty of Câteau Cambrésis between France and Spain ended the war. It marked a major change in European politics and a new alignment along confessional rather than dynastic alliances. By the end of the sixteenth century Europe was divided into two hostile camps of Protestants and Roman Catholics.[1]

The event which almost coincided with Lachlan Mor's birth and was to have a profound effect, both on his career and the future of his country, was the establishment of the Protestant religion in Scotland. The immediate cause of the outbreak of violence that brought about the end of Roman Catholicism in Scotland is usually seen as the return of John Knox in May 1559. It is however hard to avoid the conclusion that an explosion was inevitable, Knox or no Knox,[2] for the party of the revolution, the Lords of the Congregation, were protesting as much about the influence of Frenchmen on the regent, Mary of Guise, as they were in favour of the reformed religion.

If the reformed religion had a profound effect on Lachlan Mor's loyalties, it was war that shaped his career. At his birth Scotland was experiencing a bitter civil war and warfare, actual and anticipated, was to dominate his life.

Warfare changed dramatically in the sixteenth century. Change, however, came late to Scotland, which was, in a European context, a relatively unimportant country on the periphery. It was in Italy that the move from medieval to modern war began. The fall of Constantinople to the Turks in 1453 transferred the centre of European civilisation westward. Refugees who fled to Italy reawakened a spirit of enquiry and experiment in the city states of the peninsula and released an intellectual ferment that not only included art, the study of ancient history and literature, but also embraced the study of military science.

In the middle ages the commander of an army believed it was his first duty to seek out the enemy and engage him. Elaborate manoeuvring was frowned on both by the chivalric spirit of the age, which abhorred cunning, and by the desire of feudal levies to return home as soon and as quickly as possible. However, as professional soldiers began to replace these feudal levies and when citizens became increasingly reluctant to fight, warfare changed.[3]

The captains of the independent companies of mercenaries (*condottiere*) were the first to study the theory of war. They founded military schools and they were more interested in the lessons of the ancient world than in knightly ideals. They analysed strategic and tactical problems, emphasised the interdependence of the phases of a campaign and fortified their argument with quotations from the Greek and Latin classics. Rivalry between states led to wars which were frequent and more prolonged than those of preceding centuries. They gave the student of war plenty of opportunity to witness, at first hand, the most important campaigns in Europe conducted by the leading captains and most famous troops of the day.

It was almost as though Italy was one vast military academy and the comparatively bloodless campaigns of the *condottiere* can be seen as practical demonstrations by professors of the art of war. Unlike feudal armies the *condottiere* had a reason to avoid bloodshed: as mercenaries they could easily find themselves facing enemies in one campaign, who might be their allies in the next. Campaigns became one gigantic game of chess and by the end of the fifteenth century the manoeuvring of armies became almost an end in itself.

The heroic code of the middle ages took time to die. Even as late as 1494 when Charles VIII of France set out to conquer Naples, he did so in a spirit of adventure that was little different from that of his ancestors when they embarked upon Crusades, and when the marquis of Mantua could have stopped the French in their tracks by holding the passes of the Apenines, he did not do so. His motive in delaying the attack was a chivalrous sympathy for a foe in difficulties.

Curiously, for all their study of war and emphasis on manoeuvre, the *condottiere* failed to revolutionise tactics. The roles of the different arms, cavalry, infantry and artillery, remained the same as in the past. Cavalry dominated the battlefield and infantry were regarded with contempt. Even its successes such as those of the English bowmen against the mail-clad chivalry of France had not altered this opinion. For the secret of these victories had been to keep the enemy at a distance. The archer who allowed the mounted knight to reach him was doomed.

The smallest cavalry unit was the group of six, called a 'lance'. It consisted of one heavily armed warrior or 'man-at-arms' and five more lightly armed horsemen. It was a survival from the days when the feudal knight went to war accompanied by his armed followers. There was a distinct similarity between the men-at-arms throughout Europe and heavy cavalry had the prestige of an international institution. Respect for the skills and courage of the mounted upper-class warrior led to a camaraderie of like-minded gentlemen and produced a mutual admiration society that defied national boundaries.

It was the Swiss who were to destroy this cosy international relationship. Like the Gaels of the Western Isles of Scotland, amongst whom Lachlan Mor was to be brought up, the Swiss were cattle people, the breeding and rearing of cattle being the only suitable economic activity in their narrow valleys and Alpine uplands. Their semi-nomadic system of transhumance bred a belligerent, tough, insensitive race of weapon-carrying free peasants.

The Swiss military tradition was based on a highly democratic social system which was forged in the fourteenth and fifteenth centuries, during the Confederation's struggle for independence, when the fiercely independent communities of the cantons united to drive their enemies from the Alpine valleys.

The principal weapon used by the early confederates was the halberd. It was a heavy pointed axe mounted on an eight-foot-long ash pole weighing up to eight pounds. It was wielded with both hands and was used for both slashing and stabbing, could cut through limbs, armour and cleave skulls in two. Although the halberd was murderously effective as a close-quarter weapon, it was too short to be as useful against cavalry.

As the Confederation expanded out of its narrow valleys into less mountainous country, where cavalry could operate more effectively, a new weapon was needed. The weapon chosen was the pike. It was to prove ideally suited to the Swiss. Thousands of men on foot massed together in a huge column armed with long pikes and halberds, and with experience this infantry phalanx proved itself to be more than able to defend itself on open ground against cavalry. For the first time in a millennium infantry not only regularly defeated enemy cavalry but also steam-rollered opposing enemy formations out of its way.

The pike, which was the key to these victories, was eighteen feet long. It consisted of an ash shaft tipped with a six-inch iron point. In an attack the pikes were held at shoulder level. This created a centre of gravity towards the back and helped the soldier carrying it to make a downward thrust without the point being knocked out of the way or of the recoil hitting the pikeman behind.

Wherever possible the Swiss fought on the offensive. If forced on the defensive the base of the first pike was anchored to the ground with the foot and the following three pikes levelled against the oncoming enemy at waist level or at shoulder height. The attacker was therefore faced with a bristling array of four pikes for each row, hence the name of the hedgehog for this defensive formation. If there were more than four ranks of pikes, the following ranks of pikemen held their weapons ready to step into any gap. This forest of pikes overhead acted as an umbrella against any incoming arrows and cross-bow bolts. Determined pikemen could fend off the charge of heavily armoured cavalry provided they received the charge on the points of their pikes and left no gaps for horsemen to charge through. For only rarely will a horse gallop straight at an object it cannot see how to jump or pass through.

By the time of the Swabian War 600 Zürich pikemen caught in the open by 1000 Austrian cavalry could confidently form their hedgehog and shout taunts at the enemy horsemen to attack them. The pike had revolutionised warfare in Europe in a manner that all the theories of the *condottiere* had not. Its use spread throughout the Continent.

Nineteenth-century Swiss historians depicted the Swiss *Knaben* as disciplined disinterested heroes, who fought for their country's freedom. More recent research has shown them to be selfish looters. But they dominated European battlefields for almost fifty years. They terrified their enemies and their savagery and brutality became legendary. On at least one occasion they had to be forbidden to cut out the hearts of their dead enemies. Perhaps their callous behaviour was a natural consequence of a way of life that involved them in the routine butchery of animals. Whatever the cause, their opponents, who had previously been accustomed to negotiating a ransom if captured and to the gentlemanly manoeuvrings of Italian campaigns, now faced an enemy who took no prisoners. Fallen adversaries had their throats cut.

The Swiss infantry's composure in battle was legendary. This was probably because they had faith in their own physical strength and trust in the men standing next to them in the ranks of pikemen. Companies tended to recruit from the same area and the man next to you probably came from the same canton. Swiss soldiers were also well aware that they were regarded as the best in the world and were determined to preserve their reputation.

Eventually the Swiss soldiers' opponents produced the antidote to the square of pikes. First they recruited their own pikemen organised and trained in the Swiss method. These were the hated *Landsknechts* who were mainly recruited in Southern Germany. It was however not until 1503 that the great Spanish general Gonsalvo de Cordova first used the methods that would neutralise Swiss tactics. Gonsalvo placed men with firearms on the low slopes of a hill behind a bank and ditch. The advancing Swiss were unable to cross this obstacle under fire and were forced to retreat in some disorder.

It was the improvement in firearms that destroyed the Swiss offensive square of pikes. Gunpowder had been invented at some unknown date in the middle ages. It had not initially revolutionised tactics. By the end of the fifteenth century heavy guns were used for battering down the walls of fortresses but had not affected the battlefield. Eventually however the French developed a method of transporting artillery and extended its use.

The sheer size of the pike square made it an easy target for artillery and a cannon ball ploughing through the ranks of pikemen did enormous damage. As a result the first object of the Swiss was always to overrun the enemy's guns. This task became increasingly difficult.

The earliest hand-held firearm, the arquebus (German: *hackenbusche*; English: hackbus or hackbut) also at first had little effect on battlefield tactics. They were inaccurate, had a short range and filled the battlefield with dense smoke that reminded observers of Dante's *Inferno*. Machiavelli, writing as late as 1520, still belittled the importance of gunpowder in modern warfare. Others thought differently and wished that firearms had never been invented. 'Would to God', wrote Montluc the Gascon soldier of fortune in 1523, 'that this unhappy weapon had never been devised, and that so many brave and valiant men had never died by the hands of those who are often cowards and shirkers who would never dare look in the face of those whom they lay low with their wretched bullets. They are tools invented by the devil to make it easier for us to kill each other.'[4] Gian Paolo Vitelli felt even more strongly. He was in the habit of plucking out the eyes and cutting off the hands of arquebusiers captured in battle: he deemed it disgraceful that noble men-at-arms should be shot from a distance by low-born infantrymen.

The introduction of improved firearms marked the end of medieval warfare and the now outdated rules of chivalry. It also destroyed the invincibility of the Swiss pike square as a method of attack. The end of Swiss supremacy is usually thought to be the Battle of Marignano in 1515. Despite a frenzied attack and an even more heroic withdrawal the Swiss were defeated. They never fought outside Switzerland again except as mercenaries. Marignano had proved once and for all that an army of unsupported infantry, however bravely it fought, was bound to fail before a skilful combination of infantry, cavalry and artillery.[5]

The Swiss adapted their tactics to the new requirements of the battle-field which followed the improvement in firearms. The square of pikes reverted to its original role as a defensive shelter against cavalry in the open field. Only now it sheltered arquebusiers. The pike was to play an important role on the battlefield for another two hundred years. Indeed it was the only trustworthy weapon in wet weather. Control of the battlefield however passed from the Swiss to other nations who were able to raise multi-armed forces. The French not only developed field artillery but also standardised the calibre of hand-held firearms by developing the 'caliver'. It was, however, the Spanish who became the most respected users of firearms in Europe: not so much in the open field, where the reputation of the Swiss continued to be paramount, but in ambushes and in the defence of obstacles, two operations which the Swiss and Germans refused to adapt to. The Spaniards also developed the new improved weapon called the musket. It was six feet long, fired balls weighing two ounces and its weight required it to be supported on a fork-shaped rest. It was unwieldy but had a greater killing power and a longer range than the arquebus.

Despite their defeat at Marignano the Swiss were still considered to be the best infantry in Europe. All major powers competed for their services. Unlike most mercenaries, who were often the dregs of society who had dropped out of their communities, the Swiss recruit was a permanent member of his community, who was temporarily away from home. He remained answerable to the standards of that society while on active service through his officers and colleagues and through friends and relatives when he returned home between campaigns. Veteran soldiers cemented their relationship in their role as drill-masters, who trained the next generation at foot drill and at the shooting range, which each town in the Confederation was bound to provide.

Although rigid discipline was required in the square of pikes, soldiers were treated as individuals and were otherwise permitted considerable freedom. It was an extremely democratic army. Officers, who were elected by the canton, dressed the same, lived with and fought on foot alongside the men. Discipline generally was achieved by peer group pressure rather than by the presence of the provost marshall and executioner, who nevertheless accompanied the Swiss army, as did prostitutes who were chosen by each town.

By 1549 the contingents raised for service in foreign armies were officially called regiments. Each was commanded by a colonel and bore his name. Regiments were divided into companies, often 200 strong, but the number and strength varied. It is thought that 300,000 mercenaries were raised in Switzerland during the sixteenth century.

*   *   *   *

The clans of the Western Isles and adjacent mainland, amongst whom Lachlan Mor was to live his life, were like those of the Swiss cantons, engaged in the provision of mercenary soldiers. They did so, however, on a far smaller scale than their Swiss counterparts. In 1595 it was reported that 6,000 men could be raised in the Isles, the same number of men the Swiss lost at Marignano. Swiss mercenary service is also far better documented and has received more scholarly attention than the mercenaries from the Hebrides: the bibliography of the most recent English-language study of Swiss mercenaries runs to twelve pages.[6] Most publications are in French and German. The only book known to me, devoted to the mercenaries from the Western Isles, is G. A Hayes-McCoy's *Scots Mercenary Forces in Ireland*, was written before the Second World War.[7] Other articles have followed this book but it remains a neglected subject. This is why it has been worth examining the Swiss mercenaries in some detail. There were several parallels and many differences between the mercenaries of the Swiss cantons and those of the Western Isles which will become apparent as the story of Lachlan Mor progresses.

It can hardly be a coincidence that the first references to both Swiss

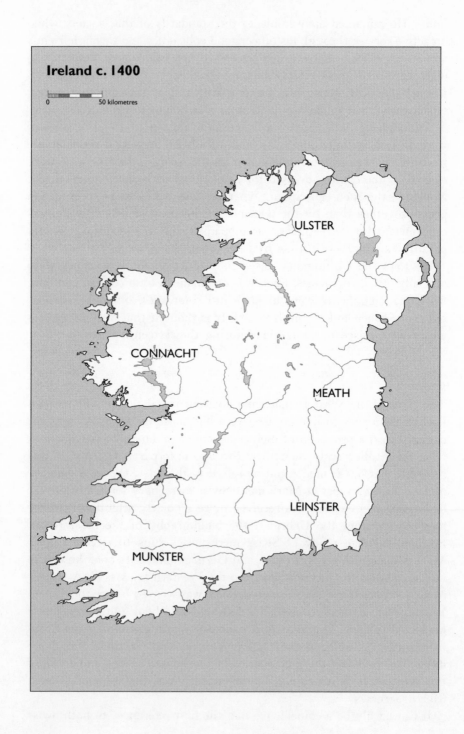

Ireland c. 1400

0   50 kilometres

ULSTER

CONNACHT

MEATH

LEINSTER

MUNSTER

and Hebridean mercenaries date from the thirteenth and early fourteenth centuries. This was a time when prolonged local and national wars, declining agricultural production and falling population affected all Western Europe. Swiss mercenaries were soon noticed throughout continental Europe. Those from the Hebrides were found solely in Ireland.

The economic and demographic problems of medieval Ireland led to a social and military reorganisation that brought a new effectiveness to the native Irish lords and kindreds. This renewed vigour, after a long period of territorial retreat, was underpinned by the hiring of large numbers of professional mercenary soldiers who were often recruited in the Hebrides and in Argyll. These Scottish troops, known as galloglass (*gallóglaigh*, i.e. foreign warriors), served alongside native Irish mercenaries known as kern (*Ceithearn*).

Although warriors from the Hebrides had been involved in Ireland in the past, it was not until the last decade of the thirteenth century that this peculiar institution from the Isles was first found in Ireland. *Gallóglaigh* appear first in the north, spread through the west and south and are found finally in Leinster. By the sixteenth century mercenary service had become hereditary amongst the descendants of the original incomers: the Macdonalds, Macsweens and Macrorys who, having backed the losing side in the Scots Wars of Independence, moved permanently to Ireland.

Gallóglaigh are often mentioned by contemporary observers, but infuriatingly it is the non-essentials that are commented on. For instance we are told that they were 'men of great stature ... courageous, even fierce, in battle ... they were dressed in coats of mail to the knee, were armed with battle-axes and were the most dependable body of troops in the Irish armies'. We are not told how many there were, under what terms they were employed or what proportion served only one master.

The term *galloglass*, foreign warrior, is only appropriate to Hebridean warriors who settled permanently in Ireland. It has recently been argued that 'certain areas of Gaelic Scotland experienced a similar process of militarisation in the late thirteenth and early fourteenth centuries', and that 'the systematic and permanent maintenance of a large military following was certainly a feature of the lordship of John of Islay, lord of the Isles, who from 1330 onwards presided over the advance of the Clan Donald'.[8]

That this theory is correct is supported by the effigies of fifteenth-century West Highland chiefs.[9] A report on the Hebrides, written in 1595, which will be referred to later, states that the islands could raise 6000 men, one third of whom 'aucht and sould be clad with attonnis and haberschonnis, and knapskal bannets'.[10] The actoun or aketon (at-tonnis) was a quilted leather jacket. The habergeon (haberschonnis) was a jacket of mail, whilst a knapscall was a steel cap or helmet. This was the proper dress for Highlanders called out 'weill bodin in feir of weir' (furnished with arms appropriate for war) to serve the king for forty days in any one year as laid down by Acts of Parliament. Unlike the lowlands, where the aristocracy were mounted on horseback, in the Hebrides the chiefs fought on foot.

It seems probable that the professional soldier was originally main-tained in much the same way in Gaelic Scotland as he was in Ireland. By the close of the fourteenth century it is clear that the maintenance of a substantial military following which lifted its supplies and wages direct from the tributary populations was an essential element in the successful exercise of power across Gaelic Scotland.[11]

Two hundred years later the government was bitterly opposed to this system and the term 'sorn' (beg) was used in a pejorative sense to describe the seizure of food for the maintenance of 'idill personis', as professional soldiers might be considered when they were not on active service. Soldiers billeted on the townships were known as *buannachan* (billeted soldiers). *Buannacht* was the pay due to them. Free quartering was provided by the peasantry in place of rent. The size and value of a chief's estate could thus restrict the number of *buannachan* he could employ.

*   *   *   *

A second wave of Scot mercenaries from the Hebrides known as 'new Scots' or 'redshanks' arrived in Ireland in the sixteenth century. They hired out their services, usually for a fighting season, did not settle and returned home in the winter. These mercenaries were also a formidable fighting force. They complemented the galloglass and together the old and new Hebridean mercenaries formed the backbone of the men avail-able to the Irish lords, and one of the English government's first actions, when it switched to a policy of conquest in 1556, was to make the hiring of Scots a capital offence.[12]

Hebridean mercenaries, like their Swiss counterparts, were respected members of their home communities. They were also notorious looters and terrified their opponents. They were also commanded by a captain. A list survives of the names of the captains of Scots and the number of men they commanded when the Scots were defeated and massacred at Ardnarea in Connaught in 1586:

Donald Gorm, son of James Macdonald of Dunyvaig	300
Alexander Carragh, his brother	400
Gillespic M'Dowell (surnamed Campbell)	400
Macalastair of Loup	300
Macfee of Colonsay	300
Alexander M'Hugh Galt (possibly a Mackay from Kintyre)	100
M'Mick Hugh Duff	100
Neil Oge M'Evee	100
Alexander M'Ranolle Boy	50

It is also noted that they were accompanied by women, boys and children, who were also slaughtered.[13]

In addition to their own companies Donald Gorm and Alexander Carragh each had command of a number of other companies, the group of men led by a captain. This command was probably a temporary grouping for a campaign and not a regiment in the Swiss sense. It is also highly unlikely that the captains were democratically elected. Captains were usually the younger brothers and cousins of the chiefs rather than the clan chief himself. The latter's role, once he had proved himself, was more likely to have been to recruit and finance the companies rather than to lead them himself, except on some very important expedition.

Some captains such as John Dubh MacConachie Campbell, tutor of Inverawe, or John Og Campbell of Cabrachan, Lochnell's younger brother, achieved considerable reputations as captains of companies of mercenaries. Their services were in great demand.

It was the potential of the clans in the Western Isles and mainland of Argyll to provide mercenaries that was to give Lachlan Mor greater influence than any other Maclean of Duart.

Notes

1. Jane E. A. Dawson, 'Anglo Scottish Protestant culture', in Steven G. Ellis & Sarah Barber (eds), *Conquest and Union*, 90.
2. Gordon Donaldson, *All the Queen's Men* (1983), 28.
3. The following four pages are based on F. L. Taylor, *The Art of War in Italy, 1494–1529* (1921) & John McCormack, *One Million Mercenaries* (1993).
4. Charles Oman, *The Art of War in the Sixteenth Century* (1937), 444.
5. Taylor, 124.
6. McCormack , 206–217.
7. Gerard A Hayes-McCoy, *Scots Mercenary Forces in Ireland., 1565–1603* (1937).

8. Steve Boardman, 'The Badenoch Stewarts I', *Northern Scotland*, vol. 16 (1996), 4.
9. K. A. Steer and J. W. M. Bannerman, *Late Medieval Monumental Sculpture in the West Highlands* (1977).
10. W. F. Skene, *Celtic Scotland* (1890), Vol. III.
11. Boardman (1996), 7.
12. W. Ball (ed), *Statutes at large passed in the parliaments held in Ireland* (1786–1804), i, 274, quoted in Hiram Morgan, *Tyrone's Rebellion* (1993), 21.
13. Hayes-McCoy, 355.

CHAPTER 2

The Macleans

Macbeth. The Prince of Cumberland! that is a step
On which I must fall down, or else I o'er leap,
For in my way it lies. Stars, hide your fires;
Let not light see my black and deep desires:
The eye wink at the hand; yet let that be,
Which the eye fears, when it is done, to see.

Macbeth Act I, Scene iv

Lachlan Mor's paternal ancestors were the Macleans of Duart. They
had risen to prominence in the Isles as stewards to the Macdonald
– lords of the Isles. They had also married into his immediate family.
I have argued elsewhere that the Macleans perhaps believed that if the
male line of the Isles family died out they would succeed to the lordship
rather than 'the bastard blood of the Isles'.

MacDomhnaill ruled the semi–independent principality of the Isles
which had been ceded to the Scots' king by Norway in 1286. It had
retained its own laws and customs, which had more in common with
Gaelic-speaking Ireland than with the rest of Scotland; its prince's title
in Gaelic was *Ri Innse Gael,* in Latin *Dominus Insularum* or 'lord of the
Isles'.

This semi–independence was a situation which the king of Scots could
not tolerate for ever and in 1496 the last lord of the Isles was forfeited.
His vast lordship passed to the crown and in 1504 the Scots parliament
decreed 'that all our soverane lordis liegis be and under his obesance
and in special all the Ilis reulit be our soverane lardis and the commoune
lawis of the realme and be nain other lawis'.[1]

In 1496 the leading supporters of the lord of the Isles were, for the
first time, brought into a direct feudal relationship with the king. It is
important to appreciate what this change meant for landowners in the
Hebrides. It is the key to understanding much of what was behind
events that occurred in Lachlan Mor's career.

Although the dominant influence in the early Scottish kingdom had
been that of the Gaelic-speaking Scots, since the reign of king David I

(1124–53) the feudal doctrine that the king was the ultimate lord of all the land came gradually to be accepted. All other landowners were 'vassals' holding their land at one remove or another from the king.[2] When one of their number died, his heir had to be 'entered' as the new vassal and pay a fine. Many chiefs failed to be 'entered' and their estates were in a state of 'non-entry'. They could be granted to anyone prepared to pay the accumulated feudal dues.

The dispossessed landowner did not have to leave the land he had once owned but often stayed on, perhaps as a 'kindly' tenant. 'Kindness' was recognised as the right of a tenant to land by long-continued occupation.[3] Contrary to what has often been said, it is clear from rent-rolls that tenants often not only retained their holdings for long periods but passed them on to their heirs.[2]

If the heir of a tenant-in-chief was a minor, i.e. under the age of 21, other feudal casualties came into play. These were the 'ward, relief and marriage' of the heir, which could again be used as a bribe to a potential ally. It was a valuable gift as the rents of the ward's estate went to the recipient of the gift. Control of the heir's marriage gave him an additional method by which to control the heir even after he came of age. Worse still, if the heir was female the owner of her 'marriage' could marry the heiress to a member of his own family and the estate was lost to the heirs-male for ever. The lords of the Isles' personal estates also passed to the crown in 1496 and were available to be rented by potential supporters. Unlike the land that was set to tenants-in-chief, crown land paid an annual rent. This rent appears in the *Exchequer Rolls*. Some of the land was let for relatively short periods of time. Much of the crown's land in the Inner Hebrides, such as Aros in Mull and most of Islay and Kintyre, was held by the local clan chief, Maclean of Duart in Mull and Macdonald of Dunyvaig in Islay and Kintyre. They in turn let it to their sub-tenants.

Maclean of Duart's proximity to the lord of the Isles brought him properties close to his master's major residences at Finlaggan in Islay and Ardtornish in Morvern. He was also given control of three important castles, Duart, Carnaburg and Dunconnel, which helped control the sea-lanes of the Inner Hebrides. Each castle had arable land to maintain it. Duart had twelve touns in the parish of Torosay. Carnaburg had five in the north-west of Mull. Dunconnel had touns in the Garvellachs, Luing, Scarba and Jura. A toun was an area of arable land on an estate occupied by a number of farmers as co-tenants.[3]

In addition Maclean of Duart was granted land in Brolas and Ard-meanach in Mull, in Morvern as well as the baillery of Tiree with two touns there to support this office. A baillery was the district under the jurisdiction of a baillie. A baillie was an officer of a barony whose main task, in the absence of the baron himself, was to hold baron-courts. These were the courts which most affected the lives of people in the countryside. They existed primarily to settle minor quarrels among the tenants and to collect the fines levied for non-attendance at the head court. They were subordinate to the courts of the sheriffs and the lords of regality and their jurisdiction stopped short of the four pleas of the crown – arson, murder, rape and robbery, although as we shall see they might have a limited right of capital punishment.

Maclean of Duart's land-holding was perhaps less valuable than that of his major rival, Maclean of Lochbuie. Duart's greater prestige came not so much from his landed property as from his closeness to his master.

Duart continued to support his old master after the forfeiture and his successors even followed the lord of the Isles' grandson, Donald Dubh, when he escaped from prison in 1501. He was however defeated and back in prison by 1506. The failure of this rebellion probably convinced Maclean of Duart that there was no future in supporting, or in hoping to succeed, the lord of the Isles.

Lachlan Mor's grandfather, Hector Mor, finally broke with the representative of the Isles family when he deserted Donald Dubh, who, after escaping from prison again in 1545, led a major rebellion in the Isles. Hector Mor was well rewarded for this change of loyalty. He received from Mary of Guise confirmation as tenant of the royal lands in Aros in the Isle of Mull, in Tiree, in Islay and in Morvern. He also obtained a charter of feu-ferm from the earl of Argyll of the strategically and economically important island of Luing.[4] Most important of all he married his daughter Katherine to the earl. This was an enormous coup. The earls of Argyll might marry their daughters to Highlanders but their sons married the daughters of their fellow lowland magnates.

The earl evidently doted on his young wife and made considerable grants of land to her.[5] She in turn consented to grants made by her husband when she is described as 'our dearest spouse Katherine nic clain Countess of Argyll'. Hector Mor became a trusted member of the earl's council and his son Hector Og married the earl's eldest daughter Lady Janet Campbell. Lachlan Mor was their only son.

Hector Mor made a bond of manrent to the fourth earl in 1543.[6] This contract made him as one of the earl's own surname. He was evidently one of the earl's closest confidants – this loyalty to Argyll is most dramatically illustrated in the earliest surviving example of Maclean of

Duart's seal. Use of a personal seal was of considerable importance at this time. It enabled its owner to authenticate his signature on grants of land as a witness and as a signatory to an agreement. It was particularly valuable in Hector Mor's case as he could not write his name in Scots.

Around the shield on this seal are grouped the objects which appear as quarterings in later Maclean heraldry – the eagle's head respectant, the galley, the red hand of the O Neills and the battlemented tower. The only actual shield it contains displays the gyronny of eight device of the chief of Clan Campbell, the earl of Argyll. Hector Mor is making the unambiguous statement that he was the earl's 'man'.

No description survives to tell us what Hector Mor looked like. There is not even a panegyric to him in the highly stylised verse of the period. Nor has anything he composed been preserved. It was at one time believed that the poem *Oran Gaoil do Nighean Mhic Domhnuill Chinntire* was made by him. It has recently been argued that this assumption is unlikely.[7] Despite this lack of evidence to make him come alive, it is clear from his actions that Hector Mor was astute, ambitious, devious and ruthless. He steered his family through tumultuous times and it was his accumulation of property and alliances that enabled his grandson to become the 'Great Maclean'.

*   *   *   *

In the sixteenth century a clan was a recognised legal entity. What exactly the Clan Maclean was is less easy to define. The literal meaning of the word *clann* is 'children'. In medieval Highland society the term was used to describe a patrilineal kindred whose members descended in known steps from a named ancestor.[8]

The Clan Maclean, as it is usually mistakenly called as opposed to Clan Gillean its correct designation, descends from *Gillean na tuaighe*, who lived in the thirteenth century. Gillean's ancestors may well have been one of the hereditary learned orders of Gaelic-speaking Scotland[9] and at least one branch of the family continued to follow this tradition into the eighteenth century.[10]

King James VI in his attempt to 'civilise' Gaelic-speaking Scotland had the Clans of the Highlands and Isles 'that has capitanes, cheiffs and chieftanes quhome on they depend ...' listed in 1587. Donald Gregory identified the 'Clan Ieane' of this list as the Macians of Ardnamurchan.[11] However, as the Macleans do not otherwise appear in it, it is possible that he is referring to the Macleans. They are firmly listed in 1594 as 'Clan Gillane' and are among 'the authors of thift, reiff (plunder), oppressioun and sorning (exacting free board and lodging by force or threats) and masteris and sustenaris of theives ... inhabiting the Hielands and Iles'.

This evidence implies that there was one 'Clan Gillane' and it is clear that its chief, the head of the surname Maclean, was Maclean of Duart. What did this mean in the context of sixteenth-century Scottish society? I know of no precise contemporary definition. It is however possible to obtain some idea from examining surviving bonds of manrent, which aimed to make a 'man' of a different surname kin to a 'lord'.

The making of bonds of manrent and maintenance was a method in late medieval and early modern Scotland by which a lord built up his following. Such bonds of manrent included four precise duties of a 'man' to his 'lord'. Firstly a 'man' bound himself never to see his lord in 'harme skaith (injury) danger nor apperand perall' without warning him of it. Other bonds stated that he would protect his lord's honour. Secondly he was to 'give and conceal counsel'. Another form was 'gyf (the lord) askis me ony counsale I sal gyf tharin the best at I can ande gyf thai ony counsale schawin me to hede it and gif that the said lord schawin to me his counsal I sall conseyl it fra al men and women on lyff and nocht schaw it agane without his commendment or leyff'. Thirdly the man was to 'ride and gang' with his lord in peace and war. Fourthly he was to 'tak his afald (sincere, honest, faithful, single minded) lele and trew part in all his actions causis and querelis lefull and honest aganis all that levis and de may'.[12]

The 'man' was therefore to be loyal and true to his chief, give and receive counsel and to support him in all his ventures. Nowhere is it mentioned that the 'lord' was to have legal jurisdiction over his 'man'. This would not matter in the case of a clansman who lived in the geographical area which was part of his barony. This however was not always the case. Clansmen could through some quirk of history be living on another chief's estate and be under his legal jurisdiction. This situation could result in divided loyalties, as it did in the case of Maclean of Boreray who lived in North Uist, under the jurisdiction of Macdonald of Sleat.

In the Gaeltachd a man acknowledged who was his chief by the paying of 'calps'. This entailed an heir handing over his best beast to the head of the kindred on his father's death. Those who agreed to pay calps obtained protection in exchange. They also undertook to visit their chief's home twice a year bringing a gift. They agreed to join their chief when he went hunting, which required considerable manpower, and when he went to war, which required even more. Calps were transferable. In the 1550s Argyll resigned the homage, manrent and service of the whole kin and surname of Maclaren, 'together with the uptaking of their calpis', to Campbell of Glenorchy.[13]

Maclean of Duart's lands had been incorporated into a free barony in 1496 when the crown took over the direct allegiance of the former vassals of the lord of the Isles. As a 'baron' Maclean of Duart had legal jurisdiction over those who lived in his barony. He did not have legal jurisdiction over other Macleans who were themselves tenants-in-chief and held their own baronies from the crown. In 1570 there were three other Maclean baronies: Lochbuie, Coll and Kingairloch.

*   *   *   *

The Macleans of Duart and Lochbuie descended from two brothers, Lachlan Lubanach and Eachan Reaganach. They were probably the first of their respective families to acquire lands in Mull. Which brother was the elder has been and still is a cause for dispute. Although Maclean of Duart was usually the more powerful and was recognised in Edinburgh as chief of the Clan Gillean, there has been a long-held tradition in the Lochbuie family that their ancestor was the elder of the two.

In 1496 it seemed possible that Lochbuie would replace Duart as the most powerful branch of the clan. The current chief, John Maclean of Lochbuie, known to folklore as 'Iain the toothless', was one of the first former vassals of the lord of the Isles to throw in his lot with the crown. As a result he was one of the first to obtain a charter to his lands and have them erected into a free barony. These lands included what appears to have been the family's original landholding in Mull, Jura, Scarba and Morvern. However, he also obtained a grant of lands in Tiree, which had previously belonged to Duart, and of lands in Lochaber claimed by both Cameron of Locheil and Maclean of Coll. In addition he received a massive grant of the lands of Duror and Glencoe. It is doubtful if Lochbuie ever occupied the latter lands and it is more than likely an example of what an ambitious, plausible and unscrupulous chief could obtain when he had the ear of an impressionable monarch.

'Iain the toothless' lived to a great age and saw in his lifetime the destruction of his hopes to dominate the Macleans. The major cause of his ruin was the continuing curse in the Lochbuie family of being divided against itself. Iain's sons fought a bitter war against their father. It was a conflict that was ably exploited by the Macleans of Duart, particularly by Hector Mor's brother Allan Maclean, better known as *Ailein nan Sop*, who burnt houses belonging to Lochbuie and killed his eldest son.[14] It was an act that was probably to have disastrous repercussions on Allan's descendants and, as we shall see, on the career of Lachlan Mor.

'Iain the toothless' was eventually succeeded by his son *Murdoch Gearr*, who only obtained control of the Lochbuie estates after a pitched battle at Gruline in Mull against his uncle Murdoch of Scallastle.

Murdoch Gearr also lived to a great age. He had at least two wives. One was the daughter of James Macdonald of Dunyvaig's formidable brother 'Sorley Boy' and one the sister of Tormod Macleod of Dunvegan.

Whether or not *Murdoch Gearr* recognised Hector Mor Maclean of Duart as his chief is uncertain. The Macleans of Lochbuie disappear from the records, from 1545/6 when they receive a 'respitt' for having joined Donald Dubh's rebellion,[15] to 1575[16] when *Murdoch Gearr* complained of his son's behaviour.

The government certainly recognised only one 'clan Gillane' in 1594, but it is less certain whether the other Hebridean chiefs did, and in the early seventeenth century one commentator talks about the two 'clan Ieans' in Mull.

*   *   *   *

The position of the next most important family of Macleans, the Macleans of Coll, is even more complicated. The Macleans of Coll's estates were in Coll itself, Mull and Morvern. They also owned the Isle of Rum. All these lands had been erected into a barony probably in 1496. The family probably descend from Lachlan the third son of Lachlan Lubanach Maclean of Duart and Mary, daughter of the lord of the Isles. The Macleans of Duart descend from the second son. The eldest son John presumably died without issue.

In 1558 Hector, known as *an cleireach beag*, the 'little clerk', succeeded his father as Maclean of Coll. Hector was a second son whose eldest brother had predeceased their father. (The third son was Neil Mor.) As a second son Hector was probably intended for the church, hence his nickname, but as he is nowhere described as 'Mr Hector' he presumably did not go to a university. He was perhaps in minor orders. As I have argued in *Warriors & Priests*, Hector, who was a poet, was ambitious and quarrelled with his brother-in-law Hector Mor of Duart. (Both had married sisters of James Macdonald of Dunnyveg.)

When Hector of Coll was in Edinburgh in 1561 Hector Mor's sons invaded Coll's outlying lands in Morvern. Coll complained to the Privy

Council. This case is at the root of the question, what was the Clan Maclean in the sixteenth century? Duart's sons claimed they were justified in punishing Coll because he refused to follow them, serve them and accompany them on cattle raids and take their part in blood feuds: duties which, as we have seen, were fundamental to the duty a clansman owed his chief.

On his part Coll claimed 'it is a veritie that he aucht him (Duart) na service, nor haldis na landis of him bot of the Quenis Majestie onelie, he being ane fre baroun as any otheris within hir Hienes realme.'[17]

Which party was correct? Certainly Coll was right in stating that he was 'ane fre baron' and he was listed as one in 'the Roll of the names of the Landlordis and Baillies of Lordis in the Hielandis and Iles ...' made in 1587.[18] As such Duart had no legal jurisdiction over him. In terms of feudal law Coll was correct, but in the older Gaelic tradition was Duart his chief?

It is perhaps significant that at this time Maclean of Coll is more often described in official documents as Lord of Coll, or by his patronymic *Macian Abraich*.[19] It is almost as though both Coll and the authorities were playing down the fact that he was a Maclean. It can however easily be shown that he was a Maclean, but a clan, like any other corporate body, was constantly changing its structure. W. D. H. Sellar has shown that several clans descending in the male line from the same individual could be regarded as distinct clans. He mentions Macsween, Maclachlan, the Macewens of Otter, Macsorleys of Monydrain who all descend from Ánrothán, an Irish prince who married the daughter of the king of Scotland.[20]

This dispute over whether or not the Macleans of Coll were part of the Clan Gillean, whose chief was Maclean of Duart, lay at the centre of the quarrel between the two families. It led directly to the murder of Neil Mor.

*   *   *   *

The third Maclean tenants-in-chief were the Macleans of Kingerloch or Kingairloch. They had an estate of some 22,000 acres mainly on the northern shore of Loch Linnhe but with outlying properties, the Isle of Carna in Loch Sunart and the superiority of Blaich on the southern shore of Loch Eil. The Macleans of Kingerloch had held their land from the lord of the Isles for the service of a galley with 22 oars,[21] which would have been essential if they were to travel to their widely dispersed estates.

Kingerloch's main estate was rough and mountainous and its few inhabitants were renowned for their skill in cattle raids and as warriors. Although the Macleans of Kingerloch descended from Eachan Reaganach, the progenitor of the Macleans of Lochbuie, after whom they took their surname *Maceachan*, they appear, by the mid-sixteenth century, to have followed Maclean of Duart. They produced a number of cadet families, principally Dochgarroch, who settled at the north end of Loch Ness and Blaich.

The origin of the Macleans of Dochgarroch is uncertain. The first member of the family to appear in the records is described as 'Alexander, *haeres* Donaldie McLeane Ferquhardi Hectoris'. *Hectoris* is here perhaps being used as a surname, in other words *Maceachan*, but who was Farquhar? The present Macleans of Dochgarroch claim that he was the brother of Hugh Maclean of Kingerloch, whom he succeeded as chief and was on record in 1509.[22]

In 1630 Alexander was served heir to his father in the eight-merk lands in Raasay and three-merk lands in Trotternish in Skye.[23] These lands in 1549 belonged to the 'Bischop of the Iles be heritage' but to 'Mcgillichallum of Raarsay be the sword'.[24] According to tradition Donald Maclean had been granted Raasay, but had failed to complete sasine. It is perhaps significant that Bishop Farquhar Maclean (1521 x 1547) was a Maclean of Kingerloch. He was perhaps the Farquhar in the above Alexander's patronymic. It is more likely that a bishop would dilapidate the church by granting land to his son rather than his brother.

When Hector Mor's maternal relations, the Macleans of Treshnish, constables of Carnaburg, died out in the male line he brought Hector Maclean of Blaich to Mull and made him constable of Carnaburg. He was perhaps succeeded in this post by his son Donald known as *Domhnall Dubh Chaistall*, who is said to have been 'a rough and hardy sort of man, but remarkably brave and faithful to his chief'.[25] Donald's sons were to play an important part in Lachlan Mor's career. One named Ewen succeeded his father as constable of Carnaburg. Another also named Ewen who had the byname *Uaibrich* succeeded to Blaich and became bailie of Garbhdarrach, Duart's vulnerable lands in Lochaber. Here he was succeeded in turn as bailie by his brother Iain Odhar Maclean of Achnadale in the braes of Lochaber.

In a society that put so much store on heredity it is not surprising that appointments such as bailies and constables became hereditary in certain families. For instance Constable of Aros Castle became the hereditary post of another family of Macleans for at least four generations whilst constable and captain of Carnaburg was to be held by *Domhnall Dubh Chaistall's* descendants for two hundred years. Although we know the names of some captains of castles who served Lachlan Mor, we do not know the names of the men who were captains of Maclean companies in the mercenary service. It is probable that they came from leading Maclean families, but extraordinarily the only Maclean described as commanding a company in Dr Hector's manuscript (see Postscript) is Allan Maclean of Auchnasaul, who led his nephew's men at *Tràigh Ghruinneart* in 1598. Unlike the mercenary captains who followed Angus Macdonald of Dunyvaig's brother at Ardnarea in 1586, no Maclean captains are listed in the Irish State Papers.

Other functionaries also became hereditary in certain families: physicians (Beatons), poets (Ó Muirgheasains), musicians (Rankins). In addition families of clerics served Duart both as chaplains and clerks. In 1558 Hector Mor's clerk was Mr John Angus, chaplain, vicar of St. Colme's who, despite his surname, was a Maclean descended from Eachan Reaganach. His family produced clergymen every generation for at least three hundred years.

*   *   *   *

Lachlan Mor's major supporters from amongst Maclean tenants-in-chief, who recognised Duart as their 'chief and master',[26] were the Macleans of Ardgour. The first Maclean of Ardgour had received his estate from the lord of the Isles in the mid-fifteenth century. Their representative in 1545 was John, who was a member of the council of Donald Dubh, the grandson of the last lord of the Isles. He was however dead by 1546 and Hector Mor was granted his son John's non-entry, ward and marriage.[27] This John must have died as a child and Hector Mor granted the lands of Ardgour to the next male heir, a second cousin named Allan.

No Maclean of Ardgour obtained an infeftment of his estate from the crown for 150 years after 1535 and the estate would have been highly vulnerable if it had not been poor rough mountainous ground and if the family had not produced a number of hard tough fighting men. Six of Allan of Ardgour's sons were formidable enough to be remembered by the seneachies.

No other families of Macleans held their lands directly from the crown in the mid-sixteenth century. There were however other families of Macleans who held from Duart or other tenants-in-chief. One of the most important were the Macleans of Boreray, said to be an Ardgour cadet who had settled in North Uist and held their lands from Macdonald of Sleat. Another family, that of Lehir in Mull, are said to have held their land for several generations, although no documentary proof has survived. They had been ousted from Lehir by *Ailein nan Sop* but still survived as substantial kindly tenants into the late eighteenth century.

Other Macleans appear as followers of Lachlan Mor. One Lachlan Odhar of Ardchraoshnish is said to have been 'a bold resolute man, he was with Lachlan Mor in all his conflicts with the Macdonalds'.[28] He was a member of the family of Ross, a family whose origins have caused much argument. Others such as Charles Maclean constable of Duart and Charles bailie of Ross [29] were evidently men of some importance at the time as they witnessed documents but cannot now be identified. Others whose names appear in complaints to the Privy Council such as 'Lauchlane McAne Dow' or 'Neill McAne McNeill' [30] were evidently followers of Lachlan Mor. They too cannot otherwise be identified.

Other Macleans will have been among Duart's 'servandis' who were members of his household. In the sixteenth century every Scottish family of standing had an enormous number of such employees. They served in return for board and lodging which a landlord, who received his rent in kind, could easily provide. Some of them were genuine domestics. Others were kinsmen or hired ruffians who were engaged because of their strong arms and their skill with weapons.

In 1531 Hector Mor was limited to a following of 40 'personis', when he was ordered to come to his sovereign's presence.[31] This bodyguard was known as the *luchd-taighe*. It attended the chief at all times whether he was at home or abroad. Its members were trained in the use of weapons, 'in wrestling, swimming, jumping, dancing, shooting with bows and arrows'. They were also expert seamen.[32]

Maclean of Duart is said to have had not less than a following of a hundred men when he wintered in Tiree. Lachlan Mor had a following of 140 men when he held his disatrous tryst with his nephew at *Tràigh Ghruinneart* in 1598.

A chief's prestige was judged by the 'length of his tail', i.e. his 'gentlemen', musicians, falconers, servants, etc. This personal following was one of the last trappings of a highland chief to disappear. As late as 1782 Hugh Maclean of Kingerloch is described as having a 'life guard' consisting of eight stout fellows, who were determined to defend their chief.[33]

To be a member of the chief's bodyguard was an honour. Young men would have vied amongst each other to be chosen for it. Martin Martin tells us that: 'Every heir, or young chieftain of a tribe, was obliged in honour to give a publick specimen of his valour before he was owned and declared governor or leader of his people ...' He goes on to say that the heir 'was usually attended with a retinue of young men of quality, who had not beforehand given any proof of their valour, and were ambitious of such an opportunity to signalise themselves'.

Notes

1. *Acts of the Parliaments of Scotland (APS)* ii, 241–2, 249.
2. W. D. H. Sellar, 'A Historical Perspective', in Scott Chrichton Symes (ed), *The Scottish Legal Tradition* (1991), 37.
3. Mairi Robinson, *The Concise Scots Dictionary* (1985) *(CSD)*, 729.
4. Scottish Record Office (SRO), SP 13/48, ATiv, 336.
5. Argyll Transcripts, made by 10th Duke of Argyll, at Inveraray Castle (AT), iv, 316.
6. AT, v, 88.
7. Helen Jane Theresa O'Sullivan, 'Developments in Love Poetry in Irish, Welsh and Scottish Gaelic before 1650', unpublished thesis in University of Glasgow's Celtic Department, July 1976. I am grateful to Colm O Baoil for this reference.
8. W. D. H. Sellar, 'Origins of clans', in D. S. Thomson (ed), *The Companion to Gaelic Scotland* (1983), 43.
9. *Warriors and Priests*, 1–19.
10. *Ibid*, 181–189; see Nicholas Maclean-Bristol & Paul Hopkins *The Lame Adventurer* (forthcoming).
11. *Collectanea de Rebus Albanicis* (1848), 38.
12. Jenny Wormald, *Lords and Men* (1983), 67.
13. E. J. Cowan, 'Clanship and Campbell Expansion in the time of Gilleasbuig Gruamach', *Transactions of the Gaelic Society of Inverness (TGSI)* (1984–86), 274.
14. *Registrum Secreti Sigilli Regum Scottorum (RSS)* (1529–42), 1527.
15. *RSS* ii, 1534.
16. *The Register of the Privy Council of Scotland (RPC)*, ii, 483.
17. *RPC*, 311–313.
18. *Collectanea de Rebus Albanicis*, 35.
19. *RSS* iv, 205.
20. 'Family origins in Cowal and Knapdale', *Scottish Studies* Vol 15: 1971, part one, 21–37.
21. J. M. Thomson & J. B. Paul (eds), *Registrum Magni Sigilli Regum Scottorum* (1882–1914) *(RMS)* vii (1609–1620), 959.
22. *Warriors and Priests*, Table 6, 181.
23. *Inquisitionum Retovoraturum Abbreviatio* (1811), 50.
24. R. W. Munro (ed), *Munro's Western Isles of Scotland* (1961), 70.
25. National Library of Scotland (NLS), Acc. 7609, 52.
26. SRO Register of Deeds (hereafter RD) 1/27 21R S V.
27. *RSS* iii, 1916.
28. 1807, 52.

29. RD1/27 H17R–19v3.
30. *RPC* iii (1578–85), 125.
31. *RSS* ii, 1030.
32. Martin Martin, *Western Isles of Scotland* (1716), 103.
33. SRO CS 237 Mc/5/28.

CHAPTER 3

MacCailein Mor

Duncan. He was a gentleman on whom I built
An absolute trust.

Macbeth Act I, Scene iv

It is impossible to understand Lachlan Mor's career without first appreciating the importance of his link with the family of Argyll which echoed his ancestor's relationship with the lord of the Isles.

The Campbell earls of Argyll were among the great magnates of Scotland. However, unlike the other two contemporary great magnate families, the Hamiltons and the Gordons, who were primarily lowlanders, who also had estates in the Highlands, Argyll was first and foremost a Gaelic prince, known in the Gaeltachd as *MacCailein Mor*, 'the son of big Colin'.

By the middle of the sixteenth century *MacCailein Mor* had replaced the lord of the Isles at the apex of the Gaelic social order. 'I shall travel with my 'complete poem' to the king of the Gael, the man who maintains the thronged court, prosperous and wealthy', sang a bard, thought to have been Maclean's, perhaps even composing his verse on the occasion of Hector Og's marriage to lady Janet Campbell.[1]

Panegyric poems such as this one praising *MacCailein Mor* were composed both by poets for their own patrons and by visiting bards. The highly stylised forms and conventions of these praise poems were used to convey the status and aspirations of the subject and when the poet proclaimed that the earl was 'King of the Gael', he was making an unequivocal statement that *MacCailein Mor* had replaced *MacDomhnaill* as leader of the *Gaeltachd*.[2]

By his alliance with the earls of Argyll Hector Mor had not only increased the Maclean of Duart's landholding. He had raised the prestige of his family to what is arguably its greatest height.

In 1558, the same year as Lachlan Mor was born, his uncle Archibald Campbell, lady Janet's half-brother, succeeded their father as the fifth earl of Argyll. Archibald is said to have been born in 1530.[3] He was to play a leading role in Scottish politics. He supported the lords of the

Congregation, Mary of Guise's enemies, in expelling the French from Scotland. But when Mary Queen of Scots returned to her native Scotland he became a favourite at court, formed a close friendship with the queen and married her half-sister. Despite his affection for Mary he was first and foremost a Protestant and a supporter of the alliance with England. He opposed both her marriages to Darnley and to Bothwell. He also acquiesced in the queen's abdication. He had, however, doubts about the propriety of Mary's removal and changed sides, not only joining the queen's party but becoming her military leader at the disastrous Battle of Langside in 1567, which resulted in Mary's flight into England, imprisonment and eventual execution.

Argyll remained one of the queen's men throughout the Civil War that raged from 1567 to 1573. Other magnates were ruined by the Civil War but although Argyll was on the losing side he came out with his power base intact. He was even given the chancellorship, the highest office in the state, as his price for being reconciled to the regent's government.

The secret of Argyll's survival lay in the brilliant use he made of his main assets, his land and its people, their galleys and their loyalty. The land with its mountains gave him a virtually impregnable fortress within which to retire in times of difficulty, whilst the long sea lochs that penetrated to the heart of Argyll enabled him to move men quickly and secretly by water to the strategically vital central lowlands of Scotland. Strategically placed castles controlled entry to these sea-lochs and pre-vented Argyll's enemies from using them to invade his territory. In addition, Argyll's position astride the Northern Approaches allowed him to dominate the sea-lanes between Scotland and Ireland and his galleys ranged as far south as Bristol and Dublin.

Argyll had his own shipwrights working for him on Loch Awe and Loch Fyne and in 1569 issued a proclamation from Largs calling all men between the ages of 16 and 60 to help him against the queen's enemies by building galleys.[4] In addition most major Campbell cadets had their own galleys, as did their allies, and in an emergency the earl could commandeer the Clyde herring boats as he did in 1568 to carry 2,000 of his men to Glasgow.

As the Scottish government had few ships and the English Royal Navy was almost always stationed on the east and south coasts of England, Argyll was in a position to dominate the Irish Sea and when, in 1568, the Dublin government heard that Argyll was building more galleys it was so alarmed that it prohibited the export of timber to Scotland.

The men who manned the galleys were his major asset. They were well-armed fighting men. Most would have taken part in clan battles and cattle raids in the Highlands. Many would have served as mercenaries in Ireland. In an emergency the earl could probably raise more than 5,000 men. Control of such numbers by one man was exceptional in the British Isles. It rivalled the capacity to recruit of both the crowns of Scotland and England and when, in 1560, the earl offered the English government 3,000 men to serve in Ireland it was double the entire English garrison that was stationed there.

Argyll was also in the unique position of owning artillery. Commoners were normally prohibited from owning the means to destroy their enemies' castles. Somehow the earls had managed to evade this prohibition and the Argylls, like the Stewart kings, seem to have had a genuine fondness for artillery. The most famous artillery piece owned by Argyll was the 'crooked gun', which accompanied the Campbell expedition to Ireland in 1555.

All these assets possessed by Argyll would have been wasted if they had been under the control of someone who had not the personality to inspire the loyalty of his subjects. The fifth earl had such a personality. *MacCailein Mor* was first and foremost the leader of the Gaelic host in battle. He had personally led his father's men to Ireland in 1555. He had also commanded them in the fighting against the French and during the retreat from Edinburgh where he had avoided a rout when he led the counter-attack which captured Leith Wynd. He had also proved himself by suppressing a mutiny among the soldiers of the lords of the Congregation, who had not received their pay.

Despite his prowess as a soldier the fifth earl was a man who preferred reason to bloodshed, and when he suppressed the mutiny John Knox recalls that the earl 'behaved himself moderately, and was so studious to pacify the tumult that many wondered as well of his prudent counsel and stoutness, as of the great obedience of his company'.[5] The mutineers had attacked the earl's men and killed one of the children who served him as a page and the earl must have used considerable powers of persuasion to prevent his men from butchering the mutineers.

The fifth earl's major military failure was at the Battle of Langside when he suffered a fainting fit, with disastrous results for the queen's army. His enemies described him as a coward for his behaviour but there is nothing in his earlier career to support such a claim. It is also doubtful if he could have commanded the respect of his Campbell chieftains if he had been a coward. *MacCailein Mor's* greatest asset was the loyalty he received from these men. Many such as Glenorchy, Cawdor and Ardkinglas were major landowners in their own right. Yet they gave the earl unswerving loyalty and obedience. This loyalty was echoed by the support he received from his non-Campbell supporters, such as Maclean of Duart, Macdougall of Dunolly and Stewart of Appin.

MacCailein Mor was not only a Gaelic prince but like any other Scottish magnate held legal jurisdiction over his vast estates. These regional jurisdictions ranged from the possession of numerous baronies, at the lowest level of the Scottish legal system, to the immense authority of a lord of regality. Technically only the king's pleas of treason and murder were excluded from this jurisdiction. In practice the distance of Argyll from the courts in Edinburgh made it necessary for the earl to perform these and many other functions of central government.

In addition the earl was hereditary sheriff of Argyll and occasionally was given special commissions of fire and sword within the Isles. He had also legal jurisdiction over more than his own region, as he was hereditary Justice-General of the whole of Scotland. In this capacity he held justice-ayres in the North, the Borders and in the western lowlands.

Although the fifth earl was often travelling around the country presiding over his courts, it is clear that he was usually to be found at court. The personal reign of Mary Queen of Scots saw the return to Scotland and to Scottish politics of a court, the first for almost twenty years. Mary's childhood, since the age of six, had been spent in France and she had been exposed to the cult of chivalry and magnificence of the Valois monarchy. This magnificence was best expressed in great renaissance festivals, such as Mary's own marriage to the Dauphin of France in 1558.

The French court was a bringer of harmony and order to the state and Mary brought its example with her to Scotland. From the autumn of 1562 to 1566 she engaged in a series of progresses throughout Scotland, which even took her to Inveraray where she wore highland dress and took part in at least one deer hunt. These journeys were a major exercise in public relations. They culminated in December 1566 in the triumphant baptismal ceremonies for her son, the infant James. This occasion was the first truly renaissance festival in Great Britain. It also acted as a means of reconciling the opposing factions within the nobility.

As a Protestant the fifth earl refused to attend the actual baptism which took place according to the rites of the Roman Church. His wife however did take part and held the child at the font. For this 'scandal' she was cited before the General Assembly and was forced to make 'public penance'.

At the formal dinner which immediately followed the baptism, the earl of Argyll did take part and as Protestant patron of the west walked in the procession beside Lord Seton, the most resolutely Roman Catholic lord of the south-east. Both carried a white staff in their hands, the traditional emblem of reconciliation of a feud.[6] It was the zenith of Mary's reign.

*   *   *   *

The rapid spread of Protestantism, at least outside the burghs, depended to a great extent on the attitude to it of the local nobility, and in the area dominated by the earl of Argyll the reformed religion had one of its foremost supporters. The fifth earl was a convinced Protestant, going so far as to destroy 'places and monuments of ydolatrie',[7] and his influence on the future of the new church in the west was to be of vital importance to its establishment in Argyll. Nor was his influence limited to his own territory, for the Campbell network reached other parts of Scotland. At the Reformation the abbot of Coupar Angus and the future bishop of Brechin were both Campbells. Both became Protestants.

Despite the fifth earl's genuine religious zeal, he was the father of several illegitimate children. He was evidently the product of his own background. He was first and foremost the leader of Gaelic-speaking Scotland and nothing separated the *Gaeltachd* from mainstream European Christian society more than its sexual mores.

The fifth earl had been brought up at a time when what has been described by scholars as Celtic secular marriage, was normal in the *Gaeltachd*. It was a carryover from the old pagan order and Christian matrimony was still no more than the exception grafted on to the older system. Secular Gaelic marriage permitted easy divorce and it was usual for both men and women in the upper echelons of Gaelic society to have a succession of spouses living at the same time.[8] This state of affairs had been tolerated by the Roman Church whose clergy in the *Gaeltachd* were often a product of such unions. It was anathema to the reformed religion.

If it was the fifth earl who gave the leadership necessary to establish the reformed church in Argyll, it was his protégé John Carswell and the other university-educated clergy, scholars and notary publics who were to spread the 'word' in the Highlands and Isles most under the earl's influence.

John Carswell is thought to have been born in 1520. He was educated at St. Andrews University, graduating as a Master of Arts in 1544. He became a notary public and as such witnessed a charter of Donald Dubh, 'Lord of the Isles', in July 1545. A month later at Carrickfergus in Ireland he drew up a notarial certificate witnessing an oath taken by Donald Dubh and his barons. In view of his later career as a servant of the earl of Argyll it is curious to find Carswell beginning his career in the opposite camp, and he may have been acting as a messenger between the earl and Hector Mor, who appears to have betrayed the uprising.

At some stage in his early career Carswell attended one of the bardic schools that still existed in Ireland and perhaps in Scotland. He learnt to master classical common Gaelic, the literary language shared by the *literati* of both Ireland and Gaelic Scotland which must have been understood by the bards' lay patrons if they were to appreciate the subtleties of the panegyrics made about them.

In September 1550 Carswell was treasurer of Lismore, perhaps his first major ecclesiastical appointment. He was to obtain many others. By 1553 he was in possession of the parsonage of Kilmartin. In 1559 he added the parsonages of Southwick and Kingarth in Bute and the chancellery of the Chapel Royal at Stirling to his portfolio. He was also to receive grants of lay property and the fifth earl made him constable of both Carnassary and Craignish castles in mid-Argyll with the necessary land to support his position. He was an early convert to Protestantism and in 1560 the newly formed General Assembly appointed him superintendent of Argyll.

In 1565 Mary Queen of Scots appointed Carswell bishop of the Isles and abbot of Iona. It was an appointment that irritated the General Assembly and infuriated the Macleans. Mr Patrick Maclean, Hector Mor's brother, was already bishop-elect of the Isles and had to be bought off with a pension. Then in May 1567, two months after his appointment had been confirmed, Mr Lachlan Maclean, Lochbuie's fourth son, appeared before the Privy Council and affirmed that he had never obtained a licence from the queen to go to Rome to purchase the bishopric of the Isles, nor other benefices pertaining to Carswell. He also promised never to molest the bishop in its peaceful possession.[9] The Macleans had evidently not given up the bishopric without a struggle.

Carswell's standing in the eyes of the reformed church must have been greatly enhanced by the appearance in 1567 of his translation into Gaelic of the *Book of Common Order*. It was a work of major literary and liturgical significance. Its appearance shortly after his election to parliament as one of the lords of the Articles in one of the busiest sections of his career adds to his achievement. It also suggests that he could not have produced his translation at such speed without the collaboration of highly educated Gaelic speakers in Argyll and the Isles. Several Macleans could be included. Leaving aside Mr Lachlan Maclean, who appears to have been more a man of action than a scholar, Carswell could have been assisted by Mr John Angus, Hector Mor's secretary, whose descendants were immersed in Gaelic culture. It was not only university-educated clergy who could have helped him. For example Hector Maclean of Coll, *an clereach beag,* has left two poems which have survived. Their language suggests that he spent some time at a bardic school and that he was an early convert to the reformed faith.[10]

Further research on the progress of the Reformation in the Highlands and Isles will probably reveal more evidence of its impact. It is however already apparent that earlier historians' comments that the progress of the Reformation was 'to be traced almost exclusively in the history of the lowlands'[11] can no longer be accepted.

John Carswell was to be remembered in Argyll. Stories about *Carsallach Mor Charnasairidh,* 'big Carswell of Carnassary', were still being told of him in the early nineteenth century. One story that survives is a biting satire that describes him as 'over capacious of stomach, as greedy as a cormorant, his well fleshed body fat with the ill-gotten riches of honest men'. The Reverend John Macinnes, writing in *Notes & Queries,* however, comments: 'we should not take this too seriously. When Carswell in his later years was fulfilling the duties of bishop ... he had perforce to uplift the church tiends ... they (the people) were naturally reluctant to part with the tenth part of the produce of land and sea and he was compelled at times to use stronger measures than kind words'.

On his deathbed in the summer of 1572 Carswell asked to be buried at Ardchattan priory. On the day of the funeral there was a violent snowstorm and his body was carried on men's shoulders the forty miles from Carnassary to Ardchattan. Thereafter it became a proverbial expression in Argyll to say of an exceptional severe snowstorm: 'there hasn't been a day like this since the Big Carsallach was buried'.[12]

It is said that Carswell was buried in a stone coffin outside what is now the kitchen fireplace at Ardchattan. Towards the end of last century a mason uncovered the coffin. The skeleton of the bishop was whole with all the joints in their place. It measured seven feet.[13]

Bishop Carswell's legacy to Lachlan Mor was the grant of a feu charter of Iona, the barony of Ross and other lands in Mull, Tiree and Islay that belonged to the church. It was a massive grant of land which could not have been made without the fifth earl's agreement. It was the culmination of Hector Mor's alliance with the earl.

The Macleans of Duart had acted as stewards and been responsible for the defence of the Abbot of Iona's lands since they had been appointed by the lord of the Isles in 1390. This arrangement worked happily in Hector Mor's lifetime and during that of his son Hector Og. It was not to do so in Lachlan Mor's time.

Maclean of Duart was not the only Maclean to obtain church lands. Sometime before Mary Queen of Scots was deposed in 1567, Mr John Angus alias Maclean, Hector Mor's secretary, obtained the 3 merk lands of Scarinish in Tiree which had belonged to the abbot of Iona.[14] Hector Maclean of Coll, *an cleireach beag*, also obtained lands belonging to the church. On 28 June 1558 'with consent of the whole convent' Hector received sasine of the lands in the east end of Coll, which belonged to the Augustinian priory of Oronsay.[15] He was also to obtain control of the west end of the island in July 1566, when Hugh Mackegane, his clerk, obtained a nineteen-year lease of Caolis, Ardnish, Friesland and the Isle of Gunna.[16]

The grant of church lands to both Mr John Angus and Hector Maclean of Coll were to be a cause of dissension in the Isles. It cannot be coincidental that both families had members murdered at the instigation of Lachlan Mor.

Notes

1. W. Gillies, 'Some Aspects of Campbell History', *TGSI* l (1976–8), 287–288, no. 1.
2. Jane Dawson, 'The fifth earl of Argyle, Gaelic Lordship and Political Power in Sixteenth-Century Scotland', *Scottish Historical Review (SHR)* LXVII, i: no. 183: (April 1988), 22.
3. Sir James Balfour-Paul (ed.), *Scots Peerage*, i (1904), 341.
4. J. MacInnes, 'West Highland Sea Power', *TGSI* xlviii (1972–4), 518–56.
5. Knox, *History*, i, 257, 260.
6. Michael Lynch, 'Queen Mary's Triumph: the Baptismal Celebrations at Stirling in December 1566', *SHR* Vol. LXIX, 1: No. 187: April 1990, 10.
7. Knox, *Works* ii, 167–8.
8. W. D. H. Sellar, 'Marriage, Divorce and Concubinage in Gaelic Scotland', *TGSI* li, 466.
9. *RPC*, i, 511.
10. Nicholas Maclean-Bristol, *Warriors and Priests*, 138–139.
11. Donald Gregory, *The History of the Western Highlands* (1881), 186.
12. John Macinnes, 'John Carswell', *Notes & Queries* iii, 3–4.
13. Angus Matheson, 'Bishop Carswell', *TGSI* xlii (1953–1959), 190.
14. *RMS* v, 1997.

15. AT V, 99.
16. *Warriors and Priests*, 154.

CHAPTER 4

Friends and Enemies

Macbeth. Blood hath been shed ere now, i' th' olden time
Ere human nature purg'd the gentle weal
Ay, and since too, murders have been perform'd
Too terrible for the ear.

Macbeth Act III, Scene iv

Lachlan Mor was at the centre of an extended family network that reached every corner of the Hebrides. First and foremost in power and influence, after his Campbell cousins, was his paternal great-uncle James Macdonald of Dunyvaig and the Glens, chief of the Clan Ian Mor, the Macdonalds *South*. It was a family which was to have enormous influence on Lachlan Mor's career.

The Clan Ian Mor descended from John Mor, second son of 'good John of Islay' lord of the Isles and lady Margaret Stewart, daughter of King Robert II. They were the most powerful clan in the Hebrides. James, who was born in about 1522, spent some of his youth at the court of King James V, as a hostage for his father's good behaviour. He received his education at court under the direction of dean Henderson of Holyrood where he is said to have been a great favourite. Irish tradition is also flattering about him: 'he was a paragon of hospitality and prowess, a festive man of many troops, and a bountiful and munificent man'.[1]

The Clan Ian Mor's patrimony was in both Scotland and in Ireland, where they held the Glens of Antrim. They were the senior and most powerful cadet of the Clan Donald. When Donald Dubh, the grandson of the last lord of the Isles, escaped from prison in 1545 and rallied his ancestor's former followers, James stood aloof from the rebellion. For his loyalty to the crown James was confirmed in his family's holdings in Kintyre, Colonsay, Islay, Jura, Rathlin Island (then considered to be part of Scotland), Uist, Sunart and Morvern, which was incorporated into the barony of Bar.[2] As a result he had his lands in Kintyre ravaged by Lennox who was then the leader of the English party in Scotland. However, when Donald Dubh died James's patriotism evaporated and many of Donald's supporters recognised him as lord of the Isles. The possibility of obtaining the English pension of 2000 crowns granted to Donald Dubh was too tempting to be resisted.[3]

James's rebellion was short-lived. On 8 August 1546 he and his brothers and other followers including Alexander Macalister of Loup, Allan Maclean of Gigha and John Macfee of Colonsay received a 'respitt' for burning the town of Saltcoats in Cunningham. In exchange James agreed to give up his claim to be lord of the Isles.

James was courted by both Mary of Guise and her rival James duke of Chatelherault, earl of Arran, the head of the Hamiltons, who were now at the peak of their power. In 1552 James received the gift of the non-entry of Macechern of Killellan, the ancient family of Mairs of south Kintyre,[4] and in 1556, in exchange for a promise to resign lands he held in Arran and to 'be ane gude frende to oure yle of Arrane' which belonged to Chatelherault, he was granted the barony of Saddell in Kintyre.[5]

The barony of Saddell was the property of the bishop of Argyll, Chatelherault's brother, who had conveyed the barony to the duke. It was now granted to James. Included in the grant was 'the place of Saddell' and James was bound to give the duke and bishop the hospitality of the house whenever they were in Kintyre.

James was not to enjoy the uninterrupted use of Saddell for long. In 1558 the earl of Sussex, lord deputy of Ireland, raided Kintyre in revenge for an incursion into Ulster by James. Sussex reported that he burnt James's 'chief house called Sandell' and a 'fayre house called Marher Imare (Machrimore) and a stronge castell called Donalvere (Dunaverty)'. Only a change in the weather and the deplorable state of his fleet caused Sussex to withdraw and save Islay from the same fate as Kintyre.

This raid underlines the basic weakness of the Clan Ian Mor. As a landowner in both Scotland and Ireland the family were neither wholly Scottish nor Irish. They were frequently used as a pawn by both governments in the often bloody undeclared war they fought in Tudor Ireland.

Despite the Scottish crown's efforts to build up James as a counter balance to the earls of Argyll in the Hebrides, it was unsuccessful. James married Agnes Campbell, the fourth earl's sister (who lent Mary Queen of Scots her highland dress when she visited Inveraray in October 1559). He joined the lords of the Congregation with 700 foot soldiers in opposition to the regent.[6]

One of Lachlan Mor's uncles by marriage was Donald Gorm Macdonald of Sleat. He was the closest in blood to the lord of the Isles and

Table 1: Some relationships between Lachlan Mor Maclean of Duest and his neighbours

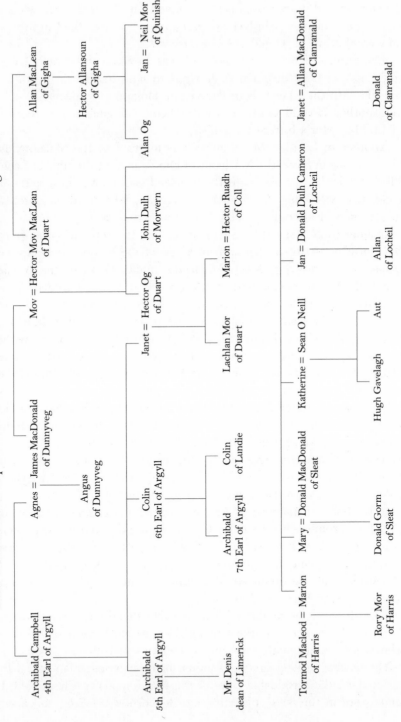

was for several years recognised by Queen Elizabeth as such.[7] He spent some time serving her in Ireland, perhaps even visited the English court and was known as Donald Gorm *Sasunach.*

The family of Sleat's landholding was in Skye and North Uist. In Skye they bitterly disputed their right to land in the Trotternish peninsula with the Macleods of Dunvegan. Donald Gorm *Sasunach's* heir, yet another Donald Gorm as well as being his cousin, was to be one of Lachlan Mor's bitterest enemies.

Another of Lachlan Mor's aunts was married to the Macdonalds of Sleat's rivals in Skye, the Macleods of Dunvegan. At the time of Lachlan Mor's birth the succession to the Macleod estates was in dispute. The legal heir was Mary Macleod of Dunvegan, who from 1562 to 1565 was a maid of honour to Mary Queen of Scots.[8]

In June 1559 Mary of Guise, in an attempt to keep him loyal, granted the ward, non-entry, relief and marriage of the heiress to James Macdonald of Dunnyveg. Mary Macleod's uncle Tormod, the Macleod heir-male, had been captured by the French allies of the regent. Argyll obtained his release and on 1st March 1559 Tormod made a bond of manrent to the earl. The latter agreed to try to establish him in his father's possessions. In return Tormod agreed not to marry without the earl's advice and to recompense Argyll and Hector Mor Maclean of Duart, Tormod's tutor, for their labours in regaining the Macleod estate and pay them the value of Mary's wardship and marriage.[9]

Four months later James Macdonald of Dunyvaig also made a bond of manrent with the earl and Argyll promised to maintain him in possession of Mary Macleod's wardship and marriage, whilst James agreed to resist any invasion by the French.[10] Despite this promise James lost this valuable piece of property and by 1566 Argyll had obtained Mary's wardship and marriage for himself.[11]

In his bond of manrent to Argyll Tormod agreed that if he failed in any of his promises he was to be 'Countit unworthy to bruik any rowmes of ane gentlemen for ewer in Scotland bot to be perpetualie deformit' and that the bond of kyndness between his house and that of the Macleans would be dissolved 'in all times coming'.[12] The Macleans and Macleods were traditional allies.

This alliance was reinforced when Duart's daughter, Marion, married Tormod. Their son was the famous Rory Mor Macleod of Dunvegan who was to be a major leader of mercenaries in Ireland.

Yet another of Lachlan Mor's aunts, Janet, married Allan son of John of Moidart, the formidable chief of the Macdonalds of Clanranald. His lands were in the isles of South Uist, Benbecula and Eigg and also on the mainland in Moidart and Arisaig. His 'caput' was the ancient castle of Eilean Tioram.

Allan's first wife had been a Macleod, the sister of Tormod. Allan is said to have deserted her to marry Lachlan Mor's aunt: a desertion which was the cause of much bad blood between the two families.

Another of Lachlan's aunts married Donald Dubh macDonald vic Ewen, Captain of Clan Cameron.

The Camerons and Macleans had been bitter enemies in the early years of the sixteenth century over the two clans' rights to lands in Lochaber and this marriage may have been the means to end the conflict.

It is unlikely that these marriages between Macleans and other major families in the Isles could have taken place without the agreement of the earl of Argyll and it is probable that they occurred at his direct command. Earlier earls of Argyll had attempted to bind the leaders of the Hebrides to their family by marrying their daughters to them and unite the island chiefs in one family unit. The problem with this method was that in Scotland at this time a woman was first and foremost a member of her father's kin and the marriage contract was not always a particularly strong form of alliance. This is why another method was needed to bind families together in one social group. This as we have seen, was the bond of manrent.

*   *   *   *

Two families of Campbells had an influence on Lachlan Mor's career as a result of incidents occurring in Hector Mor's lifetime. One was Campbell of Cawdor or Calder, the other Campbell of Ardkinglas.

The first Campbell of Cawdor was John, a younger son of the second earl of Argyll. His father had obtained the 'marriage' of Muriel the heiress of the ancient thane of Cawdor whose lands lay in Moray in north-east Scotland. In order to obtain the rich prize of the Cawdor estate for his son, the earl had Muriel kidnapped and brought to Argyll by Campbell of Inverliever. She eventually married John who became Campbell of Cawdor. He was not however satisfied with his wife's estate in Moray but made various attempts to obtain land in the Isles. In 1532 he received a grant of the lands of Muckairn from the bishop of the Isles.[13] Muckairn lies on the south side of Loch Etive. It consisted of sixteen touns which paid a rental of 125 bolls of black oats and 25 bolls of bere.[14]

On the other side of Loch Etive is the priory of Ardchattan. In the 1540s the prior designated John, Sir John Campbell of Cawdor's second

son, who is described as a noble youth, as his successor. He is likely to
have been one of Lennox's 'special friends' sent with letters to the
French king in 1543–4. If he is to be so identified, he was a sophisticated
young man who moved easily in the highest circles in the land.[15]

Mr John Campbell was nominated as bishop of the Isles in 1557, but
he probably never completed his title to the see which was vacant at
the time of the Reformation.[16] He sat in the Parliament which ratified
the Confession of Faith in August 1560. In September 1572 he succeeded
John Carswell as bishop of the Isles.[17]

Sir John Campbell of Cawdor had extended his influence by making
bonds of manrent with many of his neighbours, including Macdonald
of Dunyvaig.[18] He also made a bond of manrent with Hector Mor's
father but after he tried to dispose of his wife, Cawdor's sister, on a
rock in the Sound of Mull, Cawdor murdered him. This was an event
which was to be remembered and revenged by Lachlan Mor almost
seventy years later.

If the Campbells of Cawdor were enemies of the Macleans of Duart,
the Campbells of Ardkinglas were their allies. Ardkinglas is in the parish
of Kilmarich at the head of Loch Fyne. The family is an ancient Campbell
cadet descended from the third son of Sir Colin Campbell of Lochawe
who lived in the fourteenth century.[19] They became allies of the Macleans
of Duart after Hector Mor ransomed the Ardkinglas of the day from
James Macdonald of Dunyveg. The latter had kidnapped and forcibly
detained Ardkinglas in the islands. Mr Denis Campbell, the fifth earl's
illegitimate son, claimed that Hector Mor acted out of his love for the
fourth earl and that this was why the earl married lady Janet Campbell
to Hector Og.[20]

The ruthless and ambitious Campbells of Glenorchy were also allies
of the Macleans of Duart. A letter of Hector Og's survives, 'to my trusty
freind and cousing Colline Lord of Glenurquhey'. It is evident that
unlike his father Hector Og could write in Scots.[21]

The final major ally of the Macleans of Duart were the Macdougalls
of Dunollie. The Macdougalls were the heirs male of the ancient lords
of Lorn. Most of Lorn had passed by marriage to the Campbells, but
Dunollie held the north-west corner and the Isle of Kerrera. They were
closely related by marriage to the Campbells of Glenorchy and were
followers of the earl of Argyll.

The Macdougalls had seriously weakened their position by quarrels
within the family and through the rise of the Macdougalls of Ragray,
who were independent of Dunollie. The latter held a large chunk of the
family's old lands in mid-Argyll.

*　　*　　*　　*

To understand the background to Lachlan Mor's career one Maclean family remains to be noticed. This was the *Sliochd Ailein nan Sop*. They were Lachlan Mor's closest cousins and the next heirs if Hector Mor's descendants died without issue. *Ailein nan Sop* had acted as hatchet man for his brother. He had persecuted the Macleans of Lochbuie, seized the estate of Maclean of Lehir and been one of Donald Dubh's Council in 1545. Unlike his brother, on Donald Dubh's death he had transferred his loyalty to James Macdonald of Dunyvaig.

Ailein nan Sop or 'Allan Callit Sop', as he is identified by a clerk writing up the *Exchequer Rolls*, was formally 'Allan Maclean of Gigha', the estate of Macneill of Gigha which had been in non-entry having been granted to him in 1539.[22] Allan was dead by 1551. He was succeeded by his eldest son Hector, known as Hector Allansoun. Hector was an illegitimate son, born in 1532 and legitimated in 1547,[23] probably to enable him to succeed to his father's estates. These rights to the estate of Gigha had been challenged as early as 1540 when Annabelle Macneill, the heiress of the late Neill Macneill of Gigha, objected to the grant of non-entry to *Ailein nan sop*.

While Allan lived, the Macneills had little hope of regaining their patrimony. They tried again after his death, claiming in 1553 that the gift of the non-entry to Allan had been revoked in 1531 when it was realised that the late laird of Gigha and sixty of his men had been slain in the service of the crown by rebels in the Isles led by none other than *Ailein nan Sop*. This revocation was evidently ignored in January 1552 when Hector Allansoun received the gift of the non-entry, 'throw deceis of the said umquhile Alane'.[24]

The case of the Macneills against Hector Allansoun was heard in 1553 by William Hardy, sheriff of Tarbert, who found in favour of Hector. The royal rents on the land had however not been paid for sixty years and the sheriff was to distrain the 'moveable goods', i.e. cattle, on the lands until the royal rents were paid. Hector received a Great Seal charter of the disputed lands.[25] The sheriff had however decided that the Macneills should have full and free right of 'ingress' and 'egress' to the estate if within seven days they were able to pay Hector £16,611 18s. 4d, the sum for which it had been appraised.

This was not the end of the story.

On 9 March 1554 Neil Macneill sold his rights to Gigha to James Macdonald of Dunyvaig and his wife Agnes Campbell. Hector Allansoun evidently did not give up his inheritance without a fight. The earl of

Argyll probably was not prepared to have two of his major supporters at war with each other and his influence looms behind the agreement made on 24 April 1554, whereby Hector Allansoun agreed that he had no right to the disputed lands. Hector was 22 and spoke no English. He had therefore to have the agreement explained to him by the Justice Depute Sir John Campbell of Lundie 'in his awin language'. Hector next swore an oath on the 'holie evangelis' that he accepted the situation of his 'awin fre will uncompellit or tractit' and that he did so for his 'awin weil and proffit'. He had been paid 500 merks.

It was also agreed that as both Hector and his father Allan had had considerable expense in obtaining the non-entry of Gigha and maintaining the estate they should be repaid their expenses and discharged for any other rents they had received and for any 'guids and geir' they had taken away from Gigha or destroyed there. On their part both Hector Allansoun and his curator Hector Mor were to be 'secludit ... for ever' from the estate on pain of a fine of 500 merks. The agreement which was signed in Edinburgh was witnessed by the earl of Argyll, Donald Campbell abbot of Coupar and Colin Campbell of Ardkinglas.[26]

A clan in its looser sense might also include the clients and dependants of the leading kindred.[27] Hector Mor had in 1553 obtained the non-entry of John Macquarrie of Ulva.[28] The Macquarries were an ancient clan who had held their land directly from the lord of the Isles. They were now counted amongst the following of the Macleans of Duart.

The Macneills of Barra also followed Duart's lead. In 1587 Macneills of Barra were listed amongst 'the landlords and Baillies of landis in the Hielandis and Iles'. 'Clan Neill' is also among 'the Roll of the Clannis that has capitanes, chieffs and chieftanes quhome on they depend ...' in both 1587 and 1594. Curiously, however, neither roll states whether it is the Clan Neill of Gigha or of Barra which is referred to.[29]

Despite their independence Rorie Macneill of Barra was to describe Lachlan Mor as his 'chief and master' when in 1585 he made an obligation to the bishop of the Isles.[30] In 1595 Lachlan Mor stated that Macneill of Barra was his 'dependar' who served him 'in time of trouble with three hundred men'. He was a particularly useful follower as he was reputed to be the best seafaring warrior in the islands.[31]

The Clan Maclean was a highly complex body. It needed a man with considerable gifts to control it. It was specially in need of one in the mid-sixteenth century. For it was not for no reason that the sixteenth century is known in Gaelic as *Linn nan Creach*, the age of forays.

Notes

1. *Four Masters* V, 1605.
2. *RMS* iii (1513–46), 3085.
3. Gregory, 177.
4. *Origines Parochiales Scotiae* (1851–55) (*OPS*) ii, 1, 10.
5. SRO RD 1/1 H 313V–314R.
6. Gregory, 187.
7. *Calendar of State Papers (CSP) Ireland*, 154.
8. *Accounts of the Lord High Treasurer of Scotland*, xi , 227, 246, 349.
9. AT v, 132; *Book of Dunvegan*, 43–44.
10. Jenny Wormald, *Lords and Men in Scotland: Bonds of Manrent, 1442–1603* (1985), 185.
11. *Book of Dunvegan*, 45.
12. *Ibid*, 44.
13. AT iv (i).
14. *OPS* ii (i), 133.
15. Annie I. Cameron, *The Scottish Correspondence of Mary of Lorraine* (1927), 68–70.
16. *Scottish Gaelic Studies (SGS)*, xii, part i (1971), 96.
17. D. E. R. Watt, *Fasti Ecclesiae Scoticanae Medii Aevi ad Annum 1638 (Fasti)*, vii, 348.
18. *Lords and Men*, 255.
19. G. Harvey Johnston, *The Heraldry of the Campbells* (1977), 105.
20. Public Record Office (PRO) SP Eliz. Scotland VIII, 44.
21. SRO GD 112.39.1.4.
22. *RSS* ii, 1539.
23. *RSS* iii, 2361.
24. *RSS* iv, 1497.
25. *RMS* iv, 179–180.
26. SRO CS7/10 H 200r–201v & R D 1/3/2.
27. W. D. H. Sellar, 'Origins of the clans', in Derick S. Thomson, *The Companion to Gaelic Scotland* (1983), 43.
28. *RMS* iv, 801.
29. *Collectanea de Rebus Albanicis*, 35–40.
30. SRO RD1/27.21r & v.

CHAPTER 5

Feud with the Macdonalds

Macbeth: Is this a dagger, which I see before me,
The handle toward my hand? Come, let me clutch thee:–
I have thee not, and yet I see thee still.
Art thou not, fatal vision, sensible
To feeling as to sight? Or art thou but
A dagger of the mind, a false creation?

Macbeth Act II, Scene i

In January 1561/2 Randolph, the English agent in Edinburgh, wrote
to Robert Cecil, Queen Elizabeth's Secretary of State, that Argyll had
ridden to Glasgow to 'accord' James Macdonald and Hector Mor Maclean
of Duart, 'that lately fell out about the slaying of a man'.[1] This is the
first reference to the feud between the Macdonalds of Dunyvaig and
the Glens and the Macleans of Duart that was to dominate Lachlan
Mor's life.

The feud in Scotland in the late sixteenth century was a recognised
method of obtaining justice. It was acknowledged as such both by the
community at large and by the king himself. James might try to persuade
his subjects to abandon feuding. He did not however interfere with the
feud itself. He had neither the means nor a legal reason to do so. Even
so Scotland had, in the sixteenth century, seen a rapid growth in the
development of Scots law, law courts and the legal profession. It was
not a development which was universally applauded as litigants discovered that 'they were being asked to pay more, wait longer and receive
a judgement based more on points of law rather than on what they
regarded as justice'.[2]

There were several other reasons why men were dissatisfied with the
courts. If a crime was a capital one, then an execution was no more
acceptable to a kindred than murder would have been. Judges and assizes
were also too much a product of the feuding society in which obligation
to a friend and his kinsmen made it impossible for the law to be seen
as anything other than partisan justice.

A feud was also a method of dealing with an attack on a man's honour.

Honour and shame did not just affect an individual but his whole kin. In 1600, when the newly promoted marquis of Huntly appeared in the parliament, he demanded precedence over the earl of Angus, who had previously been ranked at the head of the earls in the order of precedence. Angus was an easygoing man, who had been instructed by the king to give way in order to prevent a quarrel. Angus's Douglas kinsmen, however, were not prepared to let him do so and 'protested never to acknowledge him hereafter, gif he did yeild that honour', which was purchased by the blood of their ancestors, and Angus was forced to stand up to both Huntly and the king.

Angus's kinsmen were making the point that to give in to Huntly would have been a signal to other men that the Douglas's were a pushover, that Angus was a weak lord and was unable to protect his family and friends. Loss of honour in sixteenth-century Scotland meant a real loss of power.

Use of feuding to settle disputes should not be overstated, however, even in the Highlands and Islands. For instance in the dispute between Hector Allansoun and the Macneills of Gigha concerning the latter's land, both parties resorted to the law,[3] in this case the sheriff court. Both parties also made sure that the result of the case was registered in the books of the Lords of Council and Session in Edinburgh and were to 'haif the strength of ane act and decreit of the lords thereof ...'[4] Hector Allansoun agreed to renounce any rights he had to Macneill of Gigha's property and Hector Mor was to see that he did so.

Compromise rather than conflict had characterised relations between Duart and Dunyvaig since the ending of Donald Dubh's rebellion, even to the extent that on 26 July 1546 Hector Mor renounced to James Macdonald all rights he had to the Rinns of Islay,[5] including the tack he had received only two months earlier of royal lands there.[6] This resignation must once again surely have been the result of the fourth earl of Argyll's influence. Maclean resentment was once again suppressed but it must have reached bursting point when on 9 March 1554 Neill Macneill sold Gigha and the rest of his property to James Macdonald and his wife Agnes Campbell, sister of the fourth earl.[7]

Gigha's estate did not just consist of the island of that name off the coast of Kintyre, it also included land in Kintyre itself, Knapdale and Islay. Islay was central to Clan Donald. One unidentified toun, 'Torlissay', had been included in Maclean of Duart's 1390 charter from the lord of the Isles. Duart's holding in Islay had increased in the late fifteenth century, when the 'caput' of his property there was close to the lord of the Isles' own castle at Finlaggan.[8]

Maclean of Duart's presence in Islay was probably always an irritant to the Macdonalds, but it was one that they were prepared to tolerate if Duart accepted that many of his lands there were held from Dunyvaig and not from the crown. Once the fourth earl was dead and his heir was more involved in politics of the court than those of the islands, Maclean discontent with what they saw as loss of face burst into flames. The spark that ignited the flame was the killing of the man that caused the fifth earl to hurry to Glasgow. Two weeks later a report reached Randolph that for the past fourteen days there had been a great convention of the 'Irish', as the islanders were considered to be. The convention was an attempt to defuse the situation. Maclean and Macdonald had however parted without agreeing. 'I see further mischief is begun', wrote Randolph's correspondent.

It was not long in coming. On 24 September 1562 the queen made a grant for seven years of 70 merks' worth of land in Islay to James Macdonald. This tack included land in the Rinns that was still occupied by Hector Mor's tenants. This was probably the new controversy between Macdonald and Maclean which Randolph reported to Cecil on 22 January 1562/3. He also reported that James was prepared to help the English in Ireland against O Neill.[9]

The quarrel between Duart and Dunyvaig now had an Irish dimension. James Macdonald was also the proprietor of the Glens of Antrim in Northern Ireland, which his ancestors had owned for almost two hundred years, despite the efforts of the English to drive them out. The Macleans had no property in Ireland but after the fourth earl's death his successor arranged to increase his influence there by marrying his widowed stepmother, Katherine Maclean, to his ally O Donnell. In May 1561 O Donnell was surprised and captured by Sean O Neill. It was believed that O Donnell had been betrayed by his wife. Whether this rumour was fact or not she became Sean's mistress.[10] It was a union which was also to have a profound effect on Lachlan Mor's career.

In September 1562 it was reported that three Macleans, kinsmen of the countess of Argyll, as Katherine Maclean was still called, were in Ulster offering O Neill 'great service' in exchange for Katherine's release. 'Great service' meant the provision of mercenaries to help O Neill in his war against the English, O Donnell and the Macdonalds. The latter had no love for O Neill, who had been married to James's daughter and had insulted him by sending her home.

In July 1563 both Maclean and Macdonald were summoned to Glasgow to appear before the queen to decide their quarrels. This meeting failed to reach a decision and they were ordered to bring documentary evidence of their claims to the Rinns of Islay to the Council. The case was heard on 24 April 1564. James was present, but Hector failed to attend, claiming that he was ill. He was ordered to pay James's costs.

When the Council finally made their ruling they decided that James was the crown tenant and that the Macleans, if they continued to remain in the Rinns, must hold their lands as vassals of Macdonald. It was a decision that infuriated the Macleans. The quarrel had now gone beyond recourse to the courts. Both James and Hector Mor were in Edinburgh on 1 January 1564/5. They were ordered to remain within the burgh on 'pane of tressoun'.[11] A week later James was ordered to keep the peace under a penalty of ten thousand pounds. Hector Mor was to leave his aggressive second son, John Dubh, in Edinburgh as a hostage for his own good behaviour.

Meanwhile James returned to Ireland with a huge body of mercenaries. He was however outmanoeuvred by O Neill and on 2 May 1565 defeated at Glenshesk. He and his brother Sorley Boy were imprisoned. James died of his wounds.

Whilst the Macdonalds were suffering at the hands of O Neill, Argyll was in arms against the queen as a protest against her marriage to the Roman Catholic Henry Stewart, Lord Darnley.

The Macleans became temporarily increasingly involved with Sean when he married his former mistress, Katherine Maclean. This event took place in late August 1565. Hector Mor was evidently present at the wedding.[12] The marriage did not last and as early as October 1565 Randolph was reporting that Maclean was in Edinburgh 'and the marriage is ended'. It was now proposed that O Neill marry James Macdonald's widow, Agnes Campbell.[13] She was however more interested in revenging her husband's death than marrying the man responsible for it.[14]

James's heir Archibald was also after revenge. He was reported to be with the earl of Argyll, who it was believed would no longer be sending mercenaries to help O Neill. This is perhaps the occasion when Archibald was reported to be coming to speak with the earl at Dunoon[15] when it is also noted that 'young Maclean is gone home with his friends'. Archibald parted good friends with the earl.

When Argyll, who had since 1560 been negotiating with Elizabeth to bring an army to Ireland in her service, made his peace with Mary she endeavoured to use his links with O Neill to stir up trouble in Ireland. Argyll, who was furious with England for ignoring him, agreed. Elizabeth was now faced with a pan-Celtic alliance which threatened her whole position in Ulster. This alarming prospect ended abruptly

when Sean, having been ambushed by O Donnell, took refuge with the
Macdonalds. He hoped to persuade them to join him. Two days of tense
hard bargaining followed. Sean and his advisers were fully aware of the
risks they ran. The volatile nature of Ulster politics and the gravity of
his own situation made the gamble worth taking. Sean however had
fatally miscalculated. The Scots suddenly fell on him and his companions,
killing all of them. It was put about that the killing followed a drunken
quarrel. Such a scenario is unlikely and it has recently been suggested
that Sidney, the Lord-Deputy, bribed the Macdonalds to assassinate O
Neill. [16] Sean's death is uncanniliy similar to that of Lachlan Mor thirty
years later, also at the hands of the Macdonalds.

Shortly before Sean's murder the Macleans raided Gigha. They burnt
houses and barns, stole cattle, killed some poor tenants and imprisoned
others.[17] Gigha now belonged to lady Agnes Campbell, James Macdonald's widow, and the raid was perhaps the result of Maclean frustration
at having lost a valuable asset. It is more likely that after their defeat
at Glenshesk it was believed that the Macdonalds were in no position
to retaliate. Whatever the cause, the earl was granted a commission of
lieutenancy against the Macleans on 28 April 1567. Three years later
at 'Carnassary' on 15 September 1570 Angus, who had succeeded his
brother as Macdonald of Dunyvaig and the Glens, and both Hector
Mor and Hector Og of Duart, submitted to the earl 'and his council'.
They agreed to abide by the earl's judgement concerning their disputes.[18]

No formal contract ending the first phase of the feud appears to
survive. If other feuds are a guide it is likely that both sides agreed not
to harm the other. The Macdonalds appear also to have accepted that
the Macleans continued to hold the Rinns which was in their possession
in April 1575.[19]

The settlement of a feud offered something to both sides. If the
Macleans remained in possession of Islay, perhaps they reaffirmed the
Macdonalds' right to Gigha. Marriages were sometimes included in a
peace settlement as a means of further binding two kindreds together.[20]
It therefore is likely that the end of the feud may have been on the
occasion when Hector Og's daughter Fynguala married Angus Macdonald. It has been argued that she was not the daughter of lady Janet
Campbell, but probably of some earlier liaison of Hector's.[21] If this is
so, by 1570 she would be old enough to marry Angus.

The earl of Argyll must have hoped that he had settled a feud that
greatly weakened his ability to recruit fighting men in the Civil War.
If he did, he was to be disappointed.

*   *   *   *

Angus Macdonald of Dunyvaig and the Glens was to be Lachlan Mor's greatest enemy. No description of him survives. It is only from his actions that it is possible to glean something of his character.

He was the second son of James Macdonald and lady Agnes Campbell. His elder brother, Archibald, is described in June 1566 as a boy of eighteen, so he must have been born about 1548. Angus could have been born the following year but he may have been even younger, as his sister the formidable Finola, known as *Ineen dubh* (*nighean dubh*) 'the dark daughter', was old enough to be married to O Donnell in 1569. Archibald, who is described as being 'not unlike his father', was dead by the end of 1566 or early 1567.

One gets the impression that their mother, lady Agnes Campbell, dominated Angus. She was one of those remarkable women in Argyll and the Isles who overwhelmed the men around them.

Agnes was a daughter of Colin 'lumpy brows', the third earl of Argyll, by an unknown mother. As Agnes is described as 'base sister' of the earl it is probable that her parents' union was not recognised by the church. She was however recognised as his sister by her brother the fourth earl and she is said to have been brought up at court.

Lady Agnes was first married to James Stewart, sheriff of Bute, who had succeeded his father in 1539.[22] She had a daughter by him but they quarrelled and she ran off only to be kidnapped and married by James Macdonald. In July 1555 her former husband, who lived until 1570, sued her for the return of a liferent of land he had made over to Agnes when they married. Agnes claimed that she had received a discharge from Stewart and that it was in the possession of her brother. She in turn, on 30 April 1557, sued the fourth earl for 300 merks of her tocher still in his hands.[23] What the result of the case was is uncertain.

Agnes had six children by James Macdonald, and when he died there was competition for her hand in Ulster. A Scots wife at the time was a highly desirable acquisition for an Irish chieftain as they were a means to obtain mercenaries. In 1569 lady Agnes and her daughter were described as being 'trayners of all Scots into Ireland as also conveighers of all commodities out of the realme, so that by these two woomen ariseth all mischief against thinglishe Pale'.[24] Eventually she married Turlough Luineach, who was now O Neill. She provided him with a Campbell bodyguard from the 1,000 men she had with her when she married him at Rathlin in April 1569. Despite her marriage to O Neill Agnes' priority was the well-being of her children by James Macdonald, and it is not unlikely that she only agreed to marry Turlough to further their careers. Agnes' sons' aim was to retain the Glens of Antrim, rather than lose it to their uncle Sorley Buidhe.

Agnes confused and infuriated the English authorities. 'And truly, sir', Sidney wrote to Walsingham, 'I found her a good counsellor to him [Turlough Luineach], a well-wisher to peace, and a reverent speaker of the Queen and majesty ... she was a grave, wise, well spoken lady, both in Scots, English, and French, and very well mannered'.

In 1575 Ralph Bagenal found her a 'verie nobell wyse woman, and as dutyfullie using herself to further the Queen's service every waye, as if she weare a naturall borne subjecte'. However, by 1577 Sidney had entirely changed his mind about her, when he wrote to the council that Turlough Luineach had become again rebellious, owing to the 'lewd counsel of his wife', who had 'a design to make her younger sons by James Macdonnell stark (strong) in Ireland'.[25] She is also accused of plotting to make Ulster a Scottish rather than an English province.

Turlough attempted to profit from his marriage by sending Agnes back to Scotland to recruit more mercenaries. When she did at last return in March 1571 Agnes wrote to Queen Elizabeth on her husband's behalf entreating the queen 'to receive my said husband O Neil in zour hienes service ...' She promised that if Turlough broke any of his promises to the queen, all those with whom she had any influence would desert him[26] In November 1571 Turlough and Agnes had another of their quarrels and she returned to Scotland, taking with her most of O Neill's mercenaries.

Notes

1. *CSP Scot* i, 1547–1593.
2. Keith M. Brown, *Bloodfeud in Scotland*, 1573–1628 (1986), 43.
3. *Warriors and Priests* (1995), 130–1.
4. SRO RD 1/3/2, 209v to 211 r.
5. SRO Macintosh Papers. G D 176, 149.
6. SRO GD 176, 149.
7. AT v, 32; SRO RD 1/3/43.
8. *Warriors and Priests*, 67–70.
9. *CSP Scot* i, 678.
10. *CSP Ireland* 172.
11. *RPC* i, 311.
12. *CSP Scot* ii, 203.
13. *CSP Ireland*, 296.
14. *CSP Scot* ii, 254.

15. SRO Breadalbane Papers GD 112/39/5/16.
16. Ciaran Brady, 'The Killing of Shane O Neill: some new evidence'. *Irish Sword* XV (1982), 116–23.
17. *Reports of the Royal Commission on Historical Manuscripts* (1870–)*HMC*, iv, 488; ATvi, 38.
18. AT vi, 15 Sept 1570.
19. AT vi, 12 Aug 1575.
20. *Bloodfeud in Scotland,* 58.
21. *SGS* Vol. xiii, 1, 60.
22. *Burke's Peerage* (1967), 397.
23. *Clan Campbell* viii, 28.
24. John Smith, 1569, quoted in Hayes-McCoy, 77.
25. George Hill, *Macdonnells of Antrim* (1873), 157.
26. PRO SP Elizabeth, Ireland, xxxi, 24.

CHAPTER 6

Hector Og

Old man. 'Tis unnatural
Even like the deed that's done. On Tuesday last,
A falcon, towering in her pride of place,
Was by a mousing owl hawk'd at and kill'd.
Macbeth Act II, Scene iv

Hector Og succeeded his father by 27 April 1571 when he witnessed a contract between the fifth earl and Donald Macdonald 'Gormeso-ne' of Sleat. In it Sleat accepted that he would lose 'the kyndnes and amitie that is betuix him' and Hector Maclean of Duart and his kin, if he failed in his duty to the earl.[1]

It is not known when Hector Og was born, but as he was old enough in 1540 to be named as heir apparent to the barony of Duart[2] it is probable that he was born before 1530. Hector Og made little impact on Maclean seanachies and perhaps he did not do so on his contemporaries. He had married lady Janet Campbell, the fifth earl's half-sister, and most of the surviving documents that mention Hector Og concern grants of land that he made to 'his beloved spouse'.[3]

In her marriage contract dated 28 October 1557 lady Janet Campbell 'in her pure virginity' received the liferent of land in Knapdale, Lochaber and Morvern.[4] After his father's death Hector Og showered lands on her. In 1573 he granted her the liferent of the 2d land of Ballichtrich in Gometra, off the coast of Mull. The following year he made over the six merk lands of Luing to her and shortly afterwards the barony of Lehir in Mull.[5] As the latter two properties are described as having a 'place' or 'mansion', they would have included houses which were rather larger than was usual at the time. Hector Og is also said to have built himself a residence in Iona situated at the head of Port-a-churreich, traces of which were still visible in the late nineteenth century. It was known as *Garadh Eachann Og*, 'the garden of young Hector'.[6]

In 1561 Hector Og had taken part in the raid on Maclean of Coll's land in Morvern.[7] In 1564 his father was reprimanded by the Privy

Council and his brother John Dubh was bound to remain in Edinburgh as a pledge for Hector Mor's good behaviour. Now that Hector Mor was dead, John Dubh was free to return to the islands.

John Dubh appears to have been a very different character to his elder brother. He is described by Mr Denis Campbell, dean of Limerick, as 'knowen to be of a craftie and subtle disposition'.[8]

In an extraordinary agreement made at the head of Lochaline in 1573 Hector Og granted his brother a tack of a vast holding of land in Morvern, Islay, Mull and Tiree. Hector Og also made John Dubh bailie over several of his own touns in Morvern and agreed that he should take his brother's advice in all weighty matters. It was also agreed that if Hector Og should send his forces into Ireland, then John Dubh should, in Hector's absence, have their command.[9]

Hector Og had given John Dubh control of the clan. Why he should have done so is not clear. He was perhaps already a sick man. His heir Lachlan Mor cannot have been more than fifteen, too young to control a turbulent clan.

John Dubh did not have control of the clan for long. His reputation, which was probably the reason he rather than Hector Og was left as a pledge in Edinburgh, alarmed the fifth earl. The latter as uncle to Lachlan Mor must also have thought that if John Dubh gained control of the Macleans there would be little chance of his nephew ever succeeding Hector Og.

The ink on the Lochaline agreement was hardly dry before John Dubh was seized by the earl's men and thrown into prison at Inchconnel or *Innis Chonnel* in Lochawe, 'quhair he has bene detenit sensyne in irnis in the maist strait and extreme maner'.[10]

The list of the witnesses to John Dubh's contract with his brother is instructive and gives a clue as to who was backing who in the struggle for power in the Clan Gillean. First listed is 'Charles Maclean, son to Allane'. He is probably the second son of Allan Maclean of Ardgour. Second on the list is 'Neill McVcAne abrych' who can only be Neil Mor using his patronymic as a surname.

This identification is supported by the extraordinary statement in the contract that Hector Og consents 'to his brother marrying the laird of Coll's daughter, if he can do so lawfully without slander or offence to the Kirk of God'. However, if he cannot marry her lawfully, he may use her at his pleasure, independent of the said Hector 'till God provide'.[11]

John Dubh is said to have had children by three wives.[12] Under the old pre-Reformation dispensation he could well have had them concurrently. However if, as seems likely, John Carswell and his colleagues had done their job effectively in the Isles, such arrangements were no longer acceptable.

It would appear from the wording of this contract that Hector Og was a supporter of the reformed church. It is also highly unlikely that the fifth earl would have agreed that his sister should marry anyone who was not a Protestant. It is also perhaps significant that Hector Og's marriage contract was witnessed by John Campbell, commendator of Ardchattan, and by Mr Alexander Campbell, dean of Moray, who both became Protestant bishops.

Hector Og evidently shrugged his shoulders over his brother's matrimonial arrangements. It is however certain that Hector Maclean of Coll, *an cleireach beag*, agreed to the 'marriage'. Not only was his brother Neil Mor a witness to the contract but there is surviving contemporary documentary evidence that refers to the affair. This evidence is an inventory of the 'Laird of Coll's writs' found at Inveraray Castle and published by duke Niall in the *Celtic Review* in October 1912.

One document listed is 'ane contract of mariage betuix John Dow and the laird of Coilles dochter'. The second is 'ane acquittance of Johne dow Mcclanes of twa hundryth merks in parte payment of ye tocher gude giffin with his concubine and apperand spous Margaret McClane', the 'tocher gude' being Margaret's dowry provided by her father for which John Dubh gave a receipt. The third writ is 'ane obligatioun of Johne dowis maid to abyd at the laird of Colles counsall baith be se and land'.

It is likely that the contracts were made at the same time as John Dubh's agreement with Hector Og, particularly as another writ is 'ane obligatioun of hector Mcclanes and Jon dowis for the soume of Vc merks (500) to be payit for Neill brother to ye laird of Coill'.

Hector Og and John Dubh probably had little other opportunity to act together.

It is curious that neither *an cleireach beag* nor his son Hector Roy witnessed the agreement at the head of Lochaline. However, Hector senior was by now an old man and had not even presented his own case to the Privy Council in 1564, whilst Hector Roy, who is known to have died young,[13] does not appear on record after 1564.[14] He may already have been sick, in which case it was perfectly natural that Neil Mor should act for his brother. Five hundred merks, an extremely large sum of money, may have been his price for accepting the contract.

Two of the writs listed in the inventory have so far come to light, one at Inveraray[15] and the other at the Scottish Record Office.[16] It is possible others will turn up, in which case it may be possible to prove that Neil Mor was backing John Dubh in May 1573.

One man was significantly not included in the witnesses to the agreement at the head of Lochaline. This was Hector Allansoun, Lachlan Mor's foster father. John Dubh was later to complain to the Privy Council that the fifth earl was persuaded to imprison him by Hector Allansoun. Certainly he had most to lose by the return of John Dubh.

Hector Allansoun had witnessed the bond of 1571, which marks Hector Og's succession and which, again significantly, was not witnessed by John Dubh. Also as Lachlan Mor's foster father Hector Allansoun was bound to protect his foster son's interests against the ambitions of a 'wicked uncle'.

It was also in Hector Allansoun's own interest to have John Dubh incarcerated. The 1540 royal charter to Duart had stated that *Ailein nan sop*'s descendants were to be the next heirs to the barony of Duart if Hector Mor's descendants were to fail.[17] Hector Allansoun had every reason to see that John Dubh remained in *Innis Chonnel.*

*   *   *   *

Meanwhile the Civil War had come to an end, as the supporters of Mary Queen of Scots reluctantly accepted that Mary's son the infant James was King James VI. James Douglas earl of Morton, the able and unscrupulous murderer of Darnley, was regent and the fifth earl was made chancellor. It was the highest office in the state and his price for being reconciled with the regent's government. Months later he was dead 'of the stone'.

The fifth earl left no legitimate issue and was succeeded by his half-brother, Colin Campbell of Boquhan. The sixth earl was a very different man to his brother. He is described by a contemporary as being 'religious and of good nature but weak in judgement and overmuch ledd by his wyf'. This formidable woman was Agnes Keith, the widow of the assassinated regent the earl of Moray. She had kept Queen Mary's jewels, 'thre greit dyamontis ... with ane greit jewell in the forme of ane H set with dyamontis'.[18] The jewels should have passed to the new government. The countess of Argyll however claimed that her late husband had not been paid for his expenses when he was regent. These royal jewels were to be a cause of dissension between Argyll and Morton.

One of the sixth earl's first actions was to make a progress through his regality holding courts in Lorn, Argyll and Cowal. In Lorn he hanged some 'eight score' who were convicted of slaughter, murder, theft or sorcery regardless of their 'estait or vocatioun'. He established ministers and readers in each parish, agreed stipends 'and had the prayeris, ministratioun of the sacramentis and forme of discipline after the ordour of Geneva translatit out of Englis in the Erische toung be Maister Jhone Carswale lait bishope of the Ylis'.[19]

During his progress the sixth earl also settled, for the time being, the feud between Angus Macdonald of Dunyvaig and the Macleans. The feud had flared up again over the Rinns of Islay and Angus besieged the castle of Lochgorm which was held by Hector Allansoun as bailie of the Rinns. During the seige the Macleans had carried away cattle from the Isle of Jura which belonged to Duncan, son of Mr Archibald Campbell.[20]

In December 1574 Hector Allansoun made a bond of manrent to the sixth earl which referred to earlier bonds of maintenance made by the fourth and fifth earls to his father. In his bond Hector is described as Hector Maclean of Ardlung, a property in the Isle of Luing. Hector's bond also referred to his duty to Maclean. His chief was not to require any men's loyalty for much longer for Hector Og was dead by 12 April 1575.

*   *   *   *

If the Macleans followed the normal practice of fosterage in the Highlands, it is likely that Lachlan Mor remained with Hector Allansoun until he was at least six and perhaps as old as nine. He would have brought cattle with him to his foster father. These would have been kept at Hector Og's expense and returned with their 'product' when Lachlan's time as a foster child came to an end. Hector Og would also have given Hector Allansoun's wife a silver brooch to be worn on her breast or a necklace to commemorate her role as foster mother. These gifts were highly prized.[21]

After he left Hector Allansoun's charge it appears that Lachlan was placed in the fifth earl's custody,[22] probably at Inveraray during the Civil War and then at Stirling where the earl had a house. It was probably during his time at Inveraray that Lachlan learned to write in both Scots and Gaelic. Examples of his handwriting in both languages survive and clearly he was well taught. He writes in a competent Gaelic hand and handles the literary dialect with confidence. The surviving letter in Gaelic is in the literary dialect and script. It is one of the few examples of such a letter written by someone who was not a member of the professional learned orders of contemporary Gaelic society to have survived. At the end of the sixteenth century the professional learned orders still included literary men, poets, genealogists and historians as well as musicians, physicians, ecclesiastics and perhaps lawmen.[23] Lachlan Mor was considered to be a cut above the normal Hebridean chief. A contemporary says that 'becaus Maclaynis educatioun was cevile, and brocht up in the gude lawis and maners of Scotland from his youth, it may be he hes had double consideratioun, one be kynd, and another be art of honest deliberatioun'. It was also believed that one of the causes of his feud with Angus was the latter's jealousy of Maclean.[24]

It is possible that Lachlan Mor learnt to write in Gaelic in Hector Allansoun's household. As we have seen, Hector did not speak Scots in his early twenties. He also could not write, at least in Scots. On several occasions when he witnesses a document he signs 'with my hand led on the pen ...'[25] An inability to sign one's name in Scots did not necessarily mean illiteracy in Gaelic, it merely meant an inability to write in the current secretary hand.[26] John Bannerman argues that 'the key to literacy in Gaelic among the laity lies in bardic poetry'. There had to be an audience for this poetry and it is inconceivable that it was not intended to be fully intelligible. If the poet required training to become proficient in his work, so did his audience to fully appreciate the results thereof. Because literacy was an integral part of that training, it could be assumed, even if no other evidence existed, that the ability to write Gaelic was likely to be relatively common, at least in the upper levels of lay society to whom the bard addressed the bulk of his output.

Whilst Lachlan was in the custody of the fifth earl 'for his better securitye in his country', the government of the Macleans was in the hands of his mother lady Janet Campbell and his foster father and when on 12 April 1575 Lachlan made a bond to repay Duncan Campbell for the cattle stolen from Jura during the siege of Lochgorm it was noted as being made at the desire of 'ane noble and potent lord Colin earl of Argyll ... our master and our freynds namlie Hector McClane allansoune'.[27]

Hector Allansoun strengthened his position by marrying lady Janet.[28] No contemporary evidence survives for this marriage but it is unlikely that Colin would have agreed to his sister forming a relationship that did not have the Kirk's approval.

Lady Janet appears to have had a daughter by Hector Allansoun. She married Neil Mor and, as we have seen, according to one version of the events leading up to his murder she reprimanded her husband for suggesting that 'her brother' could break his word. It is however possible that she was Hector Allansoun's daughter by another woman or even that she was Lachlan Mor's foster-sister.

*   *   *   *

During the Civil War the royal rents due from Hector Og for Morvern, Aros and Tiree had not been paid. In February 1576 the sixth earl agreed to become responsible for them. At about the same time Argyll probably purchased Lachlan Mor's 'ward and nonentrie, relief and marriage', although the 'gift' was not registered until 1581.[29]

At about the same time a quarrel arose between Colin of Argyll and John earl of Athol, which was not only to affect the remainder of Morton's regency but the subsequent history of the Macleans. The earl of Argyll was hereditary justice-general of Scotland. Mary Queen of Scots had, however, given Athol a commission of justiciary over his own territory . Colin demanded that this commission be annulled. Argyll was determined that the rule of law, which had been neglected during the Civil War, should be obeyed in his bounds. He was also jealous of his hereditary rights.

The immediate cause of the quarrel occurred when Athol refused to hand over two Stewarts, against whom Argyll alleged various crimes. At some time Athol seized two Camerons, whom he charged with murder. Argyll, who claimed the Camerons were his dependants, demanded that they should be handed over to him.[30]

Nowhere had the rule of law broken down so badly during the Civil War as it had in Lochaber. In 1569 Donald Dubh, captain of the Clan Cameron, had been murdered by his cousin John Dubh MacEwen mhic Ewen. The following year John Dubh Cameron's brother Donald of Erract was in turn murdered.[31] It was some of his murderers who were seized by Athol.

Argyll was not short of rivals at court. It was probably thanks to his enemies that on 15 February 1575–6 John Dubh Maclean's complaint about his imprisonment by Argyll was heard by the regent and the lords of the Secret Council.

John Dubh Maclean was represented by Mr Thomas Harvey, who had been imprisoned as a supporter of Queen Mary.[32] Morton and the Council considered the case and ordered Argyll by 1 April 1576 to obtain sufficient security that John would behave himself as a dutiful subject. Thereafter he was to set John at liberty. On 4 May at Holyrood the case again came before the regent and Council.[33] On this occasion, in addition to Mr Thomas Harvey, John Dubh was represented by Mr Lachlan Maclean, fourth son of Murdoch Maclean of Lochbuie.

They complained that, despite the regent's ruling, Argyll had no intention of releasing John Dubh. He had refused the offer of surety for John by Murdoch Maclean of Lochbuie, 'ane honest man' and a baron with an estate valued at more than £20,000. The earl however claimed Lochbuie's surety was insufficient and demanded that John Dubh's sister Katherine, the dowager Countess of Argyll, also stood surety.

Katherine Maclean had been the fourth earl's last wife. He had settled land in liferent on her in the barony of Craignish. Colin demanded that Lochbuie's whole estate and dame Katherine's liferent in Craignish should be the surety for John Dubh and would forfeit to Argyll if John Dubh misbehaved. John Dubh's procurators considered that these conditions 'are not ressonabill'. The Council agreed and Argyll was ordered to present John to them on 10 July 1576, 'as the said Erll will answer on his obedience'.

The feud between Argyll and Athol now began in earnest. On 23 June it was reported to the Council that 'of late slauchter and otheris enormities happynit betuix the friendis, servandis and dependaris of the erllis of Ergyle and Atholl'. They were commanded to desist and 'to compeir personalie with thair friendis and servandis in peciabil manner, not exceeding thre scoir persones, with ilk of thame on the 16 Nov. next'.[34]

Meanwhile Argyll had other problems to resolve in his regality concerning the longstanding feud between Clanranald and Macleod of Dunvegan. The situation was complicated by the fact that Allan, son and heir of John Moidartach, who seems to have led the Clanranald in his father's old age, had quarelled with his elder brothers Allan Og and Angus.

These elder sons' mother was a Macleod and they sided with her kin against their father's friends and dependants. On 14 September 1576 the Clanranalds represented by John Moidartach, himself and his son Allan met Argyll's commissioners at Ardlung. These commissioners were all Campbells. John Moidartach and Allan gave a bond of manrent to the earl. They also agreed to resign the lands of Glenelg to Macleod and to refer all differences between them and Macleod to the earl. In exchange Argyll was bound to maintain and defend them and to 'do diligence' on Macleod, presumably to leave them in peace. They also agree to enter into the earl's service, join with the Macleans and as soon as Lachlan Maclean of Duart 'or his deputes and friend are sent to the North Iles' take part with the 'Clan Layne and the rest of his Lorships dependers wherever they are ordered to'.

Clanranald was also to deliver 'Donald mak allan vic eain gotten upone Janet Makclayne' to Lachlan who was in turn to deliver him to Argyll as a pledge for their good behaviour. This Donald, whose mother was a daughter of Hector Mor, was eventually to become captain of Clanranald. He was probably the cause of his half-brother's resentment. Lachlan and Hector Allansoun, described as 'Baillie of the Rinns of Islay', were to be cautioners for Donald's delivery. The Clanranalds also accepted that the Macleans would invade their territory if they broke any of the conditions in their bond of manrent. This bond underlines the fact that the Macleans were now acting as if they were kin to Argyll.

Notes

1. AT v.
2. *RMS* iii, 2065.
3. AT v, 1 Jan 1573/4.
4. *RMS* iiv (1546–1580), 1240; AT v, 28 October 1557.
5. AT 8 February 1572/3; 1 January 1573/4; 11 February 1573/4.
6. J. P. Maclean, *A History of the Clan Maclean* (1889), *JPM*, 90.
7. *RPC* i, 311.
8. State Papers (SP) Elizabeth. Scotland LVIII, 46.
9. AT, 14 May 1573; *HMC* 6th Report, 625 prints part of this agreement. It does not list the witnesses.
10. *RPC* ii, 491.
11. AT 14 May 1573.
12. SRO NLS MS 7609, 57.
13. SRO NLS MS 7609, 38.
14. *RPC* i, 311.
15. AT, 28 June 1558.
16. GD 111/4/2.
17. *RMS* iii, 2065.
18. *RPC* ii, 330.
19. *CSP* (Calendar of State Papers) 1574–1581, 28.
20. AT 12 April 1575.
21. J. L. Campbell, *A Collection of Highland Rites & Customs*, 82.
22. PRO SP Ellizabeth. Scotland LVIII, 46. Mr Denis Campbell states that he had known Lachlan Mor for 26 years when he wrote his report for Sir Robert Cecil in 1596. It is therefore probable that he came to Inveraray in 1570 when he was 12.
23. John Bannerman and Ronald Black, 'A Sixteenth-Century Gaelic Letter', *SGS* xiii, part i, 62.
24. Anonymous, *The Historie and Life of King James the Sext* (1825), 217, 219.
25. AT 12 April 1575.

26. John Bannerman, 'Literacy in the Highlands', in Ian B. Cowan & Duncan Shaw (eds), *The Renaissance and Reformation in Scotland* (1983), 229.
27. SP Elizabeth. Scotland LVIII, 46; AT vi.
28. National Library of Scotland (NLS) Acc 7609, 13.
29. SRO PS 1/48.
30. Donald Gregory, *The History of the Western Highlnads* (1881), 214–5.
31. Pitcairn's *Criminal Trials* i, 33. These murders are discussed at length in John Stewart of Ardvorlich, *The Camerons*, 269–276.
32. *RPC* ii, 491.
33. *RPC* ii, 519–521.
34. *RPC* ii, 533, 546.

CHAPTER 7

Lachlan Mor's Coup d'état

Macbeth. If it were done – when 'tis done –
then 'twere well
It were done quickly.

Macbeth Act I, Scene vii.

John Dubh was probably released from his captivity at *Innis Chonnel* Castle towards the end of 1576. His release altered the balance of power in the Clan Maclean. It also occurred at a crucial moment in Lachlan Mor's adolescence. He was now eighteen and must have been increasingly frustrated by his uncle Colin's control of his actions. This frustration was probably focused on his immediate governors, his mother and his foster-father.

There would not have been a shortage of those wishing to persuade him to cast off his curators. Mr Lachlan Maclean, Lochbuie's son, who probably still felt that his family's honour was compromised by the murder of his uncle and ravaging of his estate by *Ailein nan Sop*, had been at the forefront of the attempt to obtain John Dubh's release from *Innis Chonnel*. Katherine Maclean, countess of Argyll, and her latest husband John Stewart of Appin also appeared to have been in John Dubh's camp. Hector Allansoun was outmanoeuvred. Significantly he does not appear as a witness to any agreement after the great convention at Ardlung in September 1576.

In March 1577 the plotters struck. Mr Lachlan persuaded a gatekeeper, perhaps at Ardlung, to betray his charge. Hector Allansoun was seized in his bed and transported to Duart where he and his son Allan Og were incarcerated and held in irons. The sixth earl was probably furious at the overthrow of his sister and client, whom he was bound by his bond of maintenance to protect. There was however little he could do openly, as he had too many problems with Athol to risk alienating the Macleans. In the short term at least Lachlan had to be placated.

On 11 July 1577 a great convention was held at Inveraray to ratify the agreement made at Ardlung between the earl's commissioner and Clanranald. On this occasion Tormod Macleod of Dunvegan himself was present to accept Clanranald's surrender of Glenelg. Macleod also agreed to act as cautioner for the good behaviour of Clanranald's rebellious sons, Allan Og and Angus.

Much was made at the convention of the importance of Lachlan Mor. His 'assistance and counsell' to the earl are specifically mentioned. It is almost as though Argyll was going out of his way to boost his nephew's ego. Hector Allansoun is not mentioned.

John Dubh was now his nephew's closest confidant. On 26 September 1577 at Dunoon in the presence of Lachlan Maclean of Duart, 'my chief', who was a witness, John Dubh made a bond of manrent to the earl.

In the meantime Argyll's feud with Athol was over. As early as July 1577 the English agent Bowes reported to London that Athol believed that the regent was not seriously trying to reach a settlement between him and Argyll. Instead Morton was hoping to prolong the feud for his own purposes. The two earls decided to call the regent's bluff. Their first action was to sign a bond jointly to assist the master of Mar, the king's guardian, to defend the king. This bond was signed on 22 October 1577, although it is unlikely that it was made public for some time.

Colin's increased truculence was apparent in November when David Harper, a messenger, attempted to deliver royal letters to the earl, who was hunting at Loch Eck in Argyll. Instead of allowing the messenger to come near him the earl 'spurred his horse' away from Harper. When Argyll was at a distance from him, Harper saw the earl stop and speak to some of his servants. They returned and beat him up.

The regent was not lacking in means to curb Argyll. The earl and his kinsman, John Campbell of Cawdor, had agreed to bring the two Camerons who had murdered Erracht before the Council. This they failed to do. In January the regent 'with advise of the saidis Lordis' fined the cautioners £1000.

Colin had not attended the Council since 6 August 1577. He also failed to answer Harper the messenger's complaint against him. Worse was to come. In February 1577–8 word reached Edinburgh that Argyll had sent out a proclamation to his vassals to assemble to invade Glengarry. The regent in turn sent letters to Lovat and other lairds in the north-east Highlands to go to Glengarry's assistance and on 20 February a letter was sent to Lachlan Maclean of Duart ordering him not to join Argyll.

On 2 March 1577–8 Argyll arrived in Stirling to be cordially welcomed by the master of Mar. Athol was believed to be heading there too. The following week a convention summoned by Argyll and Athol assembled at Stirling. Morton had been outmanoeuvred. On 8 March he was dismissed as regent.

It is probable that the alliance between Argyll and Athol was to be strengthened by marriage. Huntly's heir married Argyll's eldest daughter. In this case financial arrangements which accompanied the marriage contract may also have been used to cover compensation without loss of face.

According to Dr Hector Maclean, the eighteenth-century historian of the clan, the king proposed a match between Lachlan Mor and the Athol heiress. Lachlan, however, on his way home to prepare for the wedding, visited the earl of Glencairn, where he fell in love with his daughter Margaret. By marrying her he lost the great estate of Athol.

Unfortunately for the accuracy of this story there was no Athol heiress for another generation and Dorothea Stewart the heiress, who carried the estate of Athol to Murray of Tullibardine, could not have been born until 1580, the year in which her parents were married. But it is clear from contemporary evidence that Lachlan married contrary to the wishes of his uncle Colin. Mr Denis Campbell writes that Lachlan, 'unadvisedly matching himself with William earl of Glencairn's daughter without the privitye or consent of earl coline ... procured his high displeasure'.[1]

Colin had good reason to be furious. Not only did he own Lachlan's 'marriage' but Glencairn, although a staunch Protestant, was not an ally of his. Glencairn also had had ambitions in Kintyre and Islay where he had been the late king's governor and had endeavoured 'to use good husbandri' there to the king's behafe ... being a soyle in dede for the most parte fertil and pleasant, in comparison of most parte of these countryes'.[2] In doing so Glencairn was infringeing on Argyll's sphere of influence.

Glencairn's marriage contract with Lachlan Mor has survived. It is dated 30 December 1577. Lachlan agreed to give Margaret Cunningham ten thousand merks' worth of land within the sheriffdom of Lennox, Renfrew or baillery of Cunningham 'or other landis neir thereto adjacent in the Lowlands'. Land in the Highlands and Islands was evidently not acceptable.[3]

The sixth earl was not a man to take Lachlan Mor's defiance lying down. He had lost face and in a society where a man's honour was of paramount importance, shame could only be redeemed by the shedding of blood.

Lachlan was later to claim that in March 1577/8 the earl conspired with John Dubh to murder him. The plot to murder Lachlan was apparently one part of the plot to teach the Macleans a lesson, for

Argyll also persuaded Angus Macdonald of Dunyvaig, assisted by 'certayne forayne enymeis' from Ireland, to invade Maclean's property in Islay. The castle of Lochgorm was besieged by 1200 men. In addition the earl sent the laird of Lochnell's brother and John MacConachie of Inverawe with two hundred men by land, supported by a galley, to assist Angus.

Lachlan must now have decided that the gloves were off and that he would eliminate Argyll's allies in Mull and put the fear of God into any waverers. He struck first against Hector Allansoun's family who were still at large. On 15 April 1578 his servants seized Donald, son of Hector Allansoun's brother John Dowrache, and incarcerated him in Carnaburg. Ten days later his men invaded Coll. They surprised the garrison at Breacachadh and 'mannit and stuffit the said castell in weir lyke manner'. Coll's tenants were thrown 'out of their awin roumes, housis and boundis ... and put to extreme povertie'.

At the same time Hector Allansoun and his son Allan Og were transported to the castle of Coll where Lachlan 'maist cruelie and unnaturallie causit streik the heid fra the umquhile Hector'. Mr Denis Campbell states that Hector Allansoun 'by due course of lawe was beheaded by McIllaine (i.e. Maclean)'. If so he was probably executed on Hangman's Hill across the machair from Breacachadh Castle, which is reputed to be the place of execution of the barony of Coll. What Hector Allansoun's crimes were is not stated. Allan Og was thrown into the dungeon.

Why Lachlan should have made an example of Maclean of Coll is not clear. No documentary evidence survives to show that Hector Maclean of Coll was an adherent of either Argyll or Hector Allansoun. On the evidence already noticed it would seem more likely that Coll was allied to John Dubh. It is however possible that John had already discarded Margaret.

It is also possible that Hector Allansoun had made a subsequent alliance with Hector Maclean of Coll. Marion, daughter of Hector Og Maclean of Duart and Lady Janet Campbell, married Hector Maclean, younger of Coll. It is unlikely that they were married before the second half of the 1570s as Marion could not have been born before 1558. In view of subsequent events it is certain that the marriage took place before Lachlan's coup d'état. It is therefore more than likely that the marriage was intended to cement relations between Hector Allansoun and the Coll family. Instead it almost caused its ruin.

Argyll was not only having problems in the Isles. He was also having them at court. At Stirling on 27 April 1578 the earl of Mar accused his uncle, Argyll's ally the master of Mar, of exceeding his powers. In the ensuing mêlée the master's son was mortally wounded. As a result the earl of Mar displaced his uncle in charge of the king. The scene was set for a return to power of the earl of Morton and the eclipse of Argyll.

Meanwhile Argyll was doing his best to ruin Lachlan. In July Duart's servant, Fergus McBreon, was arrested as he was travelling through Argyll and held in Carrick Castle. This was the beginning of a concerted campaign to cut Mull off from the lowland markets where Lachlan's friends and tenants could sell their cattle. Proclamations were made at ports and landing places where the cattle were landed which stated that Maclean's goods were to be impounded.

Lachlan reacted in November by raiding the earl's ally George Montgomery's Isle of Meikle Cumbrae in the Clyde and seized a boat belonging to Adam McKy whom he imprisoned in Dumbarton. In both these raids Lachlan was assisted by John Smollett, burgess of Dumbarton, who had witnessed Lachlan and Margaret Cunningham's marriage contract and appears to have been increasingly in Lachlan's confidence.

Argyll in turn counter-attacked and John Og Maclean, who is probably Hector Allansoun's nephew, now described as Argyll's servant, rescued Adam.

On 18 December the earl took more drastic action when he seized Lachlan's secretary, John Achincross, and detained him and two other servants of Duart and held them in irons. The same month he struck at the Isle of Luing, which was attacked by 200 men. 500 cattle, 200 horses and 1200 sheep were carried off and Lachlan's servants, including George Smollett the captain of Luing, were held to ransom.

On 29 December Lachlan petitioned the king at Stirling. He complained that Argyll had tried to get John Dubh to murder him and of all the other mischief the earl had caused. It is not clear whether or not Lachlan was personally present to present his petition. He probably was not. However, Argyll was at the Council on 29 December and as no copy of the complaint survives in the *Records of the Privy Council*, it is likely that he had Lachlan's complaint removed from the records.

Details of Adam Mcky's complaint, which were heard the same day, were recorded and the Lords decided that as Adam was now at liberty both Lachlan and John Smollett should be absolved of the charge. James master of Glencairn, Lachlan's brother-in-law, however agreed to stand caution to present the other Macleans charged at the Tolbooth in Edinburgh in January to answer the charges against them. The following day the master of Glencairn again stood caution in £500 for Lachlan himself, guaranteeing that 'Janet Lady Dowart and her tenants shall be harmless of him'. Lachlan evidently still regarded his mother as being committed to her late husband Hector Allansoun. Such disputes between a widow and children were not uncommon in Scotland.[4] Female land-owners were seen as a soft target by acquisitive neighbours and their own family. Lady Maclean was a considerable landowner. For her and others like her the best defence lay in a new marriage and Janet was soon married again, this time to Tormod Macleod of Dunvegan. They were married by 3 December 1583 when he made her a grant of 24 merks of land in Glenelg in liferent.[5]

Glencairn could now be excused if he wondered how good a bargain he had obtained when his sister married Lachlan. However, the master himself was no shrinking violet. In 1576 he had ambushed the laird of Houston and taken him prisoner and killed two of his servants. Later he agreed to his rival the earl of Eglinton's assassination: an event that was the beginning of a feud that was to tear Ayrshire apart. It was also to last for more than 20 years.[6] On 16 June 1578–9 the Glencairns were bound to guarantee that Lachlan would not molest John Campbell, bishop of the Isles. On this occasion their surety was for £5000.

If Lachlan had hoped that his complaint against Argyll would make him the aggrieved party in the eyes of the council, his case was weakened by his uncle's actions. In January 1578–9 John Dubh raided Gigha. Gigha was still held in liferent by lady Agnes Campbell, lady Tyrone. This much-married lady was not only Colin's aunt, she was also the mother of Angus Macdonald of Dunyvaig. She was thus doubly fair game as far as the Macleans were concerned.

The Macleans devastated Gigha. Not only did they kill 'nyne of the maist honest men with the said yle, togidder with twa women, without pitie or compassioun of their estait', they also carried away 500 cattle, 1300 horses and mares and 2000 sheep and destroyed houses and corn. Others raided Inishowen in Ireland to punish O Docherty for his assist-ance to Argyll in raiding Lachlan's land in Islay.

Lachlan's crimes were now to catch up with him. On 10 April 1579 Mr Thomas Craig appeared as procurator for Hector Maclean of Coll to complain of Lachlan's seizure of his castle and lands and treatment of his tenants. 'Unless', Mr Thomas complained, the lords of the Privy Council 'provide sum present and sum more remedie of this inordinat oppressioun and outrage the said Hectour wil be utterlie wrakit for ever.' He also made the point that Coll was a 'frie subject, na wayis is astrictit to the said Lachlane, nor he havand na manner of jurisdiction or auctoritie above the said Hectour'.

Although Lachlan was 'oftymes callit', he did not compear and was put to the horn. Complaints by Allan Og, Hector Allansoun's son, Donald son of John Dowrache and lady Tyrone followed. On each occasion Lachlan was denounced and again put to the horn. Lachlan was now an outlaw and his estate was forfeit.

Lachlan Mor had brought down a hornets' nest about his head. It could be argued that he was led astray by his turbulent uncle John Dubh. It could also be said that he was merely proving himself to his clan, showing that he was afraid of no one. This was particularly important if, as Doctor Hector Maclean (see Postscript) stated, Hector Allansoun had spread the rumour that Lachlan was a weak, effeminate character who was unfit to lead the clan. It does however seem equally likely that Lachlan gloried in his bad behaviour, that he was naturally unstable and violent and that, unlike his uncle the fifth earl, he preferred bloodshed to reason.

*   *   *   *

Lachlan Mor's marriage to Margaret Cunningham had effectively destroyed the policy the Macleans of Duart had followed for a generation. Since 1543, when Hector Mor had made his bond of manrent with Argyll, the Macleans of Duart had been consistent in allying themselves with the earl. Even when Hector Mor joined Donald Dubh's rebellion, he did so only to destroy it.[7]

This policy had been highly successful, as had Hector Mor's policy of marrying his daughters to other leading islanders. As the dean of Limerick wrote, the Macleans' faction 'was thought muche the stronger' than Dunyveg's 'by reason of his consinguinitie with the principall lords of the islands'.[8]

According to the dean, James Macdonald of Dunyvaig had married lady Agnes Campbell to obtain the earl's favour. However, 'this policie ... did gaine him no creditt or trust'. Furthermore James's children by Agnes, 'following altogether the disposition of theire father, have the same regard of us [Campbells], being perswaded that upon eny advantage, if they were not kept under, they wold utter theire malice; their inclination being prowd, vaine glorious, disdainefull and treacherous, still affecting to re-establishe the dignetie of McDonell'. Argyll had as a result favoured Maclean in his feud with Dunyvaig.

Lachlan Mor had thrown away these advantages and the sixth earl 'did countenance Angues McConell against him, almost duringe his life'. Lachlan Mor had also broken the laws of the kingdom. More important in the eyes of his fellow Gaels, he had broken the almost sacred duty he owed to his foster-father. The dean might argue that Hector Allansoun was executed 'by due course of lawe', but Gaelic society must have shaken its head in horror.

Denis Campbell says that this action was 'by the procurement and practise of John his uncle'[9] whose influence is stamped on all the events that had happened since Lachlan and Margaret's marriage contract was signed at Irvine in 1577. John Dubh's hatred of Hector Allansoun is easy to understand. His vicious behaviour towards Maclean of Coll is more difficult to interpret unless his marriage with Coll's daughter had broken down.

The savagery on both sides in the short but vicious feud between Lachlan Mor and the sixth earl suggests that beneath the relative calm in the Isles during Hector Mor's long career, anger was simmering away. The mid-sixteenth century was a time of major climatic change throughout northern Europe. By the 1570s the 'little ice age' had probably begun to take its toll of the agricultural resources of the Hebrides. More land was required to provide the same food as in the past. Traditional genealogies suggest that leading families had a large number of children. If this pattern was repeated throughout Hebridean society, it is probable that the population was rising. These pressures would have encouraged raiding, desire for more land and general instability. The quarrel between earl Colin and Lachlan Mor had triggered off an explosion.

A feud of such intensity could not continue for long or the Isles would have descended into total anarchy. Lachlan Mor evidently was forced to hand back Coll's castle and estate to him and Allan Og, Hector Allansoun's son, was released from his captivity.

On 27 August 1579 a great convention of the clans was held at Inveraray. Allan Clanranald and his young son agreed to send in pledges and although the earl wished them to return home, they remained at Inveraray. Lachlan Mor and Angus agreed to cease hostilities until 'Hallomes nixt'. There was however 'na assurance betuix McClane' and the earl, other than that the latter gave Lachlan 'a license to pass hame to his kynd and cuntrie', provided that he gave up John Dubh, Rorie Macneill of Barra and 'twa of his friendis'.[10] These two friends, i.e. his kinsmen, were Allan Og and 'Lauchlan McConnell wracheneich'[11] who is perhaps Lachlan Odhar Maclean of Ardchraoshinish.

If these pledges were not handed over, the earl was to 'pas with ane armie upon clan lein'.[12] Lachlan Mor evidently later did come to terms with the earl and agreed that if he did not keep to his agreement with him the earl should deal with the pledges 'at his pleasure'.

Lachlan also agreed to hand over to the earl by charter and sasine forty merklands worth of land to be chosen by Argyll. This land was to remain in the earl's hands until Lachlan made reparations for the armed incursion into Ulster against O Docherty.[13] Lachlan was also forced to sell other land to pay his debts and on 24 February 1579–80 he sold the four merklands of the Isle of Torosay, off Luing, to Duncan Macdougall fiar of Dunollie. Later that year he sold him a further twelve merklands in Luing and on 28 August 1580 sold another four merklands there to Archibald Campbell of Melfort.[14]

The earl's 'countenance' of Angus took a practical form. In June 1579 he had acted as Angus's cautioner when the latter agreed 'to fortife, mentyne and defend Johnne bischop of Ilis ... [and] pas with our forssis throw all the Ilis with him to caus all otheris within the boundis mak him paymint or ellis thair reddiest gudis and geir'[15] would be seized. Angus also agreed that if the bishop decided to 'comprise', i.e. take back, any church land Lachlan Mor had received in Islay or Kintyre, then he would take a just infeftment of these lands 'as men of law can devyse' and would pay the bishop as high a rent as had ever been paid for them in the past.[16] The bishop was a Campbell of Cawdor, the ally of Dunyvaig. Angus, with the earl's encouragement, was striking the Macleans of Duart where it hurt most in their holding of land.

Lachlan Mor's holding of church land was certainly vulnerable. In 1573, as part of the General Assembly's plans to reorganise the finances of the Kirk, the bishop had been instructed to produce the rental of the bishopric of the Isles, abbacy of Icolmkill and priory of Ardchattan.[17] This return was not registered in the official records. A copy however was discovered by Donald Gregory in 1834 in the charter chest of Sir John Campbell of Airds and Ardnamurchan, Bart. Airds was a cadet of Campbell of Cawdor. It is published in *Collectanea De Rebus Albanicis*. Some of the lands listed were those granted to Hector Mor by John Carswell. Their rents had been paid to the bishop in Hector Mor and Hector Og's time.[18] They had not been paid during Lachlan Mor's minority,[19] nor when he gained full control of his estate. His friends now began to molest the bishop's servants[20] who were prevented from uplifting the teinds.

In March 1579 the bishop complained of the conduct of John Dubh Maclean, bailie of Morvern, Murdoch Maclean of Lochbuie and his sons and other islanders. Angus of Dunyvaig is also accused of the same offence, as were several of his allies,[21] and it is probably as a result of this complaint that he made his obligation to the bishop the following June. It was Lachlan Mor's turn now to make peace with the bishop to forestall any further advantage going to Angus.

John Campbell had had enough of the Islands. He resigned the commend of Ardchattan to his son Alexander in June 1580 [22] and on 6 June
1581 transferred the commend of Iona to him as well.[23] It had been
agreed that John should continue to enjoy the fruits of both Ardchattan
and Iona. The agreement between father and son did not however run
smoothly.[24]

In December 1580 Lachlan Mor met the bishop of the Isles at Ardchattan to resolve their dispute concerning the rents of the lands he
held from the bishop and to make arrangements concerning the teinds.[25]
At this meeting it was pointed out that Lachlan, as hereditary bailie of
the bishopric and abbey of Iona should be defending the bishop's pri-
vileges. Instead he was doing the reverse. Lachlan now bound himself
to allow the bishop to enjoy 'the Isle of Icolmkill, landis and barony of
Ross, half the toun of Ballefuil in Tiree and the grange of Kilmorie in
Islay as any bishop or abbot ... since the first foundation of the said
place of Icolmkill'.

He also agreed to take Lauchlane Mcdonnell McConych and his galley
for service 'of the saidis landis of Rosse' and should not appoint a
stewart-depute to Ross during the bishop's lifetime. He also agreed not
to let anyone oppress the tenants of Iona and Ross or take any 'stenting,
canyow gerig service' except that 'four men out of Ross and four men
out of Iona should keep the fortalice of Carnaburg upoun their awin
expensis salang a McClane is in oisting to his returneing'. He also
agreed 'to causs the haill tyndis of Mull to be thankfullie payit to the
said Reverend fader, and that the teinds of Tiree should conform to an
assessment made by John Maclean baillie of Morvern, John Campbell
of Eriska, the bishop's son and three other jurors'. Lachlan was also to
pay the bishop a thousand merks in part payment of the 'bygone mailes
and dewitees of the Kirk landis that he owed to the bishop and to the
said abbey of Iona since he became bishop'.

Lachlan was also to produce the feu charter of lands belonging to
the bishopric and abbacy to Sir Newyn MacVicar Commissar of Argyll
and Dougal Macarthur notary public by 28 December 1580. In exchange
for all these conditions the bishop agreed to obtain the letters of poinding
and horning from the lords of the Secret Council and Session. Although
John Campbell had resigned the abbacy of Iona to his son, he retained
the bishopric of the Isles. In October 1582 he was complaining to the
Privy Council that he was being made to pay a tax on his benifices
although he was despoiled of his revenues and had been obliged 'to leif
the cuntre ... this long time by past'.[26] Lachlan Mor had made Mull
untenable for the bishop.

*   *   *   *

In his letter to James Menzies, laird of Weem of 29 August 1579 reporting news of the meeting of the clans at Inveraray, Alexander MacNaughton of Dunderave wrote that the 'kingis grace has send to my Lord Ergile ane wryttin that came to his majestie from the Duik of Obenie [Esmé Stewart, seigneur d'Aubigny] out of France men and that the said Duik was on the seie cumind to Scotland. It is reportit that he desyris to be Erle of Lennox becaus yat he is nearest lynale dissen-dit'.[27] On 8 September Esmé Stewart arrived at Leith. His arrival marked the beginning of the end of Morton's regency.

The king, now a precocious boy of 12, quickly fell under his cousin's spell. By the end of the following year Morton was outmanoeuvred by his enemies and was accused of Darnley's murder. He was executed on 2 June 1581. Among the beneficiaries of Morton's downfall was the comptroller James Campbell of Ardkinglas, who obtained among other gifts the debt of £594. 4sh. 4d which the earl of Argyll had owed to Morton since 1576 as cautioner for the debt Lachlan owed the crown for the rents of royal lands in Morvern, Mull and Tiree.[28] On 26 July John bishop of the Isles obtained the gift of the escheat (property, possessions or goods, taken from a person by forfeiture) of several islanders including Lochbuie and Lachlan Mor, who were at the horn for the non-payment of their teinds etc for the years 1575–1578.[29] Lachlan had not kept his part of the agreement he made at Ardchattan. When the bishop made his will in October 1585 he left Lachlan Mor's estate to John Campbell of Cawdor.[30] It was another cause of enmity between the two families.

The earl had not yet finished with Lachlan for marrying without his permission. In May he summoned him before the Court of Session, claiming that he had the gift of marriage, which had been formally registered on 15 July 1581, of 'Lachlane McClane now of Dowart sone and aire of umquhill Hector Macklane of Dowart and faileing of him be deceis unmaret the marriage of any other heir or heiress maill or femael that sall happen to succeed to him in his lands and heretage with all profits thereof ...'. Lachlan therefore owed him ten thousand merks.[31] The decision of the court is not mentioned but it would appear that the two parties reached a compromise for on 16 July 1583 Lachlan signed a contract agreeing that he owed the earl 5000 merks for his marriage and other gifts.[32] He was to pay this sum to the earl's second son Colin Campbell of Lundie by 11 November 1583. If he failed to do so he would grant Lundie a charter of the annual rent of the 5000 merks from his lands in Luing. In security of this debt he gave Lundie sasine of the four merk lands of Ballechuan in Luing.[33]

Argyll was terminally ill by 11 September 1584 when Ardkinglas was granted the ward and marriage of the heritage of Archibald Campbell 'fiear of Ergyle', when it should fall to the crown by the decease of his father.[34]

*   *   *   *

The sixth earl's death must have been a relief to Maclean. His uncle's enmity had blighted his early manhood. He was probably now 26 years old, evidently happily married – there are no references to him having any illegitimate children. He dominated his environment.

Lachlan is described as being tall and fair.[35] He was a competent scholar and was to become a polished courtier. In some ways he was an ideal sixteenth-century chief and leader of a turbulent body of men. However, unlike the greatest of chiefs, one gets the feeling reading between the lines that he was already feared rather than loved.

He was also too impulsive. By alienating his uncle he had not only destroyed the basis of Maclean polity, he had also played into the hands of Angus Macdonald by allowing him to recruit one of the leading Campbell captains of mercenaries, John Dubh MacConachie, the tutor of Inverawe, as well as the O Dochertys of Inishowen. Lachlan Mor might be fearless, ruthless and 'a bonnie fechter', but he lacked the cunning that was necessary to a chief.

He was consistent in his opinions and loyalties. He was to be unrelenting in his enmity to Hugh O Neill, earl of Tyrone. He was also unswerving in his loyalty to the Presbyterian party. This consistency may have been admirable but it was pursued even when it jeopardised his own self-interest. Perhaps he was not very intelligent. Lachlan's feud with Argyll had dominated his young manhood. His feud with Angus Macdonald was to shape the rest of his life.

Notes

1. SP Elizabeth. Scotland LVIII, 46.
2. Ibid, 43–44.
3. SRO GD 39/94/104.
4. Brown, *Bloodfeud in Scotland*, 69.
5. *Book of Dunvegan*, 19.
6. *Bloodfeud in Scotland*, 85–105.

7. *Warriors and Priests*, 119–121.
8. SP Elizabeth. Scotland LVIII, 47.
9. *Ibid*, 46.
10. GD 50/128. I am obliged to Jane E. Dawson for this reference.
11. AT VII 27 August 1579.
12. GD 50/128.
13. AT VII 27 August 1579.
14. AT VII.
15. GD 1/19H 369r & v; *Collectanea*, 12.
16. *Ibid*, 13.
17. RPC ii, 286.
18. GD 1/27 f19v.
19. *RSS* 70.
20. *RPC* iii, 62.
21. *RPC* iii, 124–5.
22. *RMS* iv, 3021.
23. *RMS* v, 208.
24. *SGS* xi (i), ic3.
25. GD 1/19 H 49r–50r; *Collectanea*, 15–18.
26. *RPC* iii, 517.
27. GD 50/128.
28. *RSS* VIII, 317.
29. *RSS* VIII, 409.
30. Cosmo Innes (ed), *The Book of the Thanes of Cawdor* (1859), 186–8.
31. CS7/90, 102.
32. RD 1/28 H 21r–22v.
33. AT VII 20 February 1587–8; 9 August 1588.
34. *RSS* VIII, 2418.
35. SP Elizabeth. Scotland LVIII, 52.

CHAPTER 8

Whitehall and the Western Isles, 1584–1585

Macbeth. There's not a one of them but in his house
I keep a servant fee'd.

Macbeth Act III, Scene iv

It is clear that even before his death the sixth earl's grip on the Hebrides had slackened. We will see what a disastrous effect this had on the Islands. It also had alarming results for the English in Ireland.

In July 1584 a large number of Macleans landed at Lough Swilly. Not only did they not leave a cow in Mcsweeney's country but they brought with them two sons of Sean O Neill,[1] Hugh Gavelagh and Art O Neill. They were Sean's sons by Katherine Maclean. The elder son Hugh's name in Gaelic, *Aodh nan geimhleach*, means 'Hugh of the fetters' because his mother was a prisoner when Hugh was born (or more probably when he was conceived). Hugh and Art had probably left Ireland with Katherine after their father's murder and had been brought up either in Appin, with her last husband John Stewart, or with their cousin at Duart. Whilst she lived Katherine discouraged them from becoming involved in Ulster politics. She was however an old woman now and her sons were determined to gain at least part of their Irish patrimony.

Ireland was to dominate the rest of Lachlan Mor's career. The landing at Lough Swilly was the beginning of his involvement in Ireland. To see the reasons behind his Irish involvement it is necessary to understand something of English and, to a lesser extent, Scottish policy in Ireland in Queen Elizabeth's reign.

Ireland was England's Achilles heel. As the papal legate, David Wolfe, wrote to the Spanish king:

> He that will England win
> Let him in Ireland begin.[2]

In other words Ireland could be used as a stepping stone for a foreign invasion of the British mainland.

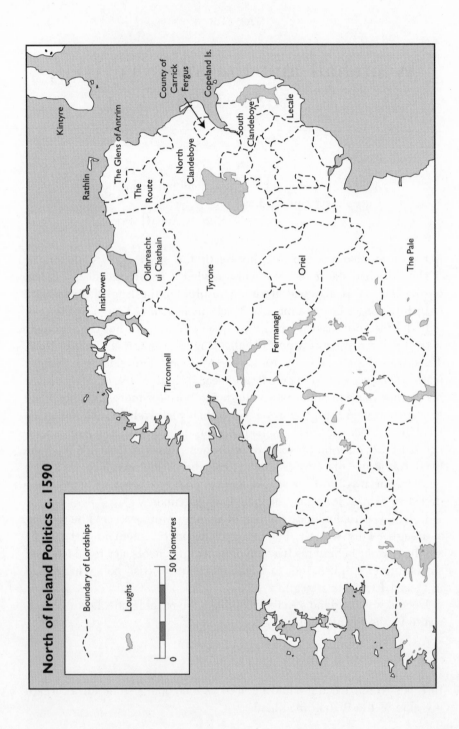

North of Ireland Politics c. 1590

- - - Boundary of Lordships

Loughs

0   50 Kilometres

Kintyre

Rathlin

The Glens of Antrim

The Route

County of Carrick Fergus

Copeland Is.

North Clandeboye

South Clandeboye

Lecale

Inishowen

Oidhreacht ui Chathain

Tyrone

Oriel

The Pale

Tirconnell

Fermanagh

The kingdom of Ireland was the most vulnerable territory held by the Tudor monarchs. Royal control was weak, its defences were minimal and it was open to disruption both by local troublemakers and foreign invaders.

In 1541 Henry VIII had assumed the title 'King of Ireland'. For the next fifteen years English policy makers sought to extend their authority over the whole kingdom. Previously English authority had been limited to the area around Dublin known as the Pale, and even here citizens were not always safe from Irish raids. The method used to extend the English crown's influence is known as 'surrender or regrant'. It was similar to the method used earlier by the Scots crown to deal with the vassals of the forfeited lord of the Isles. Basically it aimed at redefining the relationship between the crown and the Gaelic lords. Instead of the old division between the Anglo-Irish and Gaelic communities the new policy aimed at the gradual assimilation of the 'Irishry', the area under the Gaelic political and legal systems.[3]

One of the major differences between the English and the Irish systems was the method of succession to landed property. In England the heir succeeded by primogeniture, in Ireland by the Gaelic custom of election known as 'tanistry' whereby the heir was chosen in his predecessor's lifetime and although closely related to him was probably not his son.

This attempt at gradual assimilation of Gaelic-speaking Ireland was replaced in the reign of Mary Tudor by a policy of conquest and colonisation. There were three major problems facing the English in adopting this policy: the presence of Scots mercenaries in Ireland, the virtual independence of Ulster and the presence in Antrim of the Macdonalds of Dunyvaig and the Glens.

Ulster was the least anglicised part of Ireland and Dublin's influence there was at its weakest. It was dominated by the traditional rivals O Neill and O Donnell. In the middle ages O Neill had been king of much of Ulster. He still claimed tribute from his vassals such as O Cahan and all the sub-kings or *ur-righthe* of the region. The government's policy meant the end of this ancient relationship. In the future the *ur-righthe* would hold their land directly from the crown. The basis of O Neill power would be destroyed.

During the earlier period of 'liberal reform' Con O Neill had surrendered his lands to the crown and received them back again when he was created the first earl of Tyrone. At his death the two systems of inheritance came into direct conflict. The government backed Mathew who Con claimed was his eldest son. The O Neills backed another son, Sean the Tanist, who had already been elected by them during Con's lifetime. On this occasion local custom prevailed and by 1559 Sean was O Neill. He gloried in his title.

In 1566 he wrote, 'I confess she [the queen] is my sovereign lady, yet I never made peace with her but by her own seeking ... My ancestors were kings of Ulster, Ulster was theirs and shall be mine. And for O Donnell he shall never come into his country, if I can keep him out of it, nor Bagenal into the Newry nor the earl of Kildare into Dundrum or Lecale. They are mine; with this sword I will keep them ...'[4]

Sean was anathema to Dublin. He was probably murdered in 1567 on the instructions of Sir Henry Sidney. He was succeeded by his cousin Turlough Luineach. Sean had dominated his surroundings. Turlough Luineach was dominated by them. In particular he was dominated by his wife lady Agnes Campbell, and in 1575 her fellow Campbells even provided Turlough with his bodyguard.[5]

The Macdonalds of Dunyveg and the Glens presented the English government with another major problem. Although they had possessed land in Antrim since the late fourteenth century, the Macdonalds were regarded as foreigners both by the English and the Gaelic communities in Ireland. Throughout the sixteenth century they expanded their territory in Ulster and by 1584 there were two major families of Macdonalds in Ulster: Angus Macdonald of Dunyvaig in the Glens of Antrim and his uncle the formidable *Somhairle Buidh*, 'Sorley Boy', in the Route.

The military problem facing the English concerning the Macdonalds was that apart from the small garrison at Carrickfergus they had no permanent military presence in Antrim. On the other hand the Macdonalds could rapidly call for help from their supporters in Kintyre and Islay.

If the weather was clear it was even possible in Kintyre to see a signal beacon in Antrim. Reinforcements could be rushed across the north channel in less than 24 hours and the Macdonalds could rapidly have a considerable army in Antrim at their disposal. A report, almost certainly written by Captain Nicholas Dawtrey in 1597, states that Scots mercenaries 'are called over divers tymes by the great men of Ulster, with certaine smoakes maide upon the coaste of Ireland, especially upon don louse [Dunluce] in the Roate, which be highe cliffes, from whence fires and smoakes may be seene farr of, and therefore looke howe many thousand they will have come over, so many fiers they make in the night, or so many smoakes or smothers by the day ...'[6]

The Macdonalds could also withdraw to the Isles in times of trouble and Sidney's attempt to follow them there was interrupted by the weather and only partially successful.

The Scots government also used Ulster to embarrass England. It was never quite certain in Dublin whether or not the Macdonalds were receiving support and encouragement from Edinburgh.

Once Elizabeth was on the throne of England it should have been possible for the English to use the fifth earl of Argyll to spread the Protestant religion in Catholic Ulster. But Elizabeth dithered and failed to employ him. As a result the fifth earl was furious with Elizabeth and became the leader of the anti-English party in the civil war.

Elizabeth's failure to use Argyll against Sean was not just the result of her notorious dislike of spending money. She also feared that the islanders would join their fellow Irish Gaels in a pan-Celtic alliance. The fact remained that the 'redshanks' of the Highlands and Islands were far better adapted to warfare in Ireland than were the English levies and were better fighting men than the native Irish 'kerne'.

The landing by the Macleans at Loch Swilly in July 1584 was part of an attempt by Lachlan Mor to help his cousin Hugh Gavelagh to become O Neill in place of Turlough Luineach. It was also an attempt to open a second front in his feud with Angus. The possibility of an O Neill–Macdonald–Argyll alliance threatened Lachlan Mor's very survival.

Lachlan's expedition is described as being 'very well appointed of artelery and cast peces of greate and small syse. Further the brute [talk] ys here that there ys in Loghefoyll come in three greate shipps full of ordynances ...'[7] An English naval task force was however in the area and the Maclean galleys only just got out of Lough Foyle in time. They were chased ignominiously back to Scotland.

Loch Foyle was the key to the Macleans' involvement in Ulster. It is a sheltered sea loch and is only a few hours' sailing from Duart's lands at the head of Lochindaal in Islay. This journey is a far easier sail than across the dangerous north channel between Antrim and Kintyre. This is one of the reasons why these lands in Islay at the head of Lochindaal and in the Rinns were so important to successive Macleans of Duart. The sea route between Loch Foyle and Lochindaal was not only the best route between the southern Hebrides and Ulster for the traffic in mercenaries: it was also used for trade, particularly the movement of cattle. It linked in to the Maclean-dominated drove roads from the head of Lochindaal across the neck of Islay to Port Askaig and on through Jura to the markets in Mull and the mainland. Control of this route would have been of economic importance to both the Macleans and Macdonalds, a fact that was not lost on either Angus or Lachlan Mor.

Events in the Western Isles in the summer of 1584 were being watched in Whitehall by Sir Francis Walsingham, Queen Elizabeth's principal secretary of state. He was a convinced puritan, who saw the survival of an independent English state as the only means of saving Protestant Europe from the Counter-Reformation.

Walsingham was one of the new men who rose to power under the Tudors. The son of a successful lawyer, he had himself been at Gray's Inn before moving to Switzerland during Mary Tudor's reign. He had been educated at the University of Padua and had first-hand experience of Roman Catholicism and Spanish domination. He detested both. Elizabeth disliked, but respected, him.

Walsingham was one of the most efficient, cold-blooded and ruthless spymasters in the history of the English Secret Service. William Cecil, Walsingham's predecessor as principal secretary, and Robert Dudley, earl of Leicester, the glamorous courtier who wooed Elizabeth, both had their own agents. Walsingham's network was the largest. It was not only concerned with gathering intelligence, it was quite prepared to eliminate real or imagined enemies of the state at home or abroad.

An efficient extensive secret service was essential if a regime that was under threat both at home and abroad did not have a standing army. In 1570 Elizabeth had been excommunicated by Pope Pius V and officially deposed. Rebellion against her became a duty for English Roman Catholics and obedience to her a sin.[8]

On 24 August 1584 Walsingham received a report that Lachlan Maclean of Duart and 800 of his followers had passed into Ireland 'with the last O Neill's son, born of Maclane's father's sister, to put him in possession of some part of his father's living ...'[9]

Hugh Gavelagh and his full brother Art MacSean complained that Turlough had banished them as children to a foreign country (i.e. the Western Isles). In their absence he had given part of their lands to men fit only to be their followers while the rest went to ruin.[10]

The sons of Sean were not short of allies. They could rely on assistance from their cousins in Mull, whilst in Ulster they had the support of O Donnelly, marshall of Tyrone. All Sean's sons were fostered by O Donnelly as Sean had been himself, and James Carragh the chief of the O Donnellys was devoted to Sean O Neill's house.[11]

Irish men could be fostered by more than one family and Henry MacSean had also been fostered by O Cahan, O Quinn and possibly by the Macdonald galloglass family as well. Con MacSean had been fostered by O Hagan and since his mother was a Macguire was related to the most powerful family of *ur-righthe* in Ulster. He was also married to a

Macguire which increased their obligation to him. Henry and Con Mac-Sean had been imprisoned by Turlough Luineach and one of the aims of the landing at Loch Swilly was to release them. Once the expeditionary force advanced from Loch Swilly they were joined by O Donnelly and O Cahan. Turlough retreated to the Blackwater. The MacSeans were not Turlough Luineach's only rival and Hugh O Neill, earl of Tyrone, took advantage of the situation and attacked him. Hugh was the son of Mathew O Neill whom the English had wished to be O Neill instead of Sean. In the terms of his grandfather's resignation, although he was not O Neill, he was earl of Tyrone.

Hugh's attack on Turlough Luineach persuaded many of the latter's followers to transfer their loyalty to him. O Neill was forced to fall back on the crown for assistance and hand over his son Art to the lord deputy as a hostage.

The lord deputy was now Sir John Perrot, reputed to be the bastard son of King Henry VIII. He had considerable experience in Ireland as a provincial governor and a reputation as a soldier. On hearing of the Macleans' landing at Lough Foyle, Perrot immediately marched into Ulster. He did so with all the men at his disposal. The Macleans had however fled to the Isles before he reached the North and Perrot turned on the Macdonalds. Dunluce Castle, Sorley Boy's stronghold, was captured and the lord deputy set about garrisoning the north Antrim coast against the Scots.

The MacSeans strengthened their position over the summer. In October 1584 they were in a position to make overtures to the government. They had captured an English gentleman-soldier called Oliver Lambert and he was used to take their proposals to Dublin. Lambert stated that 'Hugh Gavelagh is far better beloved in the country than O Neill is and commands all at his pleasure'.[12] Turlough Luineach was forced to make an accommodation with the MacSeans and for the next twelve months their star was in the ascendant.

Meanwhile Perrot persuaded the Gaelic lords of Ulster to employ English soldiers rather than Scots. They were to be financed equally by the crown and the Gaelic lords themselves under whose command they would serve. They were also to be maintained by the local population. Sir John Norris, an extremely able and experienced soldier, who accompanied the lord deputy on his northern journey, expressed misgivings about this scheme. He believed that the maintenance of soldiers would place too great a burden on the country. It was also clear to Norris that Turlough Luineach was only interested in his own position and wanted the English soldiers to boost his declining prestige.

News of the sixth earl's death reached Dublin by mid-November. On 16 November 1584 Perrot wrote to Walsingham that 'the earl of Argyll is dead, and Angus McDonnell and M'Alane's son overrule all things in the Isles'. He had received this news from one John Sedly, who had escaped from the Isles in a little 'cockleshell' and reached the safety of the garrison at Carrickfergus.[13]

Perrot's plan to fortify the Antrim coast more efficiently in order to keep out the Scots was rejected by Elizabeth and in January 1585 Angus crossed over to Ireland to assist his brother Donald Og. He had 2000 men with him. The English authorities protested and the Scots government, whatever they were up to behind the scenes, sent a letter to Angus ordering him back to Scotland. He did not however return until March. When he did his departure seriously weakened his kin. The English took Angus's departure as a signal to attack. They did so by both land and sea. The island of Rathlin was taken by a landing party from ships commanded by Francis Drake. The Route was devastated and Angus's brother and his uncle Sorley Boy retired to Scotland.[14]

Before Angus's withdrawal from Ulster, Walsingham and Perrot had been giving serious thought to employing Lachlan Mor and the Macleans against Angus. On 14 April 1585 Walsingham wrote to Perrot that the 'Queen ... thinks it needless to put herself to the charge of giving a pension to M'Ilane'. On the same day Elizabeth herself wrote to Perrot. Instead of congratulating him on driving the Scots out of Ulster, she rebuked him for exaggerating their numbers.[15]

On 25 April 1585 Angus, at Holyrood, having declared himself an obedient subject, complained of his neighbour's behaviour towards him. As a result a proclamation was made at the market crosses of Dumbarton, Inverness and Inveraray charging the inhabitants to rise and assist Angus. At the same time Lachlan Mor and other Highland chiefs were charged with rebellion.[16]

Lady Agnes Campbell accompanied her son Angus to Holyrood, a fact that was reported by Perrot to Walsingham.[17] Agnes was in an unenviable position. Her husband Turlough Luineach had supported Perrot in his offensive against the Macdonalds. There was however no doubt which side Agnes would support. Her sons came first. But her influence had probably been reduced by the death of her nephew the sixth earl. The seventh earl, Archibald, was a minor when he succeeded.

The seventh earl's guardians were his mother Agnes Keith the dowager countess of Argyll and Moray, Sir James Campbell of Ardkinglas, the king's comptroller, John Campbell of Cawdor and Neil Campbell, bishop of Argyll. Only Cawdor was an ally of the Macdonalds. Ardkinglas was the ally of the Macleans. Angus could no longer rely on the support from the Campbells he had received during the sixth earl's last years, nor could he depend on support from the young king James VI for much longer.

The changed situation was the result of the deteriorating situation from the English point of view in the Low Countries. In July 1584 the Prince of Orange, the leader of the Protestants against King Philip II of Spain, was assassinated. The able Spanish regent, Alexander Farnese prince of Parma, besieged Antwerp. In August 1585 it fell. There was considerable consternation in Whitehall and Elizabeth was at last per-suaded to come off the fence and to send an expeditionary force under the command of the earl of Leicester to the Low Countries. England was officially at war with Spain. Troops were withdrawn from Ireland and Perrot's forward policy was put on hold.

It was also essential that Scotland was neutralised. In July 1585 a treaty was formally concluded between the English and the Scots. James became a pensioner of Elizabeth and agreed not to give aid to her enemies.

The treaty was to have instant results in the Isles. James could no longer tolerate Angus's invading Ulster. On 30 July Edward Wotton wrote to Walsingham from Edinburgh that the king had agreed that if the Macdonalds passed into Ireland 'he will permit Maclene, who is at deadly feud with Angus M'Connell, to waste and burne Sorley Boy's and Angus's country, which indeed will be the best means to revoke them'.[18] It was a complete U-turn in royal favour to the antagonists in the Isles.

Notes

1. H. C. Hamilton (ed), *Calendar of State Papers relating to Ireland (CSP Ireland)* ii (London, 1867), 520.
2. Quoted in C. Falls, *Elizabeth's Irish Wars* (London, 1950), 9.
3. Jane E. A Dawson, 'Two kingdoms or three?', in R. Mason (ed), *Scotland & England 1286–1815* (Edinburgh 1987), 115.
4. Quoted in G. A. Hayes McCoy, *Scots Mercenary Forces in Ireland* (1937), 79.
5. *CSP Ireland* ii, 173.
6. Hiram Morgan, 'A Booke of Questions and Answars concerning the Warrs or Rebellions of the Kingdome of Irelande', *Analecta Hibernica* No. 36 (Irish Manuscripts Commission, 1995), 122. This account appeared when this book was in the final stages of publication. Its evidence does not affect my own conclusions save that Dawtrey, unlike Mr Denis Campbell, thought the Irish were more than a match for the Scottish islanders.

7. SP Elizabeth. Ireland, CXI, 39 ii (quoted in *Hayes-McCoy*), 153.
8. Alan Haynes, *Invisible Power. The English Secret Service 1570–1603* (1992), xx.
9. *CSP Ireland* vii, 252.
10. PRO SP 63/112 no. 25.
11. Hiram Morgan, *Tyrone's Rebellion*, 95.
12. PRO SP 63/111 no. 25.
13. *CSP Ireland* ii, 72
14. Hayes-McCoy, 163.
15. *CSP Ireland* ii, 560.
16. *RPC* iii, 239.
17. *CSP Ireland* ii, 561.
18. *CSP Ireland* ii, 42.

CHAPTER 9

Warfare in the Isles

Malcolm. Say to the King thy knowledge of the broil
As thou didst leave it.
Sergeant. Doubtful it stood;
As two spent swimmers that do cling together
And choke their art.

Macbeth Act I, Scene ii

The feud between Angus and Lachlan Mor burst out with a new intensity in 1585. For the first time since the battle of Flodden in 1513 the Gaeltachd was without an able, energetic and ambitious man at its helm. The guardians of the seventh earl were no substitute for MacCailein Mor himself. The Isles relapsed into what is arguably its bloodiest era in early modern times and it soon spread out from the original contestants to a civil war that involved the whole Hebrides.

The immediate cause of the conflict was a misunderstanding between Lachlan Mor and one of his former allies, Macdonald of Sleat. Donald Gorm Macdonald of Sleat was Lachlan Mor's first cousin. He is said to have been educated in 'lerninge and civilitye' in the lowlands. Here he fell under the influence of Angus and they decided to consult with their friends (i.e. their relations) 'to take consultation against McIlaine'.[1]

On his return to the Isles Donald Gorm, with several galleys, set off to a convention of the whole Clan Donald both north and south to be held in Islay. Before he reached his destination a gale sprang up and the little fleet was forced to shelter at Inver-Knock-Wrich in Jura. It was in that part of the island belonging to Maclean of Duart.

Unbeknown to Sleat two of his kinsmen, with whom he had quarrelled, were shadowing him with their own men. That night they stole a number of Maclean's cattle in Jura, intending that the blame should fall on Donald Gorm. Their plan could not have worked out better. Maclean's herdsmen quickly reported the theft to Duart. Lachlan Mor was furious, 'accounting the said Donald no longer his cosen but his enemy',[2] and fell on the unsuspecting Macdonalds. About sixty of Donald Gorm's men were killed. Donald himself only escaped because he spent the night on board his galley. He fled to Skye.[3]

The Isles were a tinder box awaiting a spark and the seemingly unprovoked attack by Lachlan Mor was enough for them to burst into flame. The whole Clan Donald south and north gathered and invaded Mull. Outnumbered, Lachlan beat a tactical withdrawal to the heights of Ben More with the island's cattle, leaving the low ground undefended. His order was that the invaders were not to be attacked. However, contrary to his instructions, several young 'gentlemen' fought a spirited skirmish with the enemy and a young man of the family of Treshnish was killed.

One of Sleat's tenants, who accompanied his master in invading Mull, was Maclean of Boreray. His family had for several generations been chamberlains to the Macdonalds of Sleat in North Uist. They were thus in the unenviable position of being on the opposite side to their kinsmen. He was however a poet and, knowing his landlord's superstition, determined to use this knowledge to get himself out of his predicament.

As Sleat began his advance to the hills at a place called Licht Lee, where he hoped to outflank Duart, he noticed that Boreray was looking melancholy. Macdonald coming up to him asked 'what was the matter?' Boreray replied that he would leave him to guess the reason. 'True', said Sleat. 'I need not wonder when I consider that it is again your chief and friends that you are to fight.' 'That's not the only reason', replied Boreray and explained that he also had a dream which worried him. Macdonald demanded to know what it was. Boreray said that in his dream he had heard a voice which several times repeated to him the words:

> *A Lic-lì sin, O Lic-lì,*
> *'S ann ort-s' a bheirear an dìth.*
> *Clann-Ghilleain bheir iad buaidh*
> *Air an t-sluagh a thig air tìr.*
> *'Ghearna dhubh, 's i Ghearna dhubh!*
> *'S ann uimp' a dhoirtear an fhuil,*
> *Marbhar an Ridire Ruadh*
> *Mu'n déid lann an truaill an diugh.*

> O Lecklee, thou dread Lecklee,
> Great the carnage thou shalt see.
> The Macleans shall win the day;
> The invaders slain shall be.
> Gerna Dubh, thou hill of woe,

> Tides of blood shall round thee flow,
> Ere the gleaming swords shall rest
> The Red Knight shall be laid low.[4]

Sleat, otherwise the Red Knight, fearing the worst, ordered a withdrawal and left Mull. Lachlan Mor now had a chance to send out a fiery cross for reinforcements from his outlying clan and his supporters such as Macneill of Barra and Mackinnon. He was also joined by Boreray who changed sides. The Macdonalds in the meanwhile occupied the little Isle of Bach south-west of Kerrera in the Firth of Lorn. It was here that the Macleans struck first.

The Macdonalds were drawn up in good order on the shore ready to resist the Macleans' assault. The hail of well-directed volleys of arrows from Lachlan Mor's galleys drove them back and enabled the Macleans to get ashore. Hand-to-hand fighting now took place and the Macdonalds were routed. They fled to their galleys, leaving behind a great many dead.

It is possible that the assault on the Isle of Bach is the incident referred to in a letter of Edward Wotton to Walsingham in September 1585, which states 'there is one McClane who has a deadly feud with Angus and has lately slain many of his principal followers …'[5] Wotton was an experienced diplomat who had spent some years in Naples as Walsingham's agent and in Portugal as Elizabeth's representative. He was now her special representative in Scotland.

Wotton had written to Walsingham in August suggesting that Maclean become 'her majesty's pensioner [as] he would always be ready whenever Angus … started for Ireland, to spoil and burn their land so that fear of this would keip them at home'.[7] Lachlan Mor now made an offer himself 'to serve her majesty against Angus either in Scotland or Ireland and to reduce Shane O Neill's sons, who are his near kinsmen, to her majesty's service, if he may be made her majesty's pensioner'. Lachlan Mor claimed that he had 2500 Highlanders at his disposal and Wotton thought that a pension to him of £200 a year might save the queen £2000 per year.[7]

Lachlan Mor's offer was worth considering. The MacSeans gained strength throughout early 1585. They were to show the same insolence to the English that their father had done and 'committed divers robberies and spoils' which Turlough Luineach was unable to suppress. To prevent any further aggrandisement by the MacSeans, Hugh O Neill and Turlough's son Art took charge of central Tyrone. Official agreements, ratified after the event, attempted to put a veneer of government authority on a situation over which it exercised little or no control.[8]

It was the actions of the lord deputy Perrot which now radically changed the situation and made Lachlan Mor's offer less attractive. On a tour of the north Perrot took Art MacSean prisoner and incarcerated him in Dublin Castle with his half-brother Henry. Hugh O Neill now manipulated the situation by obtaining permission to spoil the territory of James Carragh O Donnelly, the main supporter of the MacSeans.[9] By the end of summer the MacSeans were at a low ebb.

The government now recognised the increased power which Hugh O Neill had achieved within Tyrone by a grant of his own grandfather's lands, and at a meeting of seventy lords and councillors, the Irish parliament agreed to give him 'the name, dignity and place of earl of Tyrone'.[10] Hugh was from a different background and generation to Seán and Turlough Luineach. He had been educated among the English in the Pale and fostered by an English settler. He was evidently regarded as pro-English at this time and more malleable than the drunken sot Turlough Luineach.

The decline of Lachlan Mor's allies in Ireland was not his only setback. Angus's invasion of Mull had evidently done him much damage and on 18 September 1585 the king wrote to Macleod of Harris asking him to help Lachlan Mor against the Clan Donald, who had 'already done much injury to Maclean and threatened more'.[11]

The seventh earl's guardians now tried to use their influence to resolve the dispute between Lachlan Mor and the bishop of the Isles. Earlier attempts had come to nothing and both Cawdor and Ardkinglas were at Calgary in Mull on 19 November 1585 to agree the two parties in the name of the earl.

Eventually it was accepted that Lachlan would see that the 'reverend father' was obeyed as he had been in 'Hector McClane elder of Dowart's tymes or in the tyme of Hector McClane younger within the bounds of Icolmkill, rosse, Mull and Terrey'. What this actually meant for the inhabitants of Tiree was referred to a panel of witnesses.

Lachlan also agreed to use 'his forces' to see that the bishop's rents were collected throughout the Isles, except in those parts of Islay and Jura which belonged to Angus. Other arrangements concerning the administration of the Ross of Mull were discussed. It was finally concluded that if Lachlan could find cautioners to see that he would keep his promises the bishop would discharge him from all the previous contracts made between them. Lachlan would be released from the horn and his escheat cancelled.[12]

Both sides in the feud between Maclean and Macdonald were looking for supporters. Lachlan Mor must by now have regretted his quarrel with the sixth earl. He attempted to revert to his family's old alliance with the new earl. On 23 March 1586 at Kilmarnock he entered into a bond of friendship with Duncan Campbell of Glenorchy and Sir James Campbell of Ardkinglas. Both Campbells bound themselves to try and obtain a bond of maintenance from the earl for Maclean. However, as it was pointed out in the agreement, the earl was a minor and could not enter into such a bond without the consent of his mother. They agreed to try and obtain this consent when she next came to Argyll.[13] This bond had evidently been signed at Kilmarnock to involve Lachlan Mor's brother-in-law in the search for allies as the earl of Glencairn is a witness.

Angus's search for support took a very different direction to Lachlan Mor's. In an astonishing change of direction the English government decided to reverse its policy towards the Scots in Ulster. In May 1586 it made an agreement with Angus by which he undertook to hold the land he held in Antrim from the queen. In June Sorley Boy went even further and became an Irish citizen. By doing so he obtained favourable terms for his lands between the Bush and the Bann.[14]

Angus, having secured his position in Ulster, now contrived to make peace with Lachlan Mor. Both sides agreed to lay down their arms and Maclean agreed to accept Angus as his feudal superior for the Rinns of Islay. Angus on his part gave up his son James to Maclean, the child's uncle, as a pledge for his own good will.[15] He then went to visit Duart where he was 'rycht cheirfullie welcomit be his brother in law, wha remanit thair be the space of tyme as sax dayis. And when it was persavit that Maclaynis provision was almaist spent, Angus thocht it then tyme to remove. Indeed the custome of that people is sa gevin to gluttonie and drinking without all measure, that as ane is invetit to another, they never sinder [part company] sa lang as the vivers do lest'.[16]

During these drinking sessions the guests were entertained by a bard, who might sing a panegyric in praise of the principal guest. He might also have composed less flattering verses about him behind his back. According to Mr Denis Campbell, 'certen rymes and songs ... in malice in disgrace of the McConnells' were the cause of the next stage in the tragedy. Apparently they so infuriated Angus that he decided to destroy Lachlan 'by treachery'.

Whether or not Angus intended all along to destroy his brother-in-law cannot be proved one way or another. Angus himself apparently expected treachery at Duart but as he later admitted there was no conspiracy against him there. This statement argues against the story in the *Conflicts of the Clans* that Lachlan imprisoned Angus at Duart until he agreed to hand over the Rinns to him. In fact the reverse seems to have occurred. It is more likely that both parties were genuine in their desire for reconciliation but that the mocking satire of a bard poisoned the atmosphere.

It was now Lachlan's turn to travel to Islay. He did so presumably to receive sasine of the Rinns from Angus. According to the dean of Limerick he went there in July 1586. He took with him his nephew James, whilst Angus's brother Ranald was left behind as a pledge and was imprisoned at Carnaburg.[17]

In Islay Lachlan Mor proposed to stay at his castle in Loch Gorm. It was however in a ruinous state as a result of the 1570s siege and Angus offered him alternative, more comfortable accommodation, at Mulindry. Lachlan accepted the offer. Once more the night was spent carousing and when the food and drink were exhausted the Macleans were lodged in an outhouse used as a kiln, Lachlan, as security, keeping his nephew close to him.

Meanwhile Angus had summoned two hundred of his men who surrounded the Macleans' accommodation, a kiln, which stood apart from the rest of the houses at Mulindry. When he was certain the perimeter was secure, Angus came to Lachlan's door and called to him to have one more drink. Lachlan began to suspect a trick and went to the door carrying his nephew with him on his shoulders. At the door he found Angus standing with a naked sword in his hands. James, seeing how his father and his men were armed '[cried] with a lowd voyce mearcie to his uncle for God's saik; whilk was grantit and immediatlie Maclayne was removit to a secret chalmer till the morrow'. Then Angus shouted to the rest of the Macleans within the kiln that they would save their lives if they surrendered and came out. Two only were excepted from this amnesty, one being Donald Gorm's cousin who had been instrumental in starting the feud. The Macleans, seeing that they were outnumbered, did as they were told and were all bound 'two and two together' with ropes and led away to prison. The kiln was then set on fire and the two refused amnesty were burnt to death.

The following day, contrary to the amnesty, Angus began to execute the Macleans, two being chosen to be killed each day. The executions were performed in Maclean's presence. The *Conflicts of the Clans*, which is based on Sir Robert Gordon of Gordonstoun's account written in the early seventeenth century and is sympathetic to Angus, says that the executions only began when Alan Og, Hector Allansoun's son, spread the rumour that Angus's brother had been executed at Duart. It appears that it was now that John Dubh, Lachlan's uncle, 'the eldest of the clan, renownit bayth for counsell and manheid', was executed. Lachlan himself was due to be executed next. However, 'when the day came that Maclayne should have bene brocht furthe, miserablie to have maid his tragicall end, lyke unto the rest, it pleasit Angus to lowp upon his horse, and cum furth for joy and contentatioun of mynd, evin to se and behauld the tyrannicall fact with his awin eyes. Bot it pleasit God, who mercifullie deilis with all man, and disapoyntis the decrees of the wicked, to dis-apoynt his intent for that day also, for he was not sa sone on his horse, bot the horse stumblit and Angus fell of him and broke his leg, and so was careit hayme'.

Word of what was happening in Islay eventually reached the court. The king was so horrified that he persuaded Parliament hurriedly to pass the statute known as 'Murder under Trust'. In the meantime the priority was to rescue Maclean from Angus's clutches. On 16 April 1587 it was accepted that Angus's crimes should be forgiven if he agreed to release Maclean. Hostages were to be provided in his place. These included Alexander, brother to William Macleod of Dunvegan, two sons of Mackinnon, two sons of Macneil of Barra, Alan son and apparent heir of Maclean of Ardgour and Donald son of the constable of Carnaburg Castle, all of whom appear to have been handed over to Angus.

It was now Lachlan's turn to seek revenge. He invaded Kintyre 'where be fyre, what be sworde, and what be watter he destroyit all mankynd, noyne except that come in his way, and all sort of beast that servit for any domestik use and pleasure of men: And finallie, he came to the verie place where Angus was mirrelie camping, luiking for na sik sudden invasioun for the tyme, geve he had not bene horsit incontinent, and withdrawin him self to a strong castell [Dunyvaig] which was near by, he had bene weill recompenceit for his former traiterie'. Angus retaliated by burning Tiree.

*　　　*　　　*　　　*

In 1587 by an Act of Annexations all ecclesiastical temporalities, of bishoprics and abbeys alike, were formally annexed to the crown. This did not result in a complete change in the holders of church property. Many exceptions were made and many properties were regranted to their former possessors.[18]

Among those who obtained a re-grant was Lachlan Mor, who on 19 March 1587–8 obtained a Great Seal charter of feu-ferme of the land his grandfather had obtained from John Carswell. For technical reasons the grant was made to Lachlan's son and heir apparent Hector, but there is little doubt who was the effective recipient.

It was a massive grant and specifies the rental of the lands listed in the charter. These rents were due to be paid annually to the crown. They came to what was then the considerable sum of £162. 6s. 9½d. It was made up as follows:

Lands in the Ross of Mull	£ 63.8.7½d
Other lands in Mull	£ 21.5.10d
Island of Iona	£ 22.13.4d
Lands in Islay	£ 26.15.8d
Lands in Tiree	£ 28.3.4d[19]

By this act the bishops, including John of the Isles, lost the bulk of their property and the prestige that went with them. At the same time there was a general drift to Presbyterianism.

John Campbell perhaps lived on until 1594[20] and when he died no bishop was appointed in his place. It was not to be until 1605 that another incumbent became bishop of the Isles.

That such a grant was made at the height of the Maclean-Macdonald feud makes the point that despite the feud the southern Isles were not in a state of total anarchy.

*   *   *   *

John Macian of Ardnamurchan was considered by the Macleans to have been particularly culpable over John Dubh's death. Apparently he had maliciously informed Angus that the Macleans had executed two Macdonalds when in fact they were still alive. Lachlan therefore vowed to be revenged on Macian. When he failed to achieve his aim, he resorted to 'craft and policie'.

First he let it be known that he wished to be reconciled with Macian. Then he sent a servant to let him know that he proposed that their reconciliation should be sealed by marriage. The suggestion was that Macian should marry Lachlan's mother, who was once again a widow. An alliance with the earl of Argyll's aunt, who was now in liferent a considerable landowner in her own right, was sufficient bait to ensnare Macian.

On 12 April 1588 the marriage took place at Torloisk with 'the accustomed forme and ordour of the countrey, the bankett maid, gude countenance and interteynment showne by all parteis'. Then at night the bridegroom 'was convoyed be the hand [of] the said Lachlan to his moderis awne chalmber and bed'. The wedding guests from Ardnamurchan were then escorted to their own accommodation, a barn close by, 'looking for na harme nor injurie'.

Once they were asleep the Macleans repeated Angus's treatment of their kin in Islay. Lachlan and his companions with 'hovershonis swords and durkis' entered the barn and 'in maist cruell and barbarous manner, without pitie or compassioun, unmercifullie murdreist and slew thame to the nowmer of auchtene personis, gentlemen, besydis utheris'. Lachlan then burst into his mother's room and would have killed Macian too had he not defended himself 'an the lamentable crying oute and earnest sute of the said Lachlan's mader' persuaded the assassin to spare his life. John, and his page and one of his other kinsmen, were thrown into prison where they were tortured daily.

Lachlan now received additional help from an unexpected quarter.

In September 1588, a straggler from the Spanish Armada entered Tobermory Bay in the north-east of Mull. She was an 800-ton armed merchantman from the small but important maritime republic of Ragusa in the Adriatic (the modern Dubrovnik in southern Croatia). She had been originally named the *Brod Martolosi* and had traded as far as England.

Ragusan shipbuilding and seamanship were famous and the Spanish authorities had eagerly detained and compulsorily hired several of their large ships for the Armada. The *Brod*, renamed *Santa Maria de Gracia y San Juan Bautista*, or more conveniently *San Juan de Sicilia* (since she had been detained in Sicily), retained her Slav crew of 60–70 men. She also kept her captain, Luka Ivanov Kincovic, also hispaniolised as 'Lucas de Juan'. In command of the detachment of 279 soldiers and servants was a young aristocrat Don Diego Telles Enriquez. The men came from the Spanish army's *tercios*, considered to be amongst the finest trained infantry in Europe. The *San Juan* carried at least 26 large bronze or iron cannons and smaller swivel-ball guns. Her cargo also included two enormous siege guns firing 40 pounder balls, for use after the Armada had landed.

The *San Juan*'s arrival at Tobermory was a potential bonus to Lachlan Mor in his feud with the Macdonalds. However, if he was to make use of this windfall he first had to obtain control of her. This was easier said than done, for as an English diplomat reported from Edinburgh, his 'people releave them with victell, but are not able to possess her, for she is well furnished both with shott and man'.

Lachlan Mor's immediate aim was to prevent the *San Juan* from escaping out of his hands. He therefore promised to furnish whatever the Spaniards needed, whether or not it was possible to obtain it in

Mull. In particular hundreds of square feet of canvas were needed to
make fresh sails. The Spaniards rightly distrusted the Maclean chief
and his followers. The crew later recalled that they spent a month
'repairing the ship as best we could, with much toil and in great danger
of our lives'. Don Diego, meanwhile, dined off silver at every meal,
partly perhaps to impress 'the natives'. Such behaviour would, however,
have increased the widespread and potentially dangerous impression of
the ship's wealth.

In October Lachlan Mor asked the Spanish commander for the loan
of some of his men in exchange for further supplies. Don Diego agreed
to supply a hundred soldiers armed with arquebuses under the command
of one of his junior officers. He also produced two small ship's cannon
whilst the Macleans gave hostages in exchange.

The addition of a hundred professional infantry transformed the balance of power in the vicious little war being waged between the Macleans
and the Macdonalds. Lachlan Mor used his new allies to strike at the
islands lying between Mull and Skye: Rum and Eigg occupied by the
Clanranald and Canna and Muck held by the Macian's. Amongst the
casualties on Macian's side was the eldest son of Mr John Angus, Lachlan
Mor's grandfather's secretary, who had married a Macian.

According to the government records, Lachlan Mor, 'accompanyed
with a grite nowmer of thevis, brokin men and Sornaris of Clannis,
besyedis the nowmer of ane hundreth spanyeartis tressonablie rased
fyre, and in maist barbarous, shameful and Cruell maner, burnt the same
Ilis, with the hail men, women and children being thair in til, not
spairing the pupillis and infantis, and at the same tyme past to the
Castell of Ardnamurchin, a segeit the same and lay aboute the said
Castell three dayis ...' Evidently even Spanish infantry and two small
cannon were insufficient to successfully besiege Mingary, as Adnamur-
chan's castle is better known, and the Macleans and their allies withdrew
to Mull.

Their return to Mull was marked by the most dramatic event in the
whole saga of the Tobermory galleon. On 5 November (26 October Old
Style), according to the official Spanish report, the Spaniards were taking
off the ship's gunpowder to dry it when there was suddenly a terrible
explosion forward. It was so violent that part of the forecastle was
thrown all the way to the shore. Astonishingly two or three men carried
on it (including Lachlan Mor's personal physician, who was one of the
hostages) survived. Most of those close to the blast were killed and
many others died as the ship caught fire, burnt to the waterline and
sank.

Several of the Spanish infantry had been ashore at the time of the explosion. Lachlan Mor prevented them from leaving Mull. Instead he took them into his own service and used them against his enemies in the summer of 1589. Later in the autumn, the survivors, some 60–100 men, were released. They made their way to Edinburgh and returned to Spain.

Notes

1. SP Elizabeth. Scotland VIII, 47.
2. *Ibid.*
3. *Conflicts of the Clans*, 25.
4. NLS MS. 3018, 86V.
5. *CSP Ireland* VIII, 116.
6. *CSP Ireland* VIII, 79.
7. *Ibid*, 116.
8. Hiram Morgan, *Tyrone's Rebellion*, 101.
9. PRO SP 63/118 No. 78 (1); BLO Perrot 1 H 126–129.
10. PRO SP 63/117, No. 52.
11. Gregory, 231. There is some doubt over the date of this letter. I. F. Grant, *The Macleods* says it was written in 1586. R. C. Macleod, *Book of Dunvegan* says it is dated 1588.
12. RD 1/27 H 17R–19V.
13. Wormald, *Lords & Men*, 395.
14. Hayes-McCoy, 176.
15. SP Elizabeth. Scotland VIII, 47.
16. *Historie of King James the sext*, 156.
17. SP Elizabeth. Scotland VIII, 47, 48.
18. Gordon Donaldson, 'The Scottish Church 1567–1625', in Alan G. R. Smith (ed), *The Reign of James VI and I* (1973), 48–49.
19. *RMS* (1580–93), 509–511; *Collectanea*, 161–179. For map references and details of individual holdings, see *Warriors and Priests*, 152, 157.
20. *Clan Campbell* ii, 44.

CHAPTER 10

Conspiracy, Murder and Witchcraft, 1589–1594

First Witch. Thrice the brindled cat hath mew'd
Second Witch. Thrice and once the hedge-pig whined.
Third Witch. Harpier cries:– 'tis time, 'tis time.

Macbeth Act IV, Scene i

The defeat of the Spanish Armada did not end the threat to the Protestant regimes in England and Scotland. Philip II had established a centre for the Counter-Reformation at Douai. It aimed to train young men to win the intellectual argument and regain the British Isles for Roman Catholicism.[1] At the same time the most professional army in Europe under the command of Alessandro Farnese, Prince of Parma and governor-general of the Spanish Netherlands was poised to invade Britain if favourable circumstances occurred. These two threats from Flanders were an ever present factor in the events that followed.

*   *   *   *

Whilst Macleans and Macdonalds had been murdering each other in the Isles, Hugh O Neill, earl of Tyrone, was consolidating his position in Ulster. In the spring of 1587 he travelled to court. His considerable charm impressed the queen. The findings of the land commission also favoured him and when he returned to Ireland at the end of May he probably believed that his position in Tyrone was secure and that he would soon be supreme in Ulster. If he did he was mistaken. Perrot and others in Dublin were working against him and over the next four years Turlough Luineach and the MacSeans not only halted Hugh's ambitions but actually reversed them.[2]

Despite these setbacks Hugh O Neill made one move in 1587 that was to change the future of Ulster. This event was the marriage of his daughter Rose to Hugh Roe O Donnell. Tyrone was to claim in a letter to the King of Spain that for 700 years the families of O Neill and O

Donnell had fought for supremacy in Ulster. Their rivalry had been cynically exploited by the English government.

Hugh Roe's mother was Finola Macdonald, the daughter of Sir James Macdonald of Dunyvaig and the Glens and lady Agnes Campbell. Finola, better known as *Ineen Dubh* 'dark daughter', was one of those formidable Hebridean women who changed the destiny of the Gaeltachd. She was devoted to her fellow Macdonalds and had a bodyguard of Scots mercenaries.

The potential of an alliance between the families alarmed Dublin. The lord deputy Perrot in particular regarded the marriage of Hugh Roe and Rose as detrimental to the crown's interest. In September 1587 he had Hugh Roe kidnapped and imprisoned in Dublin Castle.

The kidnapping of Hugh Roe was a disaster for his parents and their supporters. It was also to have a profound influence on what was to follow as it altered the attitude of the O Donnells to Dublin. In the past the O Donnells had been the allies of the English against O Neill. They now felt they had been betrayed. A poem addressed to Hugh Roe in captivity claims that 'the descendants of Connell have ever refrained from casting even a shot at an Englishman'.

Hugh Roe's youthful arrogance is recognised by the poet but Tirconnel was in desperate need of strong leadership which Hugh Roe could have provided. Instead it was consumed by war and strife; learned men had been evicted from their inheritances; retainers scattered throughout Ireland. Instead of spreading security Dublin was encouraging anarchy.

During 1587 Hugh O Neill also entered into an alliance with Angus.[2] In the summer he freely admitted to Perrot that he had supplied the Macdonald chief with ammunition to help him against the Macleans.[3] Tyrone probably saw this alliance as a means to prevent Lachlan Mor from helping the MacSeans. It also enabled him to hire mercenaries from Angus whom he used in the winter of 1587/8 against both Turlough Luineach and the MacSeans.

Hugh Gavelagh MacSean now withdrew once again to the Isles, where he was reported to be trying to recruit Spanish survivors from the Armada. Rumours that both Hugh O Neill and Turlough Luineach had joined up with the Spaniards against the crown were rife and exaggerated. It is more likely that any Spanish survivors from the Armada would have been used by Hugh against Turlough Luineach, or vice versa, as Lachlan Mor used them in the Hebrides. There is however evidence that Hugh rounded up a number of Spaniards at Inishowen and butchered them.[4]

In 1589 Turlough Luineach entered into an alliance with the Mac-

Seans. Hugh Gavelagh's mother Katherine Maclean, who is said to have discouraged her sons from becoming involved in Ulster, had died in 1588. In February 1589 Hugh Gavelagh returned to Ulster. On his return he wrote to the new lord deputy Fitzwilliam, who had replaced Perrot, that he had matters of great importance to the state to reveal to him.

The intelligence that Hugh Gavelagh had for Fitzwilliam was that Tyrone was in negotiations with Spain and had been aiding Angus. The Dublin authorities however had no desire to bring about Tyrone's downfall and the earl had little difficulty in denying the allegations of treating with Spain. He had never made a secret of his dealings with Angus. Hugh Gavelagh returned to Ulster in a sulk.

In July 1589 Sorley Boy reported that the Macleans were planning a descent on Ulster 'with a great number of Irish gallies'.[5] They were rumoured to be intending either to attack Sorley Boy himself or Sir John O Docherty's country. The Lord Deputy passed on the information to Lord Burghley asking him to write to the Scots king to stop them. At the same time Sorley Boy's son wrote to Tyrone to get him to try and prevent the Macleans coming ashore. There does not appear to be anything more in the records about this expedition. It probably never left the Isles. If its aim was to assist the MacSeans, it failed. They were soon in desperate need of assistance.

Turlough Luineach in one of the changes in policy which characterised his career now made peace with Tyrone The earl promptly put a price on Hugh Gavelagh's head. An illegitimate son of Maguire won the prize. Hugh Gavelagh was taken, sold to Tyrone and executed. It is said that the earl hanged him from a thorn tree with his own hands.[6] It was an act that he was to live to regret. However, for the present, with one of his major rivals eliminated Tyrone, who was in communication with Spain from at least 1589, was in a position to prepare for the rebellion known as the Nine Years War. It was to become the greatest threat to the crown's position in Ireland.

*   *   *   *

In February 1589 a Scotsman was arrested in England carrying letters to Parma from George Gordon, sixth earl of Huntly. Huntly had, at the age of fourteen, inherited what was by now the most powerful earldom in Scotland. Educated in France as a Roman Catholic, he returned home in the early 1580s and quickly identified himself with the conservative regimes of Lennox and Arran and became a major figure at court. He was a man of educated and sophisticated tastes and a sincere Catholic. He also amused James VI, who counted him amongst his closest friends, allowed him to sleep in his own chamber and made him captain of the guard.

When copies of Huntly's letters to Parma, looking forward to a second Armada, were sent to Edinburgh, Huntly was imprisoned in the castle. James however had no intention of destroying his Roman Catholic subjects. He himself was flirting with Rome and did not intend to be dominated by the Kirk. Huntly was soon released.

Huntly's major rival in the north-east, his main power base, was James Stewart, second earl of Moray. James Stewart, the younger son of Lord Doune, had arrived at court at about the same time as Huntly. He also became an ally of Arran, who obtained for him the wardship and marriage of the daughters of the assassinated lord James Stewart, first earl of Moray. By marrying Elizabeth, the eldest daughter, Stewart became the second earl. He also obtained lands which after his rebellion against Mary Queen of Scots had been forfeited by Huntly's grandfather. In doing so Moray inherited a feud with Huntly, which was exacerbated by a quarrel over the fishing rights on the River Spey. It was also complicated by the minority of the earl of Argyll, Huntly's traditional rival in the West Highlands. The seventh earl's mother was the widow of the regent Moray and the countess of Moray was thus his half-sister. Argyll was doubly tied to Moray's party in the quarrel with Huntly

The position was further complicated by the rivalries between Argyll's curators. On his deathbed in 1584 the sixth earl had nominated six curators for his nine-year-old heir: Duncan Campbell of Glenorchy, Dougal Campbell of Auchinbreck, James Campbell of Ardkinglas, John Campbell of Cawdor, Archibald Campbell of Lochnell and Neil Campbell, bishop of Argyll. They were not to be equal for the earl's will stipulated that the signature of at least two of the three principal curators, Ardkinglas, Cawdor and the bishop, were required for any matter of importance.[7]

Lochnell and Glenorchy were bitterly disappointed by being left out of the key position. Cawdor too was initially outmanoeuvred by Ardkinglas, who had been the sixth earl's principal councillor and in 1586 he made a contract of friendship with Lochnell 'because those that now keep Argyll abuse their position, preventing his friends from having access' to the earl for their lawful affairs. They agreed to support one another in repairing the abuse.[8] At the same time Cawdor made another bond with Lochnell in which they pledged each other to get Argyll into their own keeping or 'at least get him at liberty in his own house'.

Ardkinglas responded by making an alliance with Glenorchy, Montrose and renewing his friendship with Duart.

Huntly was also meddling in Argyll's affairs and in 1587 at Perth Lochnell made a bond of manrent with him. The following year Glenorchy did likewise. Rivalry between Cawdor and Ardkinglas went as far as each plotting the murder of the other.[9]

It was instability in the West Highlands caused by the feud amongst the Campbells and the king's chronic shortage of money that prevented James from attempting to resolve the feud between the Macdonalds and Maclean, and in March 1588/9 letters of remission were issued to both Angus and Lachlan, their kin and allies for all the crimes committed by them.

Three months later, in July 1589, despite the assurance he had given to Argyll's curators not to resume hostilities until May 1590, Lachlan 'with grit forces of men bodin in feir of weir' invaded the Isle of Oronsay and burnt and harried it. The Macleans then went on to Ardnave in Islay and the Isle of Gigha, all land which belonged to Angus, murdering his tenants.

Angus responded by harrying Mull, Tiree and Coll with the aid of some Englishmen, probably hired in Ireland. Despite the fact that Angus was considered to be an ally of the English, they treated him with suspicion. This suspicion increased when in November 1589 Tyrone invited him to visit. Angus was lavishly entertained. Presents were exchanged. The English authorities looked on in alarm.

Angus, Donald Gorm and Lachlan Mor refused to appear before any court to answer for their latest crimes. On the strength of their former pardon they went to Edinburgh. All three were promptly arrested and imprisoned.

In January 1590/1 they were arraigned for their 'divers crimes'. Angus threw himself on the king's mercy. Lachlan however justified his actions, stubbornly stating that he acted with the king's commission. He was eventually persuaded that this was not the way to influence James and he too 'submitted himself to the king's clemency'.[10] It was now a matter of debate whether or not their possessions should be forfeit. The problem was probably that if they were dispossessed, who would be put in their place? In February they were indicted before the tribunal and fined the enormous sum of 10,000 merks each. The king also proposed to take hostages for their good behaviour from all of them. Robert Bowes, who was now English ambassador to Scotland, noted that 'Maclean will not be able to deliver the pledges, for many of his followers have revolted and left him'.[11]

Lachlan continued to try and obtain an English pension whilst he was in ward in Edinburgh. On 25 March 1590/1 Bowes reported: 'This day Macklene sent his servant secretly to me to offer his service to her Majesty, and to make a party against Makonnell, Donald Gorum, Owrorke [O Rourke] and any others of the league'. Angus and Donald Gorm also offered their services to Queen Elizabeth. Bowes was giving a great deal of thought to affairs in the Isles and wrote to explain the background to the Maclean-Macdonald feud to Lord Burghley. Walsingham had died the previous year and Burghley had reluctantly succeeded him. However, as in the past nothing was done to secure the services of the Hebridean chiefs for England. Lachlan Mor's supporters would not wait for ever for payment, which is perhaps why his followers were said to have 'revolted and left him'. Angus, who was perhaps already in receipt of Spanish gold from Tyrone, was in a stronger position to pay his men.

The delinquents' allies amongst Argyll's curators now came to their help. Cawdor was the most effective.

In April 1590 the young earl of Argyll, 'having declaired he was past fourteen years of age', was able to choose his own curators. The Campbells were Cawdor and Lochnell. Ardkinglas was not included among the principal curators. In July 1585 he had resigned as comptroller to devote his time to looking after Argyll's estate. He was now past his prime. The next year he was dead. Cawdor, who had married Mary Keith the countess of Argyll's sister, was now in control of the earldom of Argyll. Angus and Donald Gorm were released but only after Angus had been persuaded to sell the Isle of Gigha to Cawdor and promise to pay his dues to the crown. That he was in a position to sell Gigha suggests that lady Agnes, who does not appear in the records after 1588, was dead.

Cawdor followed the earl of Argyll's traditional alliance with O Donnell. In 1590 he was reported to be lobbying the English ambassador in Scotland to release Hugh Roe.[12] Tyrone was also trying to get his son-in-law released. He visited the court in 1590 but although he persuaded the Privy Council to review the question of Hugh Roe's captivity, nothing happened. More dramatic events were required to secure the liberty of O Donnell.[13]

Sir James Campbell of Ardkinglas was succeeded by his son John, 'a man of weak and vacillating disposition',[14] whose kinsmen pressed him to follow his father's example and try to have Cawdor murdered before he ruined them all. They did not have a high opinion of their new laird and told him that his father 'was wyser nor [than] myself and as he fand the slaughter of Calder [Cawdor] to be for the weill of his hous sae I sald also follow furth the same. My answer was that it was owre great a feud to bring on my hous. Thereinafter they answerit to me that they were unhappy that had sic an man of unworthiness for a wyse and active man quhe wes my father. Bot Patrick of Auchavulling [his cousin] said an they had ane bag full of fears in place of the Laird of Ardkinglass ... and sae upon that I tuik in hand the murther of the Laird of Calder'.[15]

Ardkinglas now passed to Edinburgh to obtain Lachlan Mor's release. This he obtained in June 1591 but not before he too had obtained his pound of flesh. The price was the Isle of Luing which was sold to Ardkinglas in consideration of the 'great soumes of money' owed to his father by Duart.[16] At the same time in the presence of Alexander bishop of Brechin (old Ardkinglas's brother), the constable of Dundee and Ardkinglas, Lachlan agreed that he owed the comptroller 9,000 merks for all maills, fermes etc he owed to the king for the crop of the year.

After Lachlan Mor had been released, he and Ardkinglas were passing the Craigs of Corstorphine when they paused and drew together. Ardkinglas asked Maclean:

> were it not ane gude sport to cut him off that has led us on all thir snaris to wit the Laird of Caddel? (i.e. Cawdor)

Maclean answered:

> that there we none that aucht to be mair bent to that matter nor I for first Caddel's Gudesheir slew my Gudesheir and sen syne I haif fund him evir in my contrair in all my particulars.

Ardkinglas replied that:

> Caddel conspyrit my father's deith and now geif he leives ane zeir he will sae discredit me with my Lord Argyll that I shall not haif the moyan [influence] to doe my awin turns with his Lordship.

The two men then went on their way. When they reached the place of Ardkinglas they had further discussions. They agreed to murder Cawdor. Maclean then travelled home to Mull.[17]

The quarrel between Cawdor and Ardkinglas which split the Campbells into two camps affected a vast network of alliances. Even in Angus, where the Campbells had recently established a bridgehead on land feued to them by their relatives the bishop of Brechin and abbot of Cupar, they were divided. Ardkinglas backed the Campbell settlers. Cawdor, whose great aunt Katherine Campbell had married the master of Ogilvie, supported his cousin, the fifth Lord Ogilvie.[18]

In July 1591 the Ogilvies murdered three Campbells who were clients of the bishop. 'Look qhow you father brother is usit be the Ogilvies', Glenorchy chided young Ardkinglas when they met at Kilchurn in July 1591,[19] when Argyll held a tryst to reconcile Glenorchy and the Clan Gregor. 'I think', said Glenorchy, 'that Calder being thaire [the Ogilvies'] friend is cauld in thaire turns – quhat think ze says he, quhow I am misusit at this tyme be Calder his maintenance of the Clan Gregor?' A few days later the dead Campbells were avenged by a massive raid into Angus led by Lochnell's brother John Og of Cabrachan, his brother-in-law John Dubh McConachie, tutor of Inverawe, tenants of Glenorchy and broken men from Lochaber.[20] It was an act which could only have infuriated Cawdor. Responsibility for the raid was firmly placed on Glenorchy and young Ardkinglas and not on the earl of Argyll. As Glenorchy gloomily complained to Ardkinglas, 'If wee had beine as busie as we are wyse we had dune our turns in tyme against Calder and he had not beine to the foir to have wrocht this against us this day'.[21]

Ardkinglas and Duart were to meet again in November 1591 at Dunolly Castle in Lorn. Dunollie was the 'caput' of Duncan Macdougall of Dunolly, who was a friend and ally of Lachlan Mor. He had married an unidentified Margaret Maclean, who may possibly have been one of Lachlan Mor's half-sisters. Duncan had recently succeeded his brother and Ardkinglas' excuse for visiting Dunollie was 'to haif MacCoulis douchter in marriage'.

More than marriage was on their minds. Maclean, MacCoul (as Macdougall was called) and Ardkinglas 'passit to ane chamber and MacCouil put the sloit on the dur and John Auchavulling without the dor with ane quhyte battoune in his hand to keep all folks frae us and thair we reveilit to MacCouil this matter and speirit at him quhat wald be his pairt of this matter. He answerrit he wald tak ane part of oniething that we wald interpryse soe that we all in ane vote consentit to the perfecting of the murther'.[22]

Ardkinglas then left Dunollie for Dunstaffnage where he spent the night, sharing his bed with John Og Campbell of Cabrachan, Lochnell's brother whose mother was a Campbell of Ardkinglas and who had led the raid into Angus. John Og was also persuaded to join the conspiracy and agreed to select and brief the actual murderers. Discussion then followed on who was most suitable to perform the task. Would it be better to get men from the Isles or from Lorn? It was agreed that as the Islesmen did not know the country it was better to select someone from Lorn. Eventually it was decided that Gillipatrick Og Mackellar, a tenant and domestic servant of Ardkinglas, should carry out the actual murder with a weapon, 'a red lang hagbit', supplied by Ardkinglas. Two men belonging to Macdougall were also to be present.

*   *   *   *

At Christmas time in 1591 Hugh Roe escaped from Dublin Castle. His escape is one of the great epics of Irish history.

Curiously Hugh Roe escaped with Henry and Art MacSean O Neill, his father-in-law's enemies. They got out of Dublin Castle through the privies and down the curtain wall. A servant was waiting to guide them. They split up. The main group headed south to be stranded in Glenmalure. Art MacSean died from exposure. Lachlan Mor claimed that his cousin Art had been murdered. Henry reached Ulster only to be imprisoned by Tyrone for the length of the Nine Years War. Hugh Roe suffered from frostbite which eventually led to his big toes being amputated. Even so by January he was back in Ulster.

Soon after Hugh Roe returned to Ulster he expelled the English forces from the lordship of Tirconnell. In April 1592 the ruling sept of the O Donnells and their supporters assembled at Kilmacrenan, the traditional site for the inauguration of the O Donnell. Sir Hugh O Donnell resigned his title. It was at once conferred on Hugh Roe, who informed the Irish Council: 'I have received my father's room and his name upon the whole country by his own will and consent and the best of his chief followers, without persuasion of myself'.[23]

This is something of an understatement. The appointment of Hugh Roe was hardly a free election by the nobility of Tirconnell but was stage-managed by his mother.

The Dublin government was furious that Hugh Roe 'had taken upon him the name of O Donnell without Her Majesty's direction or consent of the State'. It was particularly irritated as immediately after his 'election' Hugh Roe had raided the territory of Turlough Luineach and spoiled his country. The government threatened to use armed force against him but lacked the capacity to do so. Instead the Irish Council accepted the situation and, to encourage him to submit, not only granted him protection but promised him a loan to cover his expenses in coming to the Pale.

At the end of July 1592 the earl of Tyrone escorted his son-in-law from Donegal to Dundalk where on 2nd August he submitted to the lord deputy. In exchange for recognition of his captaincy of Tirconnell Hugh Roe promised to remain loyal, and not to persecute his former rivals in Tirconnell and their ally Turlough Luinneach. He also agreed to pay his rents and to banish Roman Catholic priests and bishops from his territory. It was a clause he had no intention of keeping.

*   *   *   *

Even more dramatic events were taking place in Scotland. On 13 January 1591/2, at Rothesay, Angus Macdonald and John Campbell of Cawdor made a contract of friendship. If this contract had been known to the plotters it would have been the final proof, if it were necessary, that Cawdor and his network of alliances threatened all those who were in the other camp.

On 4 February 1591/2 John Campbell of Cawdor was warming himself by the fire at the house of Knipoch, belonging to his son-in-law Dugald Campbell of Glenfeochan, near the head of Loch Feochan in Lorn, when three shots were fired at him through the window. Cawdor died immediately.

A few days later Huntly, who had a commission to hunt down Francis Stewart earl of Bothwell, who had just staged an unsuccessful coup d'état against the king, left the court to cross the Forth in pursuit of Bothwell's friends including the earl of Moray. Once across the Forth he headed straight for Donibristle, the home of Moray's mother. When Moray refused to surrender, the Gordons laid siege to the house. A fire was then lit to smoke out the defenders. Patrick Dunbar, sheriff of Moray and five other men broke out from an entrance while Moray himself fled from another. Dunbar and the others were killed and after a search along the shore Moray was also taken. He was hacked to death. Huntly himself is said to have struck the crucial blow, causing the dying earl of Moray to exclaim, 'You have spoilt a better face than your own'.

*   *   *   *

Nothing is heard of Lachlan Mor for some time after the meeting of the conspirators at Dunolly. He had probably wisely and uncharacteristically returned to the islands to await events.

In Edinburgh news of Moray's murder spread rapidly. Speculation about a conspiracy was soon rife, especially when within forty-eight hours news arrived of Cawdor's murder, who it was rumoured had been 'slain in the north by the practice of Huntly'.[24]

The crown's reaction to the murder was one of official outrage and actual indifference. Huntly's commissions, including his lieutenancy, were cancelled. There was talk of pursuing him but the king did nothing, even refusing to see the murdered earl's mother and denying her the right to carry her son's corpse in a procession. He also refused to see the gruesome painting of her son's body that Lady Doune had commissioned.

Within a week of the murder both the king and his chancellor were being blamed both by Moray's friends and the people, who believed the murder to be part of a Roman Catholic conspiracy. Feelings reached a fever pitch when it was announced that a force could not be levied to pursue Huntly, because the king thought it more important to pursue Bothwell. The earls of Argyll and Atholl declared they were ready to march whilst other noblemen and ministers tried to persuade the king to go north after Huntly. Instead James rode out of Edinburgh and to the fury of the people headed west.

By going to Glasgow James had hoped to calm the situation but when he returned to Edinburgh on 22 February the crowd's anger had not abated. A coalition of differing interests was now forming for which Moray was the symbol of unity. Some wanted vengeance on Huntly, others a Protestant crusade and even the restoration of Bothwell.

Huntly however was prepared to face his accusers and offered to stand trial. This action stemmed the crowd's anger for a while, but when Huntly failed to surrender himself and occupied Perth with a small army of his men the uproar began again.

Meanwhile, before the end of March, Argyll called a convention at Dunoon to discover who had murdered Cawdor. All the leading Campbells were present. It was the first time that Ardkinglas and Glenorchy had met since Cawdor's murder and Ardkinglas described what had happened to his fellow conspirator. He also said that it was Gillipatrick Og Mackellar who had carried out the deed. Glenorchy advised him to dispose of Mackellar before he talked. He then asked Ardkinglas for a look at the bond they had both subscribed agreeing to murder Cawdor. Ardkinglas agreed to get it for him, whereupon Glenorchy said he would show Ardkinglas 'a thing that wold make me a man and would be a suretie and standing to us both ...'[25]

That afternoon when 'my Lord [was] playing at the football with Auchinbreck and uthers scholaris', Ardkinglas and Glenorchy walked to a little knoll 'and lay downe upon oure bombs our faces toward my Lord playing'. Glenorchy asked if he had the contract with him, to which Ardkinglas replied he had. 'Then he desyrit a sight thereof and I againe desyrit a sight of that quhilk he promisit to show mee, quhilk he denyit until I first shewe him his band, and I tuik it out of my sleive and gave it him in his hand quhow soon that he had markit weel that it was it he put it up into his slieve and thairefter opened the buttons of his coat and duplet and tuik out ane contract wreten in parchment ... with many tags hinging thair at of a verie fair hand wret in English without dete or witness'.[26]

The deed Glenorchy had produced was a contract agreeing not only to the murder of Cawdor and Moray but also the young earl of Argyll and his brother. It was signed by Huntly, the chancellor and Lord Maxwell as well as Lochnell, Glenorchy, Stewart of Appin and Macdougall of Dunollie. It was political dynamite, confirming the worst rumours in Edinburgh that the conspiracy went to the very top of the political establishment, perhaps even to the king himself.

At the national level the plot aimed to destroy the increasing influence of the 'Protestant' party of the Stewart earls of Moray and Bothwell and their ally Campbell of Cawdor. At the regional level its aim was no less dramatic. It proposed the destruction of the earldom of Argyll as a major force in the Highlands. The successful outcome of the conspiracy would have made Huntly pre-eminent at court and in the Gaeltachd.

As the man who had probably most to gain from the conspiracy, Huntly might be considered to be the originator of the plot. It has however much more of the mark of the chancellor, Sir John Maitland of Thirlestane, described in October 1587 as 'a heretic and an atheist, a great politician who rules the King with a rod',[27] who had probably inherited the reputation of his brother Lethington, 'Scotland's Machiavelli',[28] than Huntly the man of action. In addition to strengthening his position at court, as his reward for protecting the conspirators Thirlestane was to receive Argyll's lands in East Lothian.

Glenorchy, who claimed that 'his hous had ever fund greater friendship in other noblemen than his chieff',[29] had more to gain than the other Campbells from the dismemberment of the earldom. He was to obtain the barony of Lochawe and Benderloch. Stewart of Appin was to get Argyll's lands in Lorn, whilst Lochnell was to be recognised as earl and receive the rump of the earldom. Significantly Lachlan Mor was not mentioned by Ardkinglas although John Og Campbell of Cabrachan's wife was later to claim that his name was on the contract. He was probably not part of the wider conspiracy, a suggestion that is reinforced by the fact that Macdougall of Dunollie was to obtain the superiority of the Isle of Luing. Lachlan Mor was probably quite prepared to assist in the murder of his hereditary enemy Campbell of Cawdor. He is unlikely to have agreed to the murder of his cousin Argyll. He had perhaps made it clear to his friends that he believed he had made a mistake in feuding with the sixth earl. Glenorchy and Dunollie were probably too shrewd to mention the wider plot to him.

Glenorchy now offered Ardkinglas Argyll's lands in Rosneath if he signed the wider contract. Ardkinglas was out of his depth. He was terrified and refused to sign, at which Glenorchy 'was movit to a great raige anent me: thairefore I desyrit of him the band quhilk he had made me at Inveraray anent the cutting off of Calder ... but he plainlie refusit to give me it againe but wold keep it as ane awe band abune my head because I refusit to subscryve the same great contract concerning the cutting off of my Lord Argyll ...' [30]

It was not long before Ardkinglas was suspected of being party to Cawdor's murder. On 6 June 1592 Bowes reported to Burghley: 'The earl of Argyll, his tutors and friends have appointed to meet at Stirling this week to try out the authors of the slaughter of the Laird of Cawdor, wherein, Ardkinlass, one of Argyll's tutors, MacCoul, McClane and Glenurthie are suspected'.[31]

Ardkinglas was terrified. How much was known? Who had talked? His terror led him to consult John Og Campbell of Cabrachan's wife Margaret, daughter of Campbell of Inverawe. John Og was away in Ireland, where it was said Angus had agreed to seize and slay him.[32] As Angus and Cawdor had been allies, the motive presumably was revenge and not to suppress his evidence. Margaret's story, which was later told to those investigating the murder, is an extraordinary one which gives an insight into the beliefs and superstitions that were rife in Scotland at the time.

Ardkinglas asked Margaret how much her husband had told her of the plot to murder Cawdor. He also wanted to know how he could make sure he was not suspected and how to avoid Argyll's wrath. Even at the age of seventeen Gillespick Gruamach as the earl was nicknamed could put the fear of God into his clansmen.

Margaret was a cunning woman. She wanted to know what was going on and therefore explained that she could do nothing to help unless Ardkinglas told her all that had happened. The guileless laird admitted his part in the murder. He went to say that Gillepatrick Og believed that they could be saved by witchcraft. Mackellar had also told him that:

> all witchcraft is to be practiced in the beginning of every quarter and now the first beginning of the harvest quarter approtches and thairfore I desyre you to haif and git me intelligence of my own estate and quhat favour I may look for at my Lord's hands.

Margaret promised to help. She went to Lismore and sent a servant woman of hers to Morvern to:

> ane Nich aicherne with a chopine of acqu vitae, ane firlot of beir and an kurtiche, and desyrit to understand of her what suld becum of Ardkinglas, Gilpatrick Og and the rest of the conspirators.

The answer that the witch revealed was that they and MacCoul would be warded in Edinburgh but would eventually come home safely:

> bot she wold not tak in hand safe them any longer.

She also declared that:

> MacCoul wold escheip for a lang tyme zeit that at the last he wold pey for it and Macklane was also on the Council of the said murther.[33]

*   *   *   *

Belief in the power of witchcraft was rife in sixteenth-century Scotland. Even the king, who was educated by the leading humanist scholars of the day and was initially sceptical, became an obsessed believer. His conversion occurred after he personally examined Anny Sampson, one of the notorious North Berwick witches who was arrested in 1590. She astounded James by recounting conversations, on their honeymoon, between the king and his bride Anne of Denmark.

Anne had set sail three times for Scotland and three times she had been driven back by violent storms. They were attributed to the malign influence of witches. It was only when James travelled to Denmark himself to fetch her that she reached Scotland.

James spent that winter in Denmark and it has been suggested that the visit helped stimulate the persecution of witches in lowland Scotland.[34] The Danish reformers had labelled all those who opposed or attacked the reformed church as witches and in the hothouse atmosphere left by the Armada and Huntly's Roman Catholic plottings, Scotland was ripe for an epidemic of witch mania.

There had always been a belief in magic in Scotland. John Major, the historian, related that during his childhood in the late fifteenth century witches were well known in East Lothian. He considered them harmless, regarding them with the same dispassionate interest as he did the superstitions of the local country people and claimed that the practitioners, 'the good women to whom these customs were handed down by their ancestors are not to be condemned as sinners until they are told that such acts are wrong'.[35]

It has recently been argued that Europe was only really christianised for the first time by the twin movements of the Reformation and Counter-Reformation. It is an argument that is particularly applicable to Scotland: 'whatever may be said about the effectiveness of the pre-Reformation Church there, it is not really disputed that in the fifty years following the Reformation in those areas where Kirk sessions were set up and trained ministers sent, much of the populace was introduced through a most strenuous indoctrination of literacy, preaching and "godly discipline", to a basic Christianity and to concepts of moral behaviour which would have been quite unfamiliar to their grand-parents'.[36]

This may have been true of the Lowlands. It was not the case in the Highlands, where the Gaelic-speaking clergy, who were usually members of the old hereditary learned class, adapted the teachings of Calvin to their own culture. Unlike their Lowland brethren they did not regard all forms of witchcraft as inherently evil.

As Jane Dawson has pointed out: 'The Gaelic language had a rich vocabulary to distinguish the varieties of supernatural activity and the particular contexts in which they were employed. This enabled the Gaelic clergy to be much more discerning and to condemn black magic and sorcery but tolerate other supernatural beliefs. In particular they made a sharp distinction between witchcraft and the hereditary gift (or curse) of second sight':

> The tradition of the seer was an integral part of Highland life. The Gaelic clergy saw no reason to condemn it nor associate it in any way with the devil. They regarded the foretellings as a natural phenomenon and linked them with some of the form of prophecy found in the Old Testament.[37]

This fact explains how, as we shall see, Lachlan Mor was to be both a sincere Calvinist and one who was reputed to consult 'wise women'.

*   *   *   *

It was one thing to be suspected of murder. It was another actually to be charged with the crime. There was as yet no evidence against Ardkinglas and Glenorchy and for the present the accomplices remained at large.

It is likely that the second phase of the plot to murder the earl was now put into effect. On 24 July 1592 the earl of Argyll married lady Agnes Douglas, daughter of the fifth earl of Morton. The following winter he became dangerously ill at Stirling and it was suspected that he had been poisoned.

Although it was never admitted that there had been an attempt on the earl's life, Ardkinglas' conduct is curious. Both John Og Campbell of Cabrachan and his wife Margaret were in Stirling at the time. She was later to confess that Ardkinglas' page arrived in Stirling with letters and 'threi rois nobilis and bad the Deponer [Margaret] bid her husband drink the sam quhill mair wer sent to him'. Margaret had a long talk with the page and got a look at one letter he was carrying. It was addressed to Mr James Kirk, Argyll's secretary, and also contained the same amount of gold coins. The page told her that he had come to Stirling solely to deliver the letter and gold to Kirk. He had now spoken to him and Mr James 'had promisit to meit him ... at my Lord's clois heid and receafe from him the letters and the gold sae sun as it was nicht quhan noe person micht sie; and after that the page had deliverit the saide letters and the gold to Mr James he plenzeit [complained] and said it was owre littel for sic turns as he had tane in hand to plaisir Ardkinglas ... [and] ... geif they were knowin be my Lord Argyll it wer a sufficient caus to gar hang Mr James himself; and efter that Mr James had keipit the paige twa or thrie nichts awaiting my Lord's sickness', as it was thought 'my Lord wald but dour depairt this lyf that sam nicht that I, Glenurchye and George Balfour enterprysit that last purpose at Stirling ...'.[38] George Balfour of M'Corranstoun in Menteith was closely associated with Ardkinglas and had been one of those who had persuaded him to murder Cawdor. It would appear that he was also involved in the attempted murder of the earl.

Cawdor's family and friends had no doubt who had been responsible for the murder. On 28 March 1593 Ardkinglas was on his way to Edinburgh accompanied by four servants when he was ambushed by a party of Buchanans and broken men armed with long hagbuts, pistols and other forbidden weapons. One of his servants, Duncan Campbell, a brother of Auchavulling and another man were a little ahead of the rest of the party when they were gunned down. Duncan, who had been mistaken for Ardkinglas, was badly wounded. He was stabbed to death and then beheaded. Ardkinglas escaped.[39]

Too many people knew about conspiracy to keep it secret for long. Once the earl recovered from his illness, Glenorchy was arrested and held in Carrick Castle.

In June 1593 'a great day of law' was held in Edinburgh. Glenorchy and Ardkinglas were both formally accused of the murder. There was insufficient evidence at this time. Ardkinglas was released. He was now in a complete panic. In September 1593 he consulted John Og's wife again to demand to know whether the witch she had consulted 'usit the name of God or Christ in their practices'.[40]

John Og had been in the habit of consulting witches before he went on a journey. One of them now sent an ominous warning that John should not cross the water of Lismore 'or utherways he sald never return'.[41] It was good advice. Someone, perhaps Argyll's servitor Mr Donald Campbell, dean of Lismore, an illegitimate son of the murdered man, was hard at work seeking evidence. John Og was arrested. He was tortured 'by the boots' and confessed to his and Ardkinglas' part in the murder.[42]

Ardkinglas was arrested. He was held in Carnassary Castle where on 21 May 1594 he was examined concerning the murder of Cawdor and the conspiracy against the earl of Argyll. He made a full confession.

On 28 June 1594 Glenorchy, who was still a prisoner in Carrick Castle, was confronted with Ardkinglas' testimony . He denied everything. Although Ardkinglas confessed that he was party to the murder of Cawdor, he denied that there had been a wider conspiracy, explaining that he had invented the evidence about it in order to escape being tortured. He said that Glenorchy had nothing to do with the crime and that no one knew anything of it save John Og, Gillipatrick Og Mackellar, his brother and Duncan Campbell. The latter had been murdered by the Buchanans. The others had been executed after being tortured. Ardkinglas was released. He was not to go unscathed. On 7 February 1594/5 the earl of Argyll was granted the escheat of the estate of John Campbell of Ardkinglas, forfeit for the 'shameful and cruel murder of umquhile Johnne Campbell of Cadall'.[43]

The true extent of the conspiracy was covered up. Too many of the political establishment were implicated to allow the truth to come out.

Notes

1. Listed amongst the earliest students is an unidentified Roderick Maclean (Rodericus Maclain), described as being 'Hebridensis ex Mula', *Records of the Scots Colleges* (Aberdeen, 1906), 3.
2. Morgan (1993), 102–3, 129.
3. *CSP Ireland* iii, 397–8.
4. PRO SP 63/136 nos. 36 (2, 4), 43 (12); 137 no. 10 (2,8); CSP SP, iv 506–10.
5. *CSP Ireland* iv, 226.
6. Morgan, 107.
7. *Letters to the Argyll family* (1839), 64–65.
8. Wormald, *Lords and Men*, 394.

9. J. R. N. Macphail (ed), *Highland Papers* (1914–1934) (*HP*), i, 161.
10. *CSP Scot* x, 452.
11. *Ibid,* 469.
12. *CSP Scot* x, 518.
13. Morgan, 131.
14. Gregory, 247.
15. *HP* i, 162.
16. SRO. RD 1/36 f319v – 320r.
17. *HP* i, 164.
18. E. J. Cowan, 'The Angus Campbells', *Scottish Studies* Vol. 25. (1981).
19. *HP* i, 180.
20. RPC IV, 682–3.
21. *HP* i, 183.
22. *HP* i, 164.
23. PRO SP 63/165, no 6 (1).
24. *CSP Scot,* X, 633–634 & 636.
25. *HP* i, 184.
26. *Ibid.*
27. Robert Bruce, the Spanish agent, to Bernardino de Mendoza, *Calendar of Spanish State Papers relating to English Affairs* (London, 1899), 144.
28. Mark Loughin, 'Maitland, Machiavelli and the Propaganda of the Scottish Civil War', in A. A. MacDonald, M. Lynch and I. B. Cowan (eds), *The Renaissance in Scotland* (Leiden, 1994).
29. *HP* i, 187.
30. *Ibid,* 183.
31. CSP *Scot.* x, 684.
32. *HP* i, 159–160.
33. *Ibid* i, 105.
34. Christina Larner, *Enemies of God* (London, 1981).
35. Aeneas MacKay, *Memoir of John Major* (Edinburgh, 1892).
36. *Enemies of God,* 157.
37. Jane Dawson, 'Calvinism and the Gaidhealtachd in Scotland', in A. Pettigree, A. Duke & G. Lewis (eds), *Calvinism in Europe 1540–1620* (Cambridge, 1994), 251.
38. *HP* i, 173.
39. *RPC* V, 68–69.
40. *HP* i, 167.
41. *Ibid,* 165.
42. *Ibid* i, 170.
43. SRO PSI/67 F67R.

CHAPTER 11

The Drift to War, 1592–1594

Donalbain. To Ireland I; our separated fortune
Shall keep us both the safer: where we are,
There's daggers in men's smiles: the near in blood,
The nearer bloody.
                                    Macbeth Act II, Scene iii

The author of the most recent study of the events leading up to
Tyrone's rebellion has written that: 'The drift to war in Ulster
during 1593 and 1594 is one of the most baffling episodes in Irish
history'.[1] It was certainly a watershed in Ulster: Hugh Roe, with the
connivance of Maguire, was stamping out the last resistance of those
who challenged his 'election' as O Donnell; Tyrone with the assistance
of his sons-in-law Hugh Roe and Maguire was finally pensioning off
Turlough Luineach; the government's policy was in disarray.

Tyrone might have achieved pre-eminence in Ulster but until the
government in Dublin accepted the fact the earl was vulnerable. In the
west his allies Hugh Roe and Maguire were threatened by the ambitions
of Sir Richard Bingham. In the east the earl's rival and brother-in-law
the marshal Sir Hugh Bagenal watched for an opportunity to clip his
wings.

O Neill not only needed the government's recognition that he was
the only man through whom it could govern Ulster. He also needed
Dublin to abandon its policy of reform, which threatened every Irish
lord's power base. In order to achieve these objectives Tyrone did not
hesitate to intrigue with Spain.

On its part Dublin was becoming increasingly suspicious of the
earl. In February 1592 the privy council in London, acting on intelligence from Bingham, sent instructions for the capture of the Papist
bishops lurking in Fermanagh and Tirconnell. O Neill was ordered to
arrest them. He did nothing. To make matters worse London received
reports that the Roman Catholic Archbishop of Armagh, who was
known to be in correspondence with Spain, was promising that
foreign aid would arrive by mid-May 1592. O Neill, O Donnell as well

as other Ulstermen were said to have agreed to support the promised invasion.

The lord deputy also reported to Burghley that 'there is a rumour in Clandeboy ... that a great number of Scots are coming hither, upon a late agreement between Angus MacConnel and McAlane'.[2] He asked that Burghley would write to the King of Scots to stop the islanders from coming to Ulster.

Curt letters from Elizabeth were already on their way to James upbraiding him for his failure to arrest Huntly for the murder of Moray. Rumours of plots between the popish earls and Spain were rife. The Kirk was also on the alert and on 27 December 1592 the minister of Paisley succeeded in intercepting George Ker, brother of Lord Newbattle, and his companion David Graham of Fintry as they were sailing out of Fairlie for Spain. Ker was found to have with him letters from Huntly and the other popish earls to Father William Crichton, a Scottish Jesuit in Spain. They also had with them documents known as 'the Spanish Blanks'. These curious pieces of paper consisted of eight blank sheets signed and sealed by Huntly and his allies. Apparently they were to be filled in by Crichton with terms that would be acceptable to Philip II if he were to send an army to Scotland for the invasion of England. Another theory was that the blank pieces of paper were filled with invisible writing. The covering letter however contained the incriminating sentence 'I would you brought the rest of your friends with you that are beyond the sea'. This was taken to mean a Spanish army. Fintry and Ker were arrested. Fintry was executed and Ker tortured with the 'boots' before, amazingly, he escaped from Edinburgh Castle.

On 14 February 1592–3 Robert Bowes reported to Burghley: 'It is said that Huntly and Errol ... shall be received by Maclean into the Island of Carndburgh [Carnaburg], a very strong place amongst the West Isles where they will await to be rescued by the Spaniards'. The earl's friends were rumoured to be planning to seize the king of Scots who 'it is thought shall be weakly defended against them ...'[3]

London was now thoroughly alarmed by the threat of a Spanish invasion in both Scotland and Ireland. The move to what has become known as the Nine Years' War in Ireland was however not to be caused by Spanish intervention but by Dublin's attempt to reform Fermanagh when it had neither the support of the local magnates nor sufficient troops to ensure success. In April 1593 Captain Humphrey Willis entered Maguire's country. His objective was to set up a sheriffdom in Fermanagh. He had with him some 300 troops.

Maguire was prepared to accept a sheriffdom in his country provided the incumbent was chosen by himself. He was not prepared to accept Willis, particularly as the latter rapidly proved himself to be more interested in plunder than enforcing the law. He wrote to Angus and his bastard son Archibald for assistance. The letter, written in Gaelic, was intercepted, translated and sent by the lord deputy on 30 June 1593 to the privy council in London. It begins: 'Maguire's commendations to Angus M'Donnell, and I do send to you that there is some wars rising upon me ... [send] five or six hundred ... tall men, well armed, and I will give you meat ... moreover I think that you shall have better spoils than your wages ...'⁴ The letter is endorsed 'Let me be given to M'Gilesbig M'Angus Ilay'.

Maguire mobilised his men. He was at first hard pressed to evict Willis. Help was then forthcoming in the form of Tyrone's brother Cormac Mac Baron, with a mixed body of horse and foot. He was rapidly followed by the earl's foster brothers the O Hagans with a further 120 men armed with hagbuts. A hundred of the Macsweeney galloglass were also soon on the scene. Willis and his men took refuge in a church and they were only able to retire after Tyrone obtained safe-conduct for them.

Maguire's success encouraged him to invade Connaught to settle scores with the Binghams. He attacked Sligo and burned the Binghams' base at Ballimote. In a letter to the lord deputy Maguire complained that he had acted as he had only because his complaints of attacks by the Binghams had been ignored. Whilst Maguire was attacking Sligo, Tyrone's nephew, Brian MacArthur MacBaron, invaded South Clandeboye and attacked Bagenal's allies.

Although Tyrone had not been personally involved in evicting Willis, it is clear that behind the scenes he was aiding and abetting Maguire. He was even more obviously involved in the next incident on the road to rebellion, when in May 1593 the O Hagans murdered Phelim Mac-Turlough O Neill, lord of Killetra.

Phelim's country was strategically located around Toome on the junction of the lower Bann and Lough Neagh and commanded the main crossing point from Tyrone into North Clandeboye. It was a country that Tyrone had been trying to annexe since the late 1580s. Phelim was also a client of Bagenal's and his murder was a warning to all O Neills who had not pledged their loyalty to Tyrone.

It has been argued that these attacks on Bagenal and Bingham were not designed so much to damage their interests as to make the point in Dublin that it could only govern Ulster through Hugh O Neill.

In fact Dublin went a long way to accept the situation. But it could hardly ignore the fact that the earl was patently behind the present unrest. Tyrone was summoned to meet the council at Dundalk in September 1593. Probably to everyone's surprise he turned up. In addition to the charge of conspiring with Spain he was charged with orchestrating Maguire's revolt; and the murder of Phelim O Neill. Tyrone was able to clear himself of all the charges against him. One of the reasons behind his discharge was no doubt the fact that if he had been arrested 5000 of his men were poised to invade the Pale. Dublin was unprepared for a major incursion from Ulster, the lord deputy was sick and the government was as usual short of money and men.

One equally extraordinary result of the Dundalk conference was that the earl was given a commission against Maguire. He was to attempt to reconcile him by negotiations but if they did not succeed he was to use force.

Bagenal and Tyrone invaded Fermanagh. On 10 October 1593 Maguire made a stand at the ford on the Erne. He was defeated, losing at least 300 men. Hugh O Neill's participation in the invasion of Fermanagh was at best half-hearted. On the face of it it was extraordinary that he took part in the expedition at all. Probably to his relief the earl was wounded in the fight with Maguire, in order as one commentator stated 'so that the English would not have any suspicion of him'.

If the government in Ireland was able to accept Tyrone's innocence, London was not. The arrangements made by the council were received with disbelief. The queen considered that the allegations made against the earl at least justified his arrest; granting him a commission against Maguire was incomprehensible.

Tyrone's offer to help the government against his son-in-law was remarkably astute. It left the council with the suspicion that he just might be innocent and that the earl's accusers were wrong. It also gave him time. Had O Neill refused to co-operate, English reinforcements would have arrived in Ireland by the spring of 1594.

During 1594, when the government could put few men into the field, there was a massive increase in the power of Tyrone and O Donnell as regional overlords. Neighbouring lordships had been weakened militarily by the government's recent action in curbing their legal jurisdictions. They were now forced to give hostages, promise risings out and support bonnaughts as a sign of their dependence on the earl and his son-in-law.

Time was all-important. It allowed Tyrone to arrest his last rivals, the remaining sons of Sean. It also gave him time to recruit. In February 1594 it was reported that he had ordered a proclamation to be read in all the churches in Tyrone asking for 1900 recruits to defend his lordship.

The extra time available gave Tyrone the chance to train them. Training was essential once the use of firearms became general. It was an opportunity which enterprising Irish and Scots merchants were quick to seize, and firearms poured into Ulster. It is estimated that in Sean O Neill's time only an eighth of his army was equipped with firearms. By 1595 at least a third of the Ulster army were so armed. This transformation had mainly taken place during Turlough Luinneach's lordship. It was the earl, however, who was responsible for ensuring that the new weapons were to be used effectively. Tyrone excelled in military training and organisation. Peter Lombard the Roman Catholic propagandist claimed that the earl took a special interest in training his countrymen in the use of firearms. As a contemporary Scottish source confirms, 'he has long prepared for this war, training children, as he does now, with wood shaped like pieces for lightness and training them for shooting'. He paid for this training.[6]

Whatever his long-term preparations, it is clear that most of the training needed to weld his men together into an effective army took place during 1594. One intelligence report provides a vivid picture of this training. It tells of O Neill mustering his troops and beating with a truncheon those who were not proficient. To assist him, Tyrone hired Irish veterans from Flanders.

Part of the earl of Leicester's expedition to the Low Countries in 1586 had consisted of 600 Irish. They were under the command of Sir William Stanley. In January 1587 Stanley surrendered the fortress of Deventer to its Spanish besiegers. He changed sides, taking with him his regiment of English, Irish and Scots soldiers. Large-scale Irish military service with Spain in Flanders began with this treachery.[7]

Hugh Boye MacDavitt who had served as an ensign under Stanley returned home at the earl's request. He became Tyrone's military adviser. MacDavitt, who was highly regarded in the Spanish army, brought with him the latest ideas from Flanders. It was however Tyrone's genius to appreciate that despite his new weapons the basic characteristics of the Irish had not changed. They were experts at irregular guerrilla warfare. They were masters of the art of ambush. In the time available they could not become expert in the setpiece battles and sieges being fought in Flanders. MacDavitt and his assistants could improve weapon training and marksmanship. They could not in the time available turn the Irish kern into professional soldiers on the continental model.

In addition to his local troops Tyrone had need of reinforcements from outside Ireland. Ideally they would come from Spain, but until a

Spanish invasion took place Tyrone needed to recruit mercenaries in Scotland to have any chance of defeating the English. To prevent this happening was now a major priority of the English intelligence services and the ambassador to Scotland.

The English army had been slow to abandon the longbow that had served it so well in the wars with France. However, by the time of the Nine Years' War in Ulster archers had disappeared from Elizabeth's army and firearms, which had been introduced more slowly into the English army than into those of its continental rivals, were commonplace. By the last decade of Elizabeth's reign her footmen were usually armed with matchlock muskets, although some still carried arquebuses or calivers. Men who were equipped with these firearms were referred to as 'shot'.

Other foot soldiers in the English army were armed with pikes varying in length from twelve to eighteen feet which the Swiss mercenaries and their German equivalent the *landsknechts* had made famous by their impenetrable hedgehog columns. A few foot soldiers were still armed with halberds, a combined spear and battle-axe, whilst others called 'targets' were equipped with a sword and buckler (the round Moorish shield) after the Spanish fashion. They were placed in the rear of the pikemen with orders to rush in with their short weapons and kill the opposing pikemen when their pikes were locked with their opponents. This was also originally the role of the halberdiers, but the short stabbing sword was much more effective than the halberd when two opposing armies of pikemen clashed. By the 1590s most halberdiers acted as the bodyguard of a senior commander.

The average English company in Ireland by the late sixteenth century was nominally 200 strong. Its actual strength was only 127 men after the nominal men, whose pay went to the officers, were deleted. The breakdown of such a company into those who carried different weapons was: 67 shot, 47 pikemen and 13 targets.[8]

The English army was made up mainly of new recruits 'pressed' from the English and Welsh counties. They had little training and even less desire to serve in Ireland.

*   *   *   *

Without a standing army the English authorities relied on their intelligence services to sabotage the efforts of the enemy. The first priority of the English ambassador to Scotland was therefore to prevent Scottish mercenaries from joining Tyrone. In 1592 this post was still held by

Robert Bowes who was based at Berwick-on-Tweed. His reports to
London are a model of accurate and often lively diplomatic reporting.

In February 1592/3 Bowes had again drawn Burghley's attention to
the advantages of having Maclean as an English pensioner. More than
money was being considered to draw Lachlan Mor into the English
camp. 'For the service to be done by Maclean', wrote Bowes, 'I have
moved the king to take into his hands his (i.e. Maclean's) eldest son,
now in the keeping of Mackenzie'.[9]

Colin Mackenzie of Kintail known as *Colin Cam* had succeeded his
father in 1570. He is described as being a 'tender, feeble man but wise
and judicious and had much trouble in his tyme with the feud of neighbours'. He did however become sheriff of Inverness and a member of
the privy council.[10] His sons were to play a major role in the events
that followed the death of Lachlan Mor.

In March 1592/3 Bowes reported that Maclean, Macdonald and Donald Gorm were summoned to be forfeited by Parliament for treason
and murder. At present all three were lying low. He also reported that
the king was determined personally to subdue the Western Isles and
bring them to obedience.

In May 1593 Bowes further reported that the king had commanded
Mackenzie to hand over Maclean's son to the earl of Atholl so that
'Atholl may have the keeping of this young gentleman and the grant
of the same will enable him to do much service'.[11]

Donald Gorm of Sleat had other ideas. He was now calling himself
'King of the Isles' and had ordered Mackenzie to deliver Lachlan Mor's
son to himself. Otherwise he would 'burn and harry Mackenzie and all
his'.[12] This was not the end of the affair. On 13 June 1594 Lachlan Mor
was at Chanonry in Ross when he made a bond which referred to his
obligation to relieve Macintosh of the 5000 merks he owed to Colin
Mackenzie of Kintail. This sum was part of 30,000 merks, which Mackenzie was due to pay the earl of Huntly for the delivery of Duart's
son Hector and two other pledges at 40 days' notice.

Lachlan Mor now promised to relieve Macintosh if he were 'troubled
for this sum', when he would repay it to him. Until he did so he would
infeft Macintosh in his lands in Lochaber and give him interest of 500
merks yearly.[13] Custody of Hector was probably only finally resolved
when he married Mackenzie's daughter towards the end of 1594 or
early in 1595.

In July 1594 Bowes reported: 'I have been informed that Donald
MacConnell Gorme has gathered great forces in the West Isles of
Scotland and has passed to Mull, there to receive of the people of that

isle under Maclean to pass into Ireland to aid O Neill in his rebellion'.[14] A note in the margin gave the no doubt welcome intelligence: 'I am newly informed at this present Donald Gorme remains at Mull and Jura, that his company does not exceed 800 men and that he is there for other purposes than for Ireland'.

Bowes goes on to report that he had been advised that O Neill had been present at a meeting with O Donnell and that they had made generous offers to the islanders to join them. O Donnell was also reported to have travelled to Mull with 80 lymphads (Irish galleys) carrying 1500 'shot' and 2500 bowmen as well as another 4000 other footmen.

A few days later Mr John Colville hysterically reported that Mac-Connell, Maclean, Glengarry, Macleod and Mackenzie, 'the principals of the Isles', had joined Huntly and 'have promised him between 20 and 30,000 men if they get money'.[15]

A footnote to Bowes's letter of 21 July 1594 suggests that O Donnell might have come to Scotland to seek revenge for the late 'heryshipp' done in Lochaber by Argyll's forces. This armed incursion into Lochaber by Campbells was yet another disturbance caused by the murder of Moray and Cawdor. The Macintoshes and Grants were members of the Moray faction and were at loggerheads with Huntly even before the murders. In 1589 the earl of Huntly had decided to rebuild the Wolf of Badenoch's castle at Ruthven which controlled the northern entrance to the passes through the Mounth. It also could be used to threaten Macintosh, who was Huntly's tenant in Badenoch.

Huntly had written to Macintosh telling him to get his tenants to assist in the rebuilding by carrying stones and timber to the site. Macintosh refused; instead he frightened off the builders. In October 1592 Huntly invaded Badenoch and suborned some of the Macphersons from their loyalty to Macintosh as chief of the Clan Chattan. Macintosh's son retaliated by throwing the lime needed for building the castle into the River Spey.[16]

Eventually Huntly got his castle built. It stood on the site of the Wolf of Badenoch's motte, the artificial mound which to this day towers above the Spey dominating the route from the south to Inverness. It was garrisoned by the *Sliochd Choinnich*, the senior branch of the *Clan Mhuirich*, as the Macphersons were originally called. The Macphersons, who were staunch supporters of the earl, had acted as Huntly's emissaries when Lochnell made his bond with the earl at *Eilan-nan-Abb* in Loch Etive.[17]

In November 1593 Argyll and Macintosh had made a mutual bond

to defend each other.[18] Both the rival magnates Argyll and Huntly were
tampering with the loyalties of their enemy's subjects.

Huntly was assisted in garrisoning Ruthven Castle by the Camerons,
who had joined him in his invasion of Badenoch.[19] It was presumably
in retaliation for this raid that Argyll's men had invaded Lochaber.

Huntly and his allies had not been wasting time. In April 1594 Spanish
agents probably bringing gold with them arrived at Montrose and in
July a ship docked in Aberdeen bringing more money, messages of
support and Jesuits. To their surprise the new arrivals were promptly
arrested by the burgh's authorities. They were only released when
Huntly and the other conspirators appeared outside Aberdeen and threatened the burgh with 'ane perpetuall quarrel'. Although the money was
welcome, it was Spanish troops that Huntly, like Tyrone, required. In
August Huntly and Errol wrote to Philip II begging for military support.
Spain, at war in both France and the Netherlands, was over-exposed
and could not at this time afford to send a military expedition either
to Huntly or to Tyrone. Both men went to war knowing they had little
hope of success.

Notes

1. Hiram Morgan, *Tyrone's Rebellion: the outbreak of the nine years war in Tudor Ireland* (1993), 139. The Irish section in this chapter is based on this book
2. *CSP Ireland (CSPI)* (1585–92), 57: this appears to be the only reference to a pause in the Maclean-Macdonald feud.
3. *CSP Scot.* xi, 49.
4. *CSPI* v, 114.
6. *CSP Scot.* xi, 620.
7. Gráinne Henry, *The Irish Military Community in Spanish Flanders, 1586–1621* (1992), 19–20.
8. Hayes-McCoy (1940–1), 259.
9. *CSP Scot.* xi, 49.
10. Duncan Warrand, *Some Mackenzie Pedigrees* (1965), 11.
11. *CSP Scot.* xi, 88–89.
12. *Ibid*, 95.
13. SRO GD 176, 165.
14. *CSP Scot.* xi, 379.
15. *Ibid*, 398.
16. *Macfarlane's Genealogical Collections* i, 252.
17. *HP* i, 171.
18. AT VII, 238.
19. John Stewart of Ardvorlich, *The Camerons* (1974), 42.

CHAPTER 12

The Battle of Glenlivet,
3 October 1594

Third Apparition:
. . . Macbeth shall never vanquish'd be, until
Great Birnam wood to high Dunsinane hill
Shall come against him.

Macbeth Act IV, Scene i

James VI probably hoped until the very last minute that Huntly would make some gesture that would enable the king to be reconciled with his Roman Catholic subjects. James had no desire to become too firmly committed to the pro-English Presbyterian party or to plunge Scotland into a religious war. He could not however continue to turn a blind eye to events in the north-east of the country and on 15 July 1594 he issued a commission of fire and sword to Argyll, Atholl and Lord Forbes 'for the pursuit of the papists in the North'.[1]

The king was initially unwilling to appoint Argyll as his lieutenant. The earl was only nineteen 'bot a zouth, and not broken to business'. He also feared 'the insolency (which he thought natural to all Hylanders)'.[2] Argyll was considered to be too mighty a subject.

The now all-powerful leaders of the General Assembly of the Church of Scotland, led by Mr Robert Bruce, minister of Edinburgh, were however enthusiastic that Argyll should be appointed. Bruce himself travelled to Inveraray to persuade the earl to accept the commission. He offered much-needed cash to finance the expedition against Huntly. He also promised to persuade the king to grant Argyll Huntly's lands in Lochaber.

The threat of a highland host from the west invading Strathbogie was a double-edged weapon. Stories of Donald of the Isles' invasion which culminated in the battle of Harlaw in 1411 were probably still current in north-east Scotland and many who rallied to Huntly's banner were probably motivated more by fear for their property than any love of Rome.

Argyll's army had the characteristics of a massive raiding party. He is described as having with him 'five thousand naiked Heeland men',[3] with few experienced captains and a ragged, polyglot army many of whom were 'raskalls and poke bearers, who led and marched at raggle and in plompes without order', 'pokes' being the bag or pouch of a beggar, used for collecting meal etc, given in charity.

In fact Argyll had achieved a remarkable feat in gathering such a massive army together in so short a time. A major part of his force was made up by his own clan, including Lochnell, Auchinbreck, the tutor of Inverawe and a party even supplied by Glenorchy, although Black Duncan himself pleaded illness and was excused from joining the host.[4] It is also likely that the Cawdor Campbells were present under the leadership of Mr Donald Campbell, the murdered Cawdor's illegitimate son. Many of the army were islanders. Lachlan Mor had a large contingent of his clan and his followers including Macneill of Barra. Donald Gorm may also have brought men from Ireland to aid Argyll, whilst O Donnell was reported to have sent 500 'harqubusiers' from Ulster to assist his ancient ally.[5] It is unlikely that Bowes' report was accurate or that Donald Gorm was present in the host.

At the beginning of the Nine Years' War it was thought that O Donnell's men were not as well equipped or trained for modern warfare as were O Neill's.[6] They would therefore not have looked out of place in an army whose vanguard is described as consisting of 3000 men, 2000 of whom had firearms, 'the rest bows, Lochaber axes and swords, the latter ... all protected by coats of mail'.

The archers, according to custom and for lightness, had no armour. They were also said to have been armed with 'speares and scheildis with bulletis, dartis and bowes'. Lachlan Mor himself is said to have had 'a jacke upon him, two haberglouns [a sleeveless coat of mail] with a murrion and a Danish axe'.[7]

Argyll waited in vain for Angus Macdonald to arrive. He too probably had to bring his 500 bowmen from Ireland. He arrived too late for the battle.[8] Other Highlanders such as Mackenzie, Lovat, Ballingowan and Foulis were also late for the rendezvous.

Argyll collected troops as he marched. Macgregor perhaps joined him in Glenorchy or when the army moved down Tayside to Blair. Blair Castle commanded the southern entrance to the passes through the Mounth. The earl of Athol had been ordered to join the expedition but he refused to serve under Argyll and sent his son-in-law and eventual heir Murray of Tullibardine and 'John Dooe with 400 footmen'.[9]

The king had been highly critical of Argyll's decision to take Maclean with him. The earl however had protested that he could not leave Lachlan Mor behind as he might 'join with Glenorchy and trouble the country'. Despite Argyll's reconciliation with his kinsman he evidently did not trust Glenorchy.[10]

At Blair Argyll appointed Maclean to be 'general under him of his army' which was now estimated to be 7000 strong. Huntly attempted to dissuade Argyll from advancing. He sent Allan Cameron of Locheil (*Alan MacKendowy*) to plead for peace and 'spare the spoil and slaughter of his poor tenants and that all griefs and quarrels betwixt them be compounded by the award of the king'.[11] Huntly had however not appreciated the strength of Argyll's desire for revenge nor the intransigence of the General Assembly. Nothing could stay Argyll's advance and the highland host advanced to Badenoch.

At the head of the Spey Argyll's progress was halted by Huntly's castle of Ruthven which was garrisoned by the Macphersons. According to one source Argyll set about besieging the castle and after wasting some days failed to take it and raised the siege.[12] Another witness, however, says that Argyll did not besiege it because the Macphersons promised to deliver it up 'whenever it pleased him'.[13]

Argyll was probably now joined by the Macintoshes and the Grants. He was however altogether lacking cavalry and until he was reinforced by Lord Forbes and the rest of the anti-Huntly party in the north-east he was extremely vulnerable. He was particularly so in the upper reaches of the Spey which were probably only sparsely wooded, and away from the river itself was dry ground and excellent cavalry country.

The earl took to the high ground as quickly as possible. His column was strung out several miles long as it moved slowly across the hills between the Spey and the Avon where he hoped to meet the Forbeses. Meanwhile Huntly was gathering his forces in Strathbogie. Most of the surviving eye-witness accounts of the campaign are from those who served under Huntly and they give a graphic picture of the confederate army as they received intelligence that the enemy was scarce twenty miles from them laying waste the country with fire and sword, 'committing the greatest cruelty in murdering women, children, the aged and infirm'.[14]

Huntly's army is estimated to have been anything from 1200 strong to 4000.[15] All sources confirm that the confederates had a high percentage of horsemen. Huntly had for some time employed professional soldiers in his household and he was now to obtain the benefit of their services. He also had six field pieces under the command of Andrew Gray, who was later to distinguish himself fighting in Bohemia.

On 1 October 1594 the confederates camped for the night at Cabrach
on the upper reaches of the Deveron, posting sentries to prevent their
being surprised. Here they held a council of war which decided that the
earl of Errol should command the vanguard accompanied by Huntly's
uncle Sir Patrick Gordon of Auchindoun, Wood of Bonnington, an
ardent papist, Gordon of Gight, Innermeath, Butter of Merton and
Thomas Ker, another professional soldier plus most of the mercenaries
employed by Huntly. The army was drawn up at daybreak. According
to one account the van numbered only 200. The rest of the army was
divided into two wings, the left led by Gordon of Cluny, the right by
Gordon of Abergeldy. The rear which was commanded by Huntly himself
numbered 200.

Our anonymous Roman Catholic author remarks that that morning
'All the Catholics, who assembled, partook the holy sacrament of
penitence to expiate their sins, and this to the joy of many, but me in
particular who saw the ardour of the primitive church renewed in a
beautiful offering. Indeed, I remember, that in the plain of Cabrach, each
earl drew his sword, and swore a solemn oath to the other, that it
should not be sheathed till the enemy were vanquished, or he died in
the attempt'.[16]

The confederates then 'marched five miles through rugged difficult
roads' to Glen Fiddich. They camped at the castle of Auchindoun. That
night was spent under arms. A little before dawn the next morning the
Roman Catholics went into the castle to celebrate Mass, after which
each man's arms were blessed and consecrated. In a similar manner the
standards of the noblemen were blessed with a prayer before they set
off again.

The confederate army had marched six miles by noon. It was hard
going and it was only with the greatest difficulty that they transported
the baggage and the cannon. Although no one knew where the enemy
was, morale was high. Auchindoun and Ker were sent ahead to reconnoitre.

Whilst Huntly's army had moved to Glen Rinnes, Argyll was at
Drumin, a castle belonging to Huntly on the River Avon. It was here
that Argyll held his council of war on the night of 2 October. It is
unlikely that his army's morale equalled that of Huntly's. Lochnell
wanted to command the vanguard. Argyll however decided that his
kinsmen should remain with him in the *Staleoast* as the main body was
then called. Argyll could hardly have entrusted Lochnell with so important a task. Only weeks earlier the earl had had Lochnell's brother,
John Og, executed for his part in the murder of Cawdor. After the battle

it was said that Lochnell had sent a message to Huntly telling him to fire on Argyll's yellow standard. It is difficult to see, as neither army knew where the other was, how this treachery could have been accomplished. Another anonymous author, who was on his way to join Argyll with Mackenzie, also states that both Macintosh and Grant were in cahoots with Huntly and had betrayed Argyll.[17] The bad blood between the two chiefs and Huntly hardly makes this likely.

Our anonymous author with Huntly claims that Auchindoun's party found Argyll 'fearlessly spending his time in feasting and plunder' at Drumin. After some skirmishing Auchindoun retired to report to Huntly. Our author goes on to say that 'while we advanced in order of battle, we descried the enemy's scouts on the mountains, who hastily retreated whenever they beheld us to inform their commanders we were boldly coming up. Then a confused clamour was heard; and those foraging at a distance from the camp were recalled by a signal'.

Comments on the lack of preparation of Argyll's army can be regarded with a certain scepticism. Argyll however had a problem. He had been ordered not to engage Huntly until Lord Forbes and his cavalry joined him. His column was strung out behind for several miles and he had with him numerous camp followers including a witch. She now predicted that the following Friday (the day after the battle was to take place) 'Argyll's harp should be played in Buchan and the bagpipe should be sounded in Strathbogie'.[18] At this time the pipes were solely used by the Highlanders and not by Huntly's mainly lowland army. Argyll decided to avoid battle if possible and his vanguard rapidly seized the high ground on the western slopes of Tom Cullach which was probably considered to be too steep for cavalry. As Argyll's vanguard seized this vital high ground before Huntly's men they must either have moved exceptionally fast or Auchindoun's reconnaissance had failed to observe them. As Bowes was to report to London that Argyll only got his men into their order of battle after Auchindoun's horsemen had been sighted,[19] it would seem that the former is what happened.

All was not entirely well in Huntly's army. Errol and his horsemen had moved too fast and Huntly furiously sent word to the vanguard commander that if he did not wait for him he would leave the cannon behind and fight Argyll without him. Errol, equally irritated, replied 'it was only the forwardness of the gentlemen that were with him' and that if he could not restrain them he would await Huntly by himself.[20]

The situation was further complicated by fog which lasted all morning. The confederates however had reached the foot of Tom Cullach by ten o'clock. They took a further two hours climbing up the face 'for the ascent was mossy and so full of boggs and stones' that the horse had great difficulty in advancing. It was even worse for the carriage of the cannons. Somehow they managed.

The confederates were resting their horses and reorganising the column in an attempt to move forward again and get between Argyll and Forbes, preventing the two parts of the royal army joining together, when to their horror Huntly's men noticed Argyll's vanguard marching in over the top of the very hill that they were climbing.

Huntly had appreciated that Argyll would do his utmost to avoid a battle until he was joined by Forbes. He was therefore determined to engage the enemy as quickly as possible whatever the circumstances. They were preparing to attack Argyll's vanguard, when Huntly's men noticed what at first appeared to be 'a growing wood' moving. After more serious observation they found it to be more of Argyll's men, probably his main body, reaching the summit of Carn Tighearn. The fog was evidently playing tricks on them. What Huntly's men had actually seen is difficult to fathom but the story perhaps reinforced Holinshed's *Chronicle* and inspired Shakespeare to make the apparition in *Macbeth* predict that the king 'shall never vanquished be until Great Birnam wood to high Dunsinane hill shall come against him'.

The battle commenced with Sir Andrew Gray opening fire on Argyll's vanguard. Maclean's men saw the shot coming and divided their ranks and let it pass harmlessly between them. Encouraged by this show of disciplined fearlessness, Macneill of Barra advanced in front of the vanguard and shouted abuse at Huntly's troops, waving his sword above his head. He did not see the second shot coming. It decapitated him. As he was a great favourite with the islanders, they took his death as a bad omen and were seen 'to stagger and reel to and fro in great disorder'. The third shot hit no one but the whole vanguard dropped to the ground and refused to get to their feet until Argyll himself came up and beat them to stand.

Meanwhile Argyll's main body and rear pressed forward after the earl despite being ordered to halt. They soon became muddled with the vanguard who were still lying with their faces on the ground. Captain Ker, seeing the confusion opposite him, asked Errol to charge. Errol however was still in a sulk from the harsh words he had received from Huntly and refused.

Huntly, also seeing the moment was critical, sent a message to Ker to tell Errol that if he did not charge, Huntly himself would do so. Furious at the insult, Errol, with a cry of 'The Virgin Mary', put his

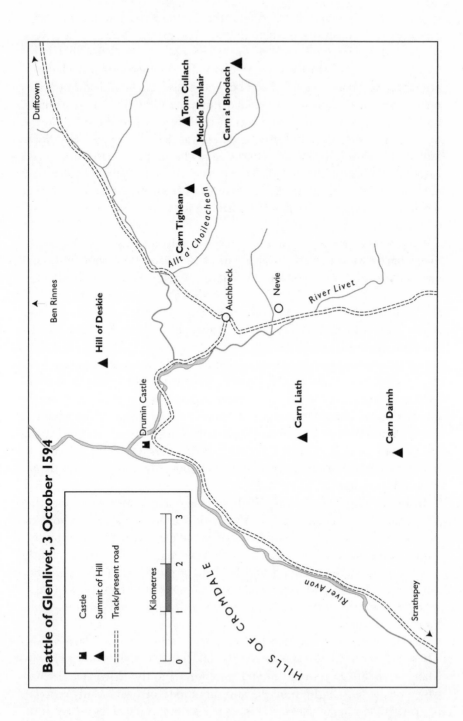

Battle of Glenlivet, 3 October 1594

Castle
Summit of Hill
Track/present road

Kilometres

0   1   2   3

Dufftown

Ben Rinnes

Hill of Deskie

Drumin Castle

Tom Cullach
Muckle Tomlair
Carn a' Bhodach

Allt a' Choileachean

Carn Tighean

Auchbreck

Nevie

River Livet

Carn Liath

Carn Daimh

HILLS OF CROMDALE

River Avon

Strathspey

spurs to his horse and charged followed by the whole confederate vanguard with 'their spears to their thighs'. The ground however was very
rough and their opponents kept up so great a volume of fire that Errol
could not break them by a frontal assault. He therefore wheeled and
attempted to break Argyll's main body and rear. As he did so Maclean's
men turned and almost surrounded him. Errol received two wounds,
both from barbed arrows. One was in the left arm and the other in the
left leg. He survived, but Auchindoun was less fortunate. His horse
bolted and threw its master. The Campbells in the Lieutenant's main
body fell on him with their dirks and stabbed him to death. Later they
cut off his head. Sir Patrick had had a fall from his horse earlier that
morning as the confederates left their camp, which had been seen as a
bad omen.

Huntly, seeing his fellow earl's danger and noticing that Maclean's
men's backs were turned towards him, now seized the opportunity and
charged. He did so, so strongly that the enemy vanguard broke and
were driven back upon Argyll's main body and rear. Chaos ensued. Led
by Lochnell, Argyll's main body fled. Both Lochnell and his brother
James were killed. Argyll wept with rage, shouting at his men as they
fled that they were traitors.

There were scattered bushes and thickets of wood on either side of
the burn of Allt Cullach and some of the Lieutenant's men used them
as cover. They fired back at their pursuers. They were to pay dearly
for their audacity and they were overrun and slaughtered. At one moment
Argyll himself was cornered. Huntly, who was eager to capture the
Lieutenant himself, rushed forward to seize him. Only the bravery of
half-a-dozen of Argyll's companions, including Maclean, saved him and
drove Huntly back.

In the thick of the fighting Tullibardine, one of those who saved the
Lieutenant, did his best to do the same for his opponent whom he
mistook for his cousin, an unidentified nobleman known as 'Cowbardy'.
Tullibardine shouted at him to withdraw and save himself. Huntly
refused to heed the warning and held his ground. His horse was shot
under him. Horse and rider collapsed in the burn. Huntly was soon
rehorsed but the initiative was lost. Argyll and his companions got
away to safety.

Lachlan Mor and his men had fought a desperate rearguard action.
They had received the whole weight of Huntly's main body's charge.
Many were killed or wounded and were forced to fly. However, Lachlan
Mor, 'disdaining flight himself, and ambitious of everlasting renown,
... rushed to the thickest of his enemies, and rescued as many from

slaughter as in the compass of his power' and most undoubtedly would have died, had not his own people forced him from the field.

Our eyewitness evidently was fighting at this corner of the battle-field. He goes on to say: 'How can I sufficiently extol his (i.e. Maclean's) soldiers? They stood singly, and rather suffered themselves to be killed, than ask quarter; Nay, we saw many individually surrounded by the horse refuse to yield, and meet death with an undaunted countenance'.[21]

One Maclean who survived was Allan of Ardtornish, John Dubh of Morvern's eldest surviving son. He was shot in the head. His life however was saved 'by the goodness of his helmet'. The force of the shot knocked him to the ground and he was only rescued from the Gordons by the bravery of Lachlan Odhar Maclean of the family of Ross.

Another witness reported that when Huntly's main body was overwhelming Maclean's vanguard, Lachlan Mor noticed Huntly's standard bearer not far off on horseback. Rushing towards him with his axe, he slew five or six men in his way. He then drove its spike into the standard bearer's horse and cut the rider in two at the waist. He carried the standard off with him.[22]

Donald Campbell, who is probably the bloodthirsty dean of Lismore, captured another standard.[23] Standard bearers were prime targets for those wanting to earn renown. Robert Fraser, the king's herald with Argyll's army, was set upon by Huntly's horsemen. Crying 'Have at the Lyon', they ran him through.[24] The king was reported to be furious. He was less upset by Argyll's defeat and is reported to have said, 'Fair fall thee, Geordie [Good for you, Huntly], sending him home like a subject'.[25] James VI was never to have any love for the seventh earl of Argyll. Others did. In Argyll's baggage captured in the battle a letter was found to the earl from his wife 'in the most affectionate terms' begging him to do nothing rash without consulting his friends and to be 'careful in avoiding snares'.

Also found were letters from Mr Robert Bruce the minister urging the earl only 'to injure Catholics' and reporting that he had spoken to the king about granting Argyll Huntly's estate in Lochaber, but that the king was 'much displeased' at the earl's arrogance, 'not being present himself' to make the request.[26]

Argyll is said to have lost 500 men at Glenlivet. Huntly lost only a dozen men. All those killed on the confederate side were however men of some importance. Many more were badly wounded. Argyll's standard was flown in triumph by the Gordons over Strathbogie Castle whilst the Lieutenant's harp and bagpipes were played as the witch predicted, although not by the men she had expected to do so. The witch herself was executed by the Gordons.

Despite Huntly's victory it was the end of the Roman Catholic party in the north-east. Neither Huntly nor his men were in a position to face the king who had moved to Aberdeen. Both Huntly and Errol went into exile. The attempt by the Roman Catholic earls in Scotland to reverse the decision of 1560 had failed. It fell to the Gaels of Ulster alone to keep militant Roman Catholicism alive in the British Isles.

Notes

1. AT vii, 265.
2. *Spottiswoode Miscellany* i, 261.
3. Calderwood, *History* v, 348.
4. AT vii, 262.
5. *CSP Scot.* xi, 453.
6. PRO SP 63/179, no 51;180, no 48 (1); 182 no 42 (1).
7. Dalyell; 145; Calderwood v, 350.
8. *Spottiswoode Miscellany* i, 260.
9. *CSP Scot.* xi, 453.
10. *Ibid*, 432.
11. *Ibid*, 453.
12. Macfarlane i, 256; Gordonstoun, 226.
13. Calderwood v, 348.
14. Dalyell i, 142 & 150.
15. *CSP Scot.* xi, 453.
16. Dalyell i, 142–3.
17. Calderwood v, 348.
18. Dalyell, i, 151.
19. *CSP Scot.* xi, 459.
20. *Spottiswoode Miscellany* i, 263.
21. Dalyell, i, 148.
22. Calderwood v, 350.
23. Alastair Campbell of Airds, *The Life and Troubled times of Sir Donald Campbell of Ardnamurchan* (nd), 8.
24. *CSP Scot.* xi, 459.
25. Hugh Campbell, *The Murders of Lord Moray and the Thane of Cawdor* (1985), 22.
26. Dalyell i, 152.

CHAPTER 13

An Intelligence Assessment from the Isles

Macbeth.
Hang out our banners on the outward walls;
The cry is still, 'They come': our castle's strength
Will laugh a siege to scorn: here let them live
Till famine and the ague eat them up.

Macbeth, Act V, Scene v

In the immediate aftermath of the battle of Glenlivet the earl of Argyll was a broken man. He had disobeyed his orders and fought without supporting cavalry. Contrary to all current military experience his overwhelmingly stronger infantry had been defeated by a relatively small body of cavalry. Coming so soon after the plots against him within his own clan, the psychological effects on a young man – he was no more than nineteen – must have been devastating. To make matters worse he was briefly imprisoned in Edinburgh Castle for the damage his men had done in the north-east.[1]

Lachlan Mor, on the other hand, was the hero of the hour. His reputation was at its height and the euphoria of just being alive, after facing almost certain death, went to his head. As the survivors of the vanguard regrouped after cutting their way through Huntly's ranks Lachlan Mor boasted that if Argyll would lend him but 500 men, in addition to his own clan, he would capture Huntly and bring him to Edinburgh in chains. Argyll was in no mood for heroics and Maclean was forbidden to proceed. The boast lost nothing in its telling. Eventually word of it reached Huntly. It was a boast that the Macleans were to live to regret.

By 7 October news of the battle had reached Robert Bowes and he immediately reported to Burghley. Not all his information was correct as he stated that 'it is supposed Maclean is slain'.[2] He also claimed that Locheil (*Alan Mackindowy*), who had fought for Huntly on horseback, had been killed.

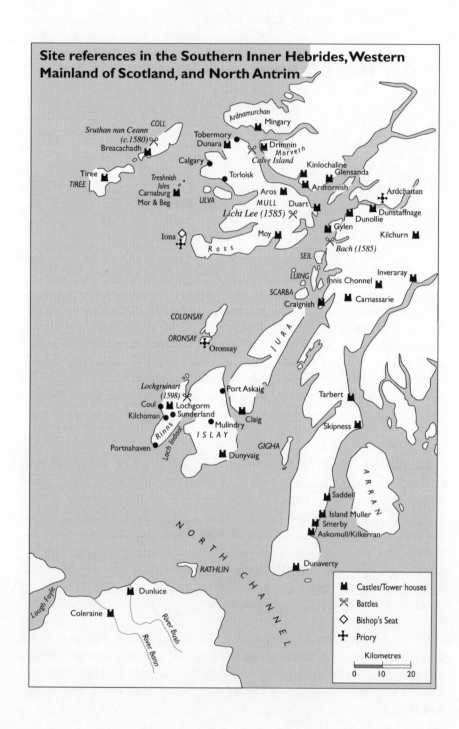

Site references in the Southern Inner Hebrides, Western Mainland of Scotland, and North Antrim

Ardnamurchan
Mingary
Sruthan nan Ceann (c.1580)
COLL
Tobermory
Dunara
Breacachadh
Drimnin
Morvern
Calve Island
Calgary
Kinlochaline
Glensanda
Tiree
TIREE
Treshnish Isles
Carnaburg Mor & Beg
Torloisk
Ardtornish
Ardchattan
Aros
ULVA
MULL
Duart
Dunstaffnage
Licht Lee (1585)
Dunollie
Iona
Gylen
Kilchurn
Moy
Ross
Bach (1585)
SEIL
LUING
Innis Chonnel
Inveraray
SCARBA
Carnassarie
Craignish
COLONSAY
JURA
ORONSAY
Oronsay
Lochgruinart (1598)
Port Askaig
Tarbert
Coul
Lochgorm
Kilchoman
Sunderland
Claig
Skipness
Mulindry
Rinns
ISLAY
Portnahaven
Loch Indaal
GIGHA
Dunyvaig
ARRAN
Saddell
Island Muller
Smerby
Askomull/Kilkerran
NORTH CHANNEL
Dunaverty
RATHLIN
Dunluce
Lough Foyle
Coleraine
River Bush
River Bonn

⬛	Castles/Tower houses
✗	Battles
◇	Bishop's Seat
✝	Priory

Kilometres
0   10   20

In the same letter Bowes reported that the Irish confederates had sent a servant to Argyll desiring that the old friendship between their houses should be renewed and that if he brought some of his men to Ireland to join them they would pay him a pension of £8,000 Scots. Argyll had expressed interest in the offer but was too involved at the time (June 1594), trying those Campbells who were plotting against him, to concern himself with Ireland. Instead the messenger wrote immediately to Donald Gorm with the same offer. As a result Donald Gorm took 1200 men with him to join O Neill and O Donnell. He had however returned to Scotland at the beginning of September, leaving 300 men with the confederates. He was now said to be with Argyll pursuing Huntly.

The following day Bowes had more information to send to Burghley. Fourteen Gordons, 'landed men of good quality', were reported to have been slain in the battle. Eleven of them were said to be guilty of Moray's murder. On the Lieutenant's side Lochnell, Tullibardine's third son and Argyll's master of the household were reported to have been killed. On the 12th Bowes sent a more detailed report of Glenlivet. It included the news that immediately after the battle Argyll had gathered his people together and for lack of victuals sent them all home with the exception of 600 specially chosen men whom he placed under Macintosh's command. Lack of supplies for his vast army had been a constant problem for Argyll. The Highland army was used to living off the country. It was not particularly fussy over where it did so and it was not until December 1596 that Lord Forbes gave the Lieutenant a receipt for full payment for 'all goods and geir spulzeit and taken away by the said earl and his friends and defenders at the time of the conflict of Balrinnes'.[3]

*   *   *   *

By mid-November 1594 the situation in Ulster had so deteriorated that the queen decided to redeploy 2,000 of her troops serving in Brittany. It was to be another four months before the first companies began to arrive in Ireland and not until May that Sir John Norris their commander, a veteran of the wars on the continent, himself arrived.[4] Meanwhile the English agents were doing their utmost to persuade King James and Argyll to stop the flow of highland recruits to Tyrone. On 12 December Roger Aston reported to Bowes that he had held discussions with the king and Argyll. The earl had promised to be answerable for all his people and the king himself had ordered the highland chiefs to report to him at Edinburgh by 17 December. He also gave Argyll permission to write to Maclean who had once again offered to 'daunt all the rest' if he had the king's remission for all 'bygones'. Angus and Donald Gorm on the other hand were 'under the doom of forfeiture'.[5]

Intelligence from his spies continued to reach Bowes throughout December. Donald Gorm and Macleod of Harris, who had patched up his quarrel with his family's old rival, were both reported to be busy recruiting men to serve with the rebels in Ireland. But by the end of the month it was reported that the men they had dispatched there 'have returned home malcontent'. The old story of Maclean's enmity towards Tyrone, over the execution of Hugh Gavelagh, is once again paraded as the reason why he was out of step with the other islanders. The latter were reported to be planning to hold a great convention to co-ordinate their actions. As it was now winter it is worth noting that the islanders were sufficiently confident in their seamanship to move about the islands and travel to Ulster, in the often lengthy pauses between winter gales. Bowes's spies were dispatched to report on the chiefs' deliberations.

*   *   *   *

It was probably at this time that one of the most important reports on the Western Isles was written. Burghley had probably asked Bowes for a detailed assessment of their military potential: the number of men each chief could command and details of their fortresses. In March 1595 a précis of this report reached Whitehall.

The author outlines the ancient means by which the Isles were administered. He writes that: 'The haill Ile of Scotland were devidit in four pairts of auld viz Lewis, Sky, Mule and Yla, and the remanent haill Isles were reknit but as pertinents and pendicles of the said four isles ...' 'But now', he writes, 'their Iles are becum under sundrie men's dominions quhair throw thai answer not to the said four principal Iles Yit thai keip the lawes and uses of the saids four principal Isles, and specialie of thair yeirlie dewtis ...' He points out that Point of Ardnamurchan divided the Isles into two distinct groups: the north included the Skye and Lewis group and the south that of Mull and Islay.

The report points out that the method of maintaining these forces is different to that of Ireland. When writing of Rathlin, which is off the Ulster coast but was then administratively considered to be one of the Western Isles of Scotland, he states that its 'zeirlie dewtie is conform to use and consuetude (i.e. custom) of Ireland'. The Irish system was to maintain a number of men in 'meit and fie', i.e. food, and a sum of money. In addition the tenants had to pay an unspecified quantity of everything they grew once a year to their master, as well as any 'taxation' he might impose. The system in the Scottish Isles was less arbitrary, if no less burdensome.

In Islay 'ilk merk land man [must] sustein daylie and yeirlie ane gentleman in meit and claith, quhilk dois na labour, but is held in as ane of their maister's household men, and man be sustenit and furneisit in all necessaries be the tennent'. Such support of a fighting man was an ancient imposition on the tenants. In the 1590s Islay was worth 360 merklands. Each merkland had to maintain one of their 'maister's household men'. This might therefore be expected to produce 360 men. We are however informed that the 'rising out' of Islay was 800 men. Who were the other 440? They could not have been 'labourers of the ground' as we are specifically told that they were not 'permittit to steir furth of the cuntrie quatevir thair maister have ado ... that the labors belonging to the teilling of the ground and wynning of thair corns may not be left undone ...'[6]

The 'household men' were professional soldiers similar to the 'Galloglaigh' in Ireland, that Dr Boardman argued must have existed in the Hebrides. They were heavy infantry clad in armour and armed with two-handed swords or 'Danish' axes, who were also adept at the long bow. In order to perfect their skills they would have had little time to do anything other than prepare for war, for they must 'be reddie at all times to his maister's service and advis'.[7]

The other 440 were probably not professional soldiers but part-timers. They were not churls tilling or tied to the ground but they could well have been cattle men, drovers, herds or just young men who were not yet ready to be professional fighting men. They would only have been mobilised in a major emergency or when the crown called out fencible men (those aged between 16 and 60), to serve in the 'host' or 'ost', the assembly of the nation's armed men called out by the sovereign for forty days' military service.

It is clear from the amount of 'silver rent' mentioned in the rental that commercial cattle farming was already well established. One of Lachlan Mor's complaints against the sixth earl of Argyll was that he was preventing Maclean's people from travelling to the lowland markets to sell their cattle.

Not every isle was as developed as Mull. Sleat in Skye, the patrimony of Donald Gorm, was 'occupeit for the maist pairt be gentlemen, thaifore it payis but the auld deutis, that is of victuall, buttir, cheis, wyne, aill and acquavitae, samekle as thair maister may be able to spend being

one nicht ... on ilk merk land'. Sleat could raise 700. This is a considerable amount considering it was only 30 merk land. There is no mention
of 'silver rent'. Sleat was clearly organised exclusively for war. It is also
said of Sleat that when Donald Gorm took his night's entertainment
from each merkland he might be accompanied by 600 men. It is therefore
hardly surprising, as John Auchinross exclaimed in July 1595, that before
he sailed for Ireland, Donald Gorm 'had vrackit his lands' in holding
these forces together.[8]

Maclean's *cudeigh* (the number of nights that a tenant had to entertain
his master) was probably no less excessive. Tiree was 'very commodious
and fertile of corns and store of gudes (i.e. cattle) ... It pertenis to great
McClane of Doward, gevin him to be McConneill (i.e. the lord of the
Isles). It was callit in all tymes McConnell's girnell; for it is tellit land,
and na girs but ley land, quhilk is maist nurischand girs of any other,
quhair throw the ky of this Ile abundis sa of milk that thai are milkit
four times in the day. The yeirlie dewtie thairof is sa great of victual,
buttir, cheis, mairtis, wedderis, and other customs, that it is uncertain
to the inhabitants thairof quhat thai should pay, but obeyis and payis
quhatevir is cravet be thair maister for thair haill duties ...'

Tiree was often the winter resort of Maclean. He had free quarters
there for himself and his retinue, who it is said were never less than a
hundred strong. His retinue included falconers who also had free quarters
for themselves and lambs for their hawks. The island had also to provide
a sail and hair tackle for a galley as part of its rent.[9] Tiree was 140
merk land. It had a 'rising out' of 300 men.

Maclean also had the rising out of Scalpay (20), his own land in Mull
(600), Gometra (20) and half Jura (50). Ulva (60) was in a different
position. Lachlan Mor's grandfather had purchased the non-entry of
Macquarrie's estate on the island and nearby 'mainland' of Mull in
1553.[10] Macquarrie's descendants had remained on the property as kindly
tenants. In November 1593 'Hector McQuoyrie in Ulva' purchased the
estate from Lachlan Mor 'for divers sums of money paid to the granter
in his necessity'. He did so only after agreeing certain conditions: that
the estate should descend to his nearest lawful male heir bearing 'the
name and arms of McQuoyrie'; he and his successors pay the sum of
£106.13.4 Scots whenever an heir inherited; and pay the 'exaction called
in Irish *Creachlig Claddich*' whenever the granter and his heirs 'happen
to visit strange parts on the bounds of Mull' as the 'other inhabitants
of the granter's lands in Mull payit together with a penny Scots yearly
at Whitsunday on the lands of Carnacallich if asked'. Macquarrie was
also bound to provide a long boat, plus sufficient victual and munition

and arms to serve Maclean as often as he was required and to do so 'at his own expence'. Finally, if Macquarrie or his heirs 'became hostill to the granter and his heirs ... then this present charter should become null and void and the lands should return to Maclean'. Sasine given at Carnacallich would suffice for the whole estate.[11]

Macneill of Barra was also a follower of Maclean,[12] who in 1585 he describes as his 'chief and master'.[13] Barra with his 'four or five small Iles that he has besides' could raise '200 gude men',[14] although Lachlan Mor claimed that he 'serves me in time of trouble with three hundred men'.[15] The dean of Limerick confirmed that Macneill of Barra was a follower of Maclean. He also stated that he 'was reputed the best sea-faringe waryer in the Ilands ... and hath bein accustomed to invade Ulla in Conoght in Irlande, beinge O Mallyes countrey and to pray in the sea coaste of Conoght, ... Thomond, Kyery, and Desmond, in Ireland'.[16]

He goes on to say that Macneill and 'Grany ny Mallye ... invaded one anothers possessions, though farre distant'. This is something of an understatement. O Malley's country and Barra were some 300 miles apart, a distance which would take a galley three days to a week to cover. 'Grany ny Malley', otherwise Grace O Malley, was the formidable female pirate who led a fleet of galleys for almost fifty years from her base in Clead Bay in what is now Co. Mayo. From here she traded with France and Spain, bringing home wine as well as carrying out piratical raids.[17]

Lachlan Mor could count on the rising out of Maclean of Coll's estate in Coll itself (140) and Quinish in Mull (50). He could also expect to have the support of Maclean of Lochbuie: 'McClane of Lochbuy has three score merk land and will raise 200 men thair on'. He also owned the mountainous island of Scarba which was four merk land. 'It is all woodis and craigis, except twa tounis, and thairfore it is better for sustentation of bestiall nor far cornes'. It could raise 17 men.[18]

Lochbuie almost disappears from the records during Lachlan Mor's lifetime. In the 1570s there had been a feud between the Lochbuie chief and his heir apparent John Maclean.[19] John had eventually inherited the estate. He was as unpredictable as his father. In 1587–8 he illegally imprisoned one of his clansmen and had been summoned to appear before the council.[20] Probably as a result of these quarrels Lochbuie had failed to maintain its position during the sixteenth century and had been reduced from being the rival to Duart for leadership of the Macleans to becoming very much the less important of the two, a fact that did not make for good relations between the two families.

Duart's powerbase had been increased by taking over the crown lands once owned by the lords of the Isles and those of the Church. 'McClane Doward callit Great McClane has the maist pairt [of Mull], extending to aucht score merk land and ten and will raise on it, with the pairt he has of the Bischop 600 men ...'[21] The bishop had 30 merk land in Mull 'but McClane Doward has it in his possession occupeit be his kin'. Iona was also 30 merk land and 'in this isle is the Bischop of the Iles principall dwelling places'. It is however unlikely that he was living there at the time. John Campbell, bishop in the Isles, was dead by 24 April 1594.[22] His son and successor was commendator of Iona but he is more likely to have been based at Ardchattan. Iona was also included in the royal rental to Maclean of 1588. There was no 'rising out' from Iona. It was however the custom for 'four men out of Rosse onlie and four men furth of ycolmkill to pas and keep the fortalice of Carnabulg upon their awin expensis salang as McClane is in oisting to his returneing ...',[23] i.e. when Maclean was called out by his sovereign for military service. This custom, as far as Iona was concerned, continued until the rebellion of 1715 when sixteen men from the island formed the garrison at Carnaburg.[24]

The sources do not deal with the mainland adjacent to the Western Isles in detail so it is not possible to obtain a complete count of the number of men that Lachlan Mor could count on. It would seem quite possible that he could just about assemble the 2,000 men he claimed to be able to raise for service in Ireland. In addition to his own property in Morvern, Lachlan Mor had control of the rising out of the men at Ardgour. On 19 November 1585 Ewen Maclean of Ardgour had described Lachlan as his 'chief and master'.[25] Sometime between that date and 27 November 1591, Ewen was murdered by mistake in his galley off the coast of Mamore. He was shot dead by some Macdonalds of Keppoch who mistook him for Cameron of Locheil as he was wearing a scarlet coat similar to one worn by Locheil. His son was a minor at the time of his death and Ewen's brother, Charles, became tutor of Ardgour. Charles was also a staunch supporter of his chief whose sister, the widow of Hector Ruadh of Coll, he had married. Charles is described as a 'bold daring and very aspiring man, he did not only live very high during his management but purposed to defraud his pupil of the estate'.[26]

Ardgour's neighbours, the Macleans of Kingerloch, although descended from Hector Reagenach the predecessor of the family of Lochbuie, appear always to have followed Maclean of Duart. They too disappear from the records at this time.

Lachlan Mor had several non-Maclean allies. In the Isles Mackinnon generally seems to have followed his lead. He had an estate in Mull, Mishnish, which was 20 merk land which had a 'rising out' of 50 men. His main estate by this time was at Strathordell in Skye.

Mackinnon could raise 160 men in Skye. In the fourteenth and fifteenth centuries the family retreated as Maclean advanced. Mackinnon now usually favoured Maclean, but determined to keep his independence.

A more enthusiastic ally was Duncan Macdougall of Dunollie. He had married an unidentified Margaret Maclean. He was a staunch Presbyterian but had been heavily involved in Cawdor's murder. He had purchased the Isle of Luing from Lachlan Mor. It is still described as belonging to 'McClane Doward [who] has it of my Lord Argile for service'. It was 40 merk land. Its 'rising out' is not mentioned. Macdougall was hereditary steward of the Isle of Lismore which had anciently been tied to Mull. It now belonged jointly to Argyll and Glenorchy. It is described as being 'very fertile for all kind of corns and speciallie for beir, and will grow alsmeule eftir one boll sowing as in the Lewis or any pairt thair with les gudeing or labour ...' It could raise 100 men.[27]

Macdougall's main estate was on the mainland. A kinsman of his did however own one of the two Shunas. It was 8 merk land and could raise 60 men. The other Shuna, off Appin, belonged to John Stewart of Appin who had married Lachlan Mor's aunt, the dowager countess of Argyll. His main estate was on the mainland. His Shuna however was only 4 merk land. It could also raise 60 men.[28]

Duncan Macdougall's castle, Dunolly, is dramatically situated upon the summit of a rocky promontory towards the north end of Oban Bay. It consists of a tower house with an associated bailey. He had another castle, which he seems to have built at Gylen in the south of the island of Kerrera.

Castles were the key to the number of men the Isles could send to Ireland. Over the previous three centuries the inhabitants of the Isles had built a formidable network of fortifications to protect themselves. The castles built of local stone had walls that were often ten feet thick. They not only dominated the landscape, they could also be defended by a relatively small garrison, allowing the rest of the 'rising out' to sally forth on an expedition sure that their women, children and cattle were secure. Beyond the major stone structure were often walls constructed of wattle and daub behind which the people's cattle would be driven in an emergency. Unless the garrison was surprised or the attackers had siege artillery, the defenders were safe. They could like Macbeth 'laugh a siege to scorn' and wait until help came or the assailants ran out of food or became sick.

Lachlan Mor had several castles. Duart in the south-west of Mull overlooking the Sound was probably the most important. It is one of the most commanding sites in the whole western seaboard, lying as it does at the intersection of three major waterways, the Sound of Mull, Loch Linnhe and the Firth of Lorn. Duart Bay immediately to the south-west of the castle provides a convenient anchorage, although galleys are said to have been kept to the south-west in Loch Don.

The original castle comprised a rectangular wall of enclosure, the entrance being situated in the south-west curtain wall. Once the Macleans obtained possession of the castle in the fourteenth century, a substantial tower house was built within the curtain wall. Major improvements are said to have been made by Lachlan Mor's grandfather. Lachlan Mor's addition would appear to have been the remodelling of the north-east verge of courtyard buildings and building a projecting stair turret at the rear.[29]

Aros Castle occupies a flat-topped promontory of rock situated at the mouth of the Aros river on the Sound of Mull. It came to Maclean when Hector Mor obtained a lease of the crown's estate in Mull in the mid-sixteenth century.[30] It was at the time the main centre of communication between the island and the Scottish mainland. In 1687 it was the major centre for the dispensation of justice in Mull and is likely to have been a century earlier.[31] The captaincy of Aros Castle became hereditary in a family of Macleans.

Carnaburg Castle in the Treshnish islands was one of the Macleans of Duart's original holdings. The site is one of great strategic importance as it commands the main inner west-coast sea lane at the southern approach to the Inner Hebrides. It was used both as a prison by Maclean of Duart and as a refuge. It was commanded by a hereditary Maclean constable who also held the Treshnish estate in the north-west of Mull.

Kinlochaline Castle in Morvern is a tower house that occupies the north end of a rocky ridge where the River Aline flows into Loch Aline. The original building probably dates from the fifteenth century and was perhaps extensively remodelled in the late sixteenth century. The castle was probably built by the Macleans of Duart, perhaps, as local tradition says, on the site of earlier buildings owned by Macinnes. It was granted in 1573 by Hector Og to his brother John Dubh and after his death held by his son Allan.

The castle in Tiree was noted in the late fourteenth century as being 'a very strong tower'. It was situated on what was once an island in Loch Heylipoll. It was demolished in the eighteenth century to make way for Island House which is now the duke of Argyll's residence on Tiree.

Maclean's castle in Islay is described as 'ane strenthie Castell ... quhilk standis in ane niche within ane fresche-water loch callit Lochgormen'. It had a violent history. It first appears on record in 1549 when Dean Munro describes it as 'the Castell of Lochgorme, quhilk is biggit in ane isle in the said fresch water loch far from land partining to Clan Donald of Kintyre of auld, now usurpit be McGillane of Doward ...'[32] It was besieged and in a ruinous state in 1578. It would seem that it had been restored in Lachlan Mor's time and the visible remains today probably date from the late sixteenth century.[33]

Although he does not make the distinction, the anonymous author of the 'Description' gives details of those who had offered their services to Elizabeth such as Lachlan Mor and those who had been allied to Angus Macdonald of Dunyvaig and Donald Gorm. We have seen that the latter could count on 700 men from Sleat. He could also call on the rising out of North Uist which was worth 60 merks and could raise 300 men. Uist is described as having 'na woods nor great rivers in it, but their is many deir ... Ilk merkland ... payis 20 bolls victual'. However, 'by all uther customes, maills and oist silver ... thair is na certane rentall'. He goes on to say that, 'the customs of this Ile are splendit, and payit at the landlordis cumming to the Ile to his cudicht'.[34]

Donald Gorm also possessed the 80 merk land of Trotternish, which 'payis yeirlie Ilk merkland thairof twa bollis meill, twa bollis malt, four mairtis, 16 wedderis, 16 dozen of pultrie, twa merkis by the auld maills and utheris dewteis accustomat'. It had an old ruinous castle, 'quhair of the wallis standis yit'.

Angus's castle of Dunyvaig or Dunivaig in Islay had played and was to play an important part in the history of the Isles. It is now in ruins. It stands on a coastal promontory on the east side of Lagavulin Bay guarding the entrance to the anchorage. It looks out to the coasts of Kintyre and Antrim, both of which are in view on a clear day. It was a place of considerable strength.

Am Fraoch Eilean, off the south-west of Jura, had another small castle called Claig, which was owned by Angus. It guarded the southern approach to the Sound of Islay.

Although Angus Macdonald of Dunyvaig took his title from his castle in Islay, his major landholding was in Kintyre and in the Glens of Antrim. Kintyre is described as being 'for the most part the King's proper land by the "forfalture" of the Lord of the Isles', but was in 1595 'presently possessed by Angus MacConnell and others of the Clan Donald of the south'.[35]

Angus had several castles in Kintyre. Dunaverty, one of his principal fortresses, occupies a conspicuous headland which overlooks the Sound of Sanda. It is a natural fortification, 'being sea-girt on three sides and approachable only from the north, where a narrow path links it to the mainland'.[36]

Dunaverty had been damaged during the earl of Sussex's raid in 1558. It had evidently been repaired and was an important military structure. Angus and his close relatives however appear to have spent more time at more conveniently situated houses such as Askomel and Kilkerran Castle which was close to what is now Campbeltown. Another fortified tower house is situated on Island Muller, a small rocky promontory on the north side of Kilchousland about 4 km north-east of Campbeltown.[58] Saddell Castle, Angus's father's residence, had been badly damaged during Sussex's raid and does not appear to have been used in Angus's time. Both Angus and Lachlan Mor carried out a great deal of work in their fortresses which were still considered to have considerable military significance.

The total number of men Angus could raise in Kintyre and the Glens of Antrim is not mentioned in the report sent to Burghley in 1595. His holding in Islay, which was valued at 90 merks, could raise 400 men. He also possessed Rathlin Island. It could raise 100 men. He could also raise 50 men in his half of Jura and another 100 in Gigha. His follower, Macduffy or Macfee of Colonsay, could raise 100 men.

The Captain of Clanranald was another Macdonald who could be expected to follow Angus. His holding on the mainland is not listed but he also possessed South Uist where he could raise 300 men. He also owned Eigg which could raise 60 men and Canna which could raise 20 men. He could raise 6 or 7 men in the Isle of Rum which belonged to Maclean of Coll but was at the time occupied by him. Another mainland-based Macdonald, Macian of Ardnamurchan, is said to have been able to raise 200 men. Sixteen able men could be raised in the Isle of Muck, which belonged to the bishop of the Isles, but was occupied by Macian.

The Isle of Lewis is listed at the beginning of the description. It was the property of Macleod of Lewis, whose principal messuage was the castle of Stornoway. He could raise 700 men in Lewis and a further 60 men in the Isle of Bernera off Lewis. He also owned Waternish in Skye which could raise a further 200 men.[37]

Old Ruaridh Macleod of Lewis seems to have died in 1595. His marital adventures had produced a turbulent brood of sons. The eldest was Torquil Connanach, whose mother was Janet Mackenzie, sister of Colin *Cam* Mackenzie of Kintail. Ruaridh disowned Torquil Connanach who, he claimed with good reason, was not his son at all but the son of the Brieve of Lewis. Ruaridh's eventual heir was Torquil Dubh, whose mother was Lachlan Mor's half-sister, the daughter of Hector Og Maclean of Duart and an unknown mother. As his parents were not married until 1573, Torquil Dubh could not have been born before 1574. He was married to a sister of Macleod of Harris.[38] The latter was by 1595 Rory Mor, whose nephew and ward died that year.[39]

Rory Mor was known as such 'not so much from his size or stature of his body – which was not remarkably large – as from the strength of his parts'. He could raise 140 men in the Isle of Harris.[40] He also owned three estates in Skye: Durinish, which was 28 merkland, which could raise 240 men; Bracadale which was 16 merkland and could raise 140 men; and Minginish which is curiously not listed in the published version of the report, but is said in the copy sent to London in 1595 to be able to provide 120 men.[41] Macleod also owned Glenelg on the mainland opposite Skye, which was claimed by Fraser of Lovat. He also disputed Donald Gorm's ownership of Trotternish and Clanranald's property in Uist.

Macleod of Harris also owned the little island of Pabbay. It was two merkland and could raise 40 men. Curiously his castle in Skye, Dunvegan, is not mentioned.

Off the coast of Skye is the Isle of Raasay, which belonged to the bishop of the Isles. In the report it is said to be occupied 'be ane gentleman of McCloyd Lewis kin, callit Gillechallum Raarsa ... It is but 8 merkland and will raise 80 men. It payis yeirlie to the bischop 16 merks, but to the capitane thairof it payis of sundrie tributes better nor 500 merks'.[42]

Whoever wrote this report had a detailed knowledge of the Isles. It was probably knowledge that the author had at first hand as he makes no mention of the account of the Isles which appeared in print in 1582. This was printed at the beginning of George Buchanan's *Rerum Scoticorum Historia*. It was an abridged version of the material Buchanan received from Dean Munro, who compiled his report in 1549.[43] Buchanan's work was anathema to the king. It was banned and it was an offence to possess a copy.

It was suggested by Skene that our anonymous description was written for King James VI.[44] It is far more likely that it was written for Sir Robert Cecil or his father. The English authorities probably had more detailed information about the Hebrides in 1595 than the Scottish government itself had.

The report also states that one third of the total who could be raised in the isles 'aucht and sould be cled with attonis and haberschonnis,

and knapskal bannets, as their lawis beir'. This is a reference to the Act
of Parliament of 1574 which specified that Highlanders were to be
differently clothed to the 'rising out' of the rest of Scotland. This breakdown of the number of mercenaries from the Isles who could descend
on Ulster was vital to Burghley in assessing the threat to Ulster.

*   *   *   *

Increasingly disturbing reports were now reaching Burghley from all
quarters. In February 1593/4 Bagenal reported from Newry that Randal
MacNeece, i.e. Raghnall son of Aonghus (Angus) son of Alasdrann
Carrach, a Scot dwelling in the Glens of Ulster, who was Angus's
governor there, had been sent by his master to inform the English
authorities that some 4000 Scots were to land at Lough Foyle or Lough
Swilly or at both shortly after Easter. These mercenaries were to
assemble in the Isle of Jura, presumably at the traditional assembly point
at Whitefarland Bay in the Sound of Islay.

According to Angus, these Scots were to serve under O Donnell,
Maguire and O Rourke. They had been recruited by Angus's cousin
James Macdonald, son of Sorley Boy, who was increasingly competing
with Angus for the leadership of the Macdonalds in Antrim. Angus also
reported that O Donnell was in correspondence with Argyll and with
Maclean. Both had promised to send men to the confederates. Maclean
had also written to Angus suggesting he do likewise, but he had refused.
The Scots now coming to Ireland were said to be followers of Argyll
and Maclean.[45] Argyll is said to have been offered as much as £10,000
Scots to provide 2000 men for the confederates, and when he proved
to be uncooperative the confederates gave Angus and Donald Gorm
advance payments in silver to bring over their men.[46]

MacNeece's scenario is not plausible. Argyll was probably by now
too immersed in the search for the murderers of Cawdor to concern
himself with Ireland. He may also have learned of the plot to murder
both himself and his brother. He would have received confirmation of
Huntly's involvement in both events.

*   *   *   *

Tyrone was officially still a loyal subject of the queen. By February
1595/6 he had come off the fence. At about 8 o'clock on the morning
of Sunday 16 February some 40 or 50 of his men from Armagh 'with
matches alight and bullets in their mouths' marched through the town

1. Archibald, 7th Earl of Argyll. He avenged his cousin Lachlan Mor's death.

2. Queen Elizabeth of England enthroned between Lord Burleigh (left) and Sir Francis Walsingham. Sir Lachlan planned to invade Ulster on her behalf.

3. Sir Robert Cecil, Elizabeth's Principal Secretary of State. As pennypinching and prevaricating as his mistress, he held Lachlan Mor's fate in his hands.

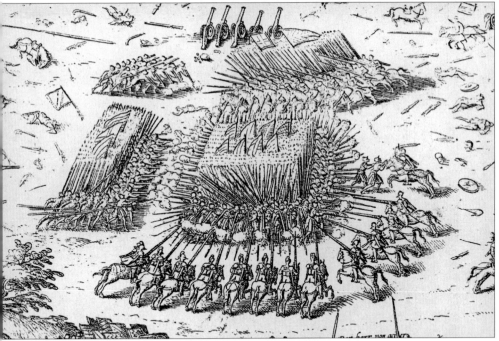

4. Hedgehog formation from a contemporary engraving of the Battle of Moncontour, 1569. Swiss squares faced attackers with bristling pike points. This formation was copied by the English in Ulster and by Sir Lachlan Mor at the Battle of Glenlivet, 1594.

5. An English army on the march in Ireland, 1581. Cavalry, pikemen and calivermen probably adopted this formation at Clontibret in 1595.

6. King James VI of Scotland in 1595. He disliked Sir Lachlan after the latter sided with the ministers of the Church of Scotland on 17 December 1596.

7. King Philip II of Spain, Elizabeth of England's great antagonist. Although he realised Spain could not send a second Armada to assist the Roman Catholic rebels in Ireland, he manipulated them and his spies persuaded them not to make terms with the English.

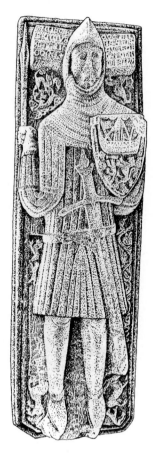

8. Effigy (left) of Bricius McKinnon from Iona, showing armour worn still by the Islesmen in the sixteenth century, such as the pointed helmet (bascinet) and quilted knee-length tunic (aketon).

9. Carving of the 'Rodel Ship', the type of galley or birlinn used off the western seaboard.

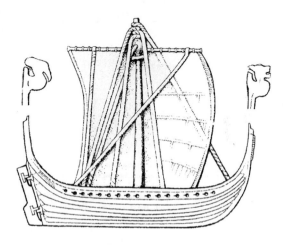

10. The first known Maclean seal, that of Hector Maclean of Duart, 1546. The shield displays the gyronny of eight device of the Chief of the Clan Campbell, the Earl of Argyll, to whom Maclean signed a bond of manrent in 1543.

11. The entrance to Strathbogie Castle (now Huntly). The panels, dated 1602, are the
Marquis of Huntly's coat of arms, below the coat of arms of James VI and Queen
Anne, above which are panels (since vandalised as being 'idolatrous') whose symbolism
proclaimed the Catholicism of the Gordons.

12. Sir Duncan Campbell of Glenorchy. He was an ally of Sir Lachlan and one of the plotters in the conspiracy to murder Campbell of Cawdor and the Earl of Moray. He was also an English spy.

13. Duart Castle, on the Sound of Mull, before and after restoration.

of Blackwater and charged the gate of the wooden stockade of the fort there. They were rapidly through the gate and got between it and the door of the stone castle inside the stockade.

The garrison was only five strong, two of whom were wounded in the first assault. They did however kill thirteen of the assailants and the surviving defenders with their swords drove the remaining enemy from the stockade. There were many more rebels outside and in the afternoon a woman was sent to the fort to beg that the garrison surrender and prevent further bloodshed.

Eventually after some bluster Blackwater was surrendered. The fort was destroyed. It was not surrendered, the lord deputy wrote despairingly to Burghley on the 28 March, for want of 'victual or munitions'. The Ulster rebels were just better trained than they had been in Sean O Neill's day. He also reported that he had sent two pinnaces to intercept the Scots coming to Ulster.[47]

Lachlan Mor was now in an extremely strong position to bargain with the English. The situation in Ulster was deteriorating. His reputation both as a soldier and a commander was at its zenith. Negotiations were carried out both by Lachlan himself and his confidential clerk John Auchinross. On 25 March the latter wrote to Bowes that his master had commanded him to 'speak to your lordship anent the rebellious doing of Tyrone, O Donnell and their assisters who, with the assistance of the Clan Donald and others in Scotland mind to make great insurrection against her Grace'.[48] He reported that 'O Donnell had written divers times to Maclean, craving his assistance' and that 7–800 Macdonalds had been in Ulster the previous July and August. Donald Gorm had made a band with Tyrone and O Donnell on behalf of himself and Angus, and since Donald Gorm's return to Scotland they had also made a band with Huntly. They had not however joined him and would not do so or return to Ireland until they had made peace with Maclean.

As part of their negotiations with him the Macdonalds had promised to obtain the release of Lachlan Mor's eldest son who was still in Mackenzie's custody. They offered to discuss their controversy over the Rinns of Islay. They further proposed that Lachlan Mor's heir should marry Angus's daughter and that the latter's son marry Maclean's daughter.[49]

Another English agent, James Campbell, younger, of Lawers, reported on 7 April that Angus had now even offered Maclean all the lands he claimed in Islay if he would join them.[50] Instead of such an alliance that might have united the Isles Maclean proposed that he and Argyll prevent the other islanders from going to Ireland. He wrote to Bowes himself

from Duart on 22 April with more intelligence about his neighbours.[51] He also agreed to invade Ireland himself with his own clan and
the Campbells. They would 'pursue the rebels on the one side while
her Highness's army pursue them on the other side ...'[52] He also suggested that the queen should send three or four of her ships with
provisions to Maclean's galleys whilst they were in Ireland. This plan
was to be the basis of Lachlan Mor's negotiations with Burghley and
Sir Robert Cecil over the next two years. It had certain attractions for
them. It was certainly a proposal that was taken seriously.

Meanwhile the situation in Ireland, as far as the English were concerned, was getting worse. Reluctantly Burghley, who had no wish for
war, drafted the proclamation in April declaring Tyrone a traitor. He
stressed the earl's 'cruel tyranny in hanging Hugh Gavelagh', the son of
Sean O Neill, 'without any crime',[53] which as it had been stressed in
Auchinross's letter was perhaps a sop to Lachlan Mor. Before the proclamation could be issued it was learned that the castle of Enniskillen
had fallen to the rebels and that the garrison had been put to the sword.
They had capitulated on the promise that their lives would be spared.[54]

Notes

1. Calderwood v, 361.
2. *CSP Scot.* xi, 457.
3. AT vii, 273.
4. *CSP Ireland* v, 315.
5. *CSP Scot.* xi, 495.
6. W. D. Lamont (1966).
7. Stephen Boardman, in *Northern Scotland*, Vol. 16 (1996).
8. *CSP Scot.* xi, 647.
9. Niall D. Campbell, 'An Old Tiree Rental of the year 1662', *SHR* ix (1912), 343–44. I am grateful to Professor R. A. Dodgshon for sending me a copy of this rental.
10. *Warriors and Priests*, 145.
11. AT vii, 243.
12. *CSP Scot.* xii, 35.
13. SRO RD 1/27 H 21 R & V.
14. Skene, *Celtic Scotland* iii, 430.
15. *CSP Scot.* xii, 25.
16. PRO SP Eliz. Scotland lviii, 72, 49.
17. Wallace Clark, *The Lord of the Isles Voyage* (1993), 46–54. I am grateful to the author for a copy of this book.
18. *Celtic Scotland* iii, 434.
19. *RPC* ii, 483; iii, 37.

20. *RPC* iv, 263. According to John Drummond, *The Memoirs of Sir Ewen Cameron of Locheill* (1842), 46, which was probably written in 1733, Hector Maclean of Lochbuie fought for the Macdonalds against Lachlan Mor at *Tràigh Ghruinneart*. Locheil was so angry with Lochbuie for siding against 'the head of his Clan' that he captured him and kept him in chains for six months thereafter.

21. *Celtic Scotland* iii, 434–5.

22. *Clan Campbell* ii, 44.

23. SRO RD 1/19 H 49r–50r; *Collectanea*, 16.

24. SRO SC 54/22/52.

25. SRO RD 1/27 H 21r & v.

26. NLS MS 3018 H 39 R.

27. *Celtic Scotland* iii, 435.

28. *Ibid*, 436.

29. Royal Commission on the Ancient and Historical Monuments of Scotland (RCAHMS), *Argyll* Vol. 3, 191–3.

30. *Warriors and Priests*, 122.

31. 'Law and Order in Mull in 1687', *West Highland Notes & Queries* Series 2, No. 4 (October 1989), 15–16.

32. Munro, *Western Isles*, 56.

33. RCAHMS *Argyll* Vol. 5, 282–3.

34. *Celtic Scotland* iii, 430.

35. *CSP Scot.* xi, 255.

36. RCAHMS *Argyll* Vol. 1, 157.

37. *Celtic Scotland* iii, 429, 432–3.

38. I. F. Grant, *The Macleods* (1959).

39. Donald Mackinnon and Alick Morrison, *The Macleods* (1969), 23.

40. *Celtic Scotland* iii, 430.

41. *CSP Scot.* xi, 253.

42. *Ibid.*

43. R. W. Munro, 'Roll Call of the Isles', *West Highland Notes & Queries* (March 1988), Series 2, Nos. 1, 5.

44. *Celtic Scotland* iii.

45. *CSP Ireland*, 1592–96, 217.

46. *CSP Scot.* xi, 457–8, 476–7, 581, 650.

47. *CSP Ireland*, v, 298, 308.

48. *CSP Scot.* xi, 551.

49. *Ibid.*

50. *CSP Scot.* xi, 573.

51. *Ibid*, 581.

52. *Ibid*, 557.

53. *CSP Ireland* v, 310.

54. *Ibid*, 317.

CHAPTER 14

War in Ulster, 1595

Lay on, Macduff;
And damn'd be him that first cries 'Hold,
Enough!'

Macbeth Act V, Scene viii

On 24 May the lord deputy wrote to Burghley that Tyrone had 6,000 men under arms and that they were better trained than the queen's forces.[1] That this statement was true was soon to be confirmed.

On 25 May 1595 marshall Bagenal set out from his base at Newry to resupply Monaghan. He travelled only eight miles that day and in the evening Tyrone appeared outside his camp with a troop of a hundred horse. He was evidently only there to observe Bagenal's position, for when the marshall 'with some gentlemen and horse' challenged him he forced the earl 'from one hill to another'. Tyrone had no intention of fighting that night and Bagenal returned to his camp.

The next morning the marshal set off again. Throughout the day he was constantly sniped at by Tyrone's men, who now had infantry with them. Eventually the relief column reached Monaghan. The 'victuals' were delivered and as much 'munitions' as could be spared. The following day Bagenal's force, which included fourteen companies and horse sent from the Pale, attempted to return to Newry. They were under constant attack all the way. The earl had the advantage of a bog on each side of the track along which Bagenal's men moved and from which Tyrone's men kept up a steady fire, attacking the columns with both horse and on foot as an opportunity presented itself.

Tyrone himself had been in the thick of the fighting. At Crossaghy half a mile east of Clontibret Church, where the track entered the bog, the earl's men ambushed the royal army, pounding them with fire for three hours. Ammunition was running low and the English pikemen, 'for lack of shot to save them, began to waver'. Bagenal was in a desperate position. At this moment the earl himself appeared on the other side of the stream and he was recognised by Segrave, a Palesman serving with the English horse, who spurred his horse into the stream

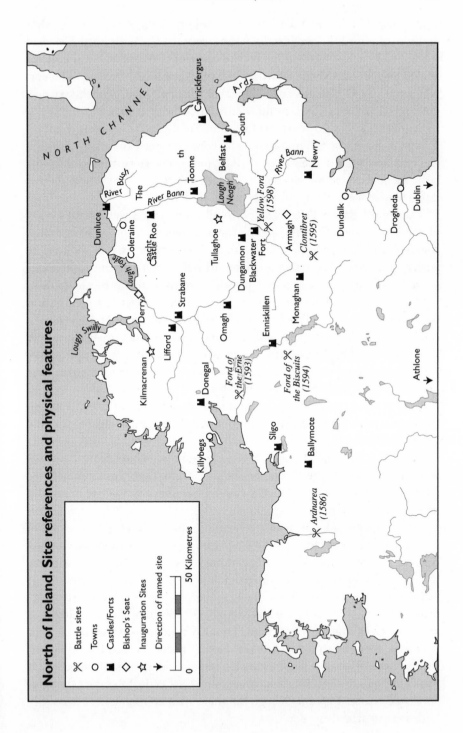

North of Ireland. Site references and physical features

Legend:
- ✗ Battle sites
- ○ Towns
- ◼ Castles/Forts
- ◇ Bishop's Seat
- ☆ Inauguration Sites
- → Direction of named site

0 — 50 Kilometres

NORTH CHANNEL

Ards
South
Carrickfergus
Belfast
River Bann
Newry
River Bush
River Bann
The
Toome
Lough Neagh
Yellow Ford (1598)
Armagh
Clontibret (1595)
Dundalk
Drogheda
Dublin
Dunluce
Castle Roe
Coleraine
each
Tullaghoe
Dungannon
Blackwater Fort
Monaghan
Lough Foyle
Derry
Strabane
Omagh
Enniskillen
Lough Swilly
Lifford
Kilmacrenan
Donegal
Ford of the Erne (1593)
Ford of the Biscuits (1594)
Athlone
Killybegs
Sligo
Ballymote
Ardnarea (1586)

and charged Tyrone. Forty troopers followed him. Some were shot
down in the ford. Segrave rode on and reached the earl. Both men had
a lance and each splintered his on the corselet of the other. In the mêlée
Segrave grabbed Tyrone and they fell together to the ground. The earl
was saved by O Cahan's son. He struck the Palesman with his sword,
cutting off his arm. Tyrone finished him off with his dagger.

Segrave had not however died in vain. For a crucial moment the Irish
appear to have lost the initiative. The column forced their way through
the bog and fought their way to Ballymacowen. Here they picked the
best defensive position available, shared out their powder and melted
down Bagenal's pewter dishes to make bullets.

That night Bagenal's men stood to all night and it was a weary body
of men who set off again at six the following morning. Eventually,
'wearied and hungry', the army returned to Newry. It was so short of
ammunition that Bagenal was unable to risk sending it the eight miles
from Newry to Dundalk as the passes were now in the rebels' hands.

This was the first action against the English in which Tyrone himself
was actively engaged. It is known as the Battle of Clontibret. Bagenal's
report of 29 May from the safety of Newry made depressing reading.
It shocked the Dublin government to realise what they were up against.
Tyrone was thought to have had 1,000 horse and 14,000 foot with him,
including '300 shot in redcoats like English soldiers'.

The earl had used his cavalry and shot to devastating effect. English
commanders present, who had experience of Flanders, compared Tyrone
with the Prince of Parma.

Efforts to prevent the earl receiving reinforcements from Scotland
were renewed. 'If the Scots be holden from him this summer his
[Tyrone's] end will be soon', Sir Robert Salesbury wrote optimistically
from Newry in June.

The English had one major advantage in that they had control of
the sea. It was therefore possible to send the ammunition required to
Newry. It would also be possible, thought Sir John Norris in a letter
to his patron Sir Robert Cecil dated 4 June 1595, to open a second front
by sending a force from England to Lough Foyle. If such a force were
provided with all necessaries and victuals for four months, it could cause
havoc in O Donnell's country and 'spoil the enemy's harvest'.

Norris thought that his brother Henry would be ideally suited for
such a task if he had 'some captains acquainted with that country'. It
was a proposal that must have given the Cecils food for thought,
particularly after Captain George Bingham with 200 soldiers successfully
raided Tory island by sea.

More bad news for the English was on the way. On 7 June Sir Richard Bingham wrote from Athlone to Cecil that his cousin Captain George Bingham had been sitting at his table in his chamber in Sligo Castle writing letters when Ulick Burke, his cousin's ensign bearer and 20 of his company, had fallen on him and seized the castle. Sligo was essential to the control of Connaught. Its loss was another devastating blow for the English.[2]

It had been known for some time to the English that many Islesmen were planning to cross over to Ireland in May 1595. They had been delayed and on 23 June Bowes' agent George Nicolson reported that Argyll had told him the previous Tuesday that Donald Gorm had 2,000 men ready to pass into Ireland and that others were ready, whom he could not prevent from crossing over. He also wrote that Donald Gorm had quarrelled with his brother-in-law, the formidable Rory Mor Macleod of Harris, which might cause mischief among the Islesmen.

Unfortunately Argyll had not even been able to prevent some of his own men from joining the rebels. One was Duncan Campbell of Danna who had fallen foul of the law in Scotland.[3] The other recalcitrant Campbell was John Dubh Campbell, tutor of Inverawe, known as Mac-Conachie, who had won himself a formidable reputation as a captain of mercenaries in Ireland. He had been reported as having been killed at Glenlivet, which alarmed O Neill, but had survived. He had come to Argyll and been given armour and other presents. He was not satisfied. He now demanded land from Argyll in exchange for staying at home. When his request was refused 'he departed without leave or farewell'. 'Our rebels', the earl complained, 'little care now for her majesty, the King or himself' and think of nothing but 'their own advantage'. Nicolson pleaded that Maclean only needed money to keep him loyal and the encouragement of 'some fit person to travail on this matter, which has been over long deferred already and will be too soon, I fear past remedy'.

Nicolson proposed to use John Cunningham, the Edinburgh merchant, to communicate with Maclean. He was to travel to Argyll where Maclean was at present. Nicolson was also in communication with Mr George Erskine, the earl of Mar's brother. Erskine, who was Argyll's confidential clerk, promised to get his master to negotiate with Maclean. Neither Erskine nor the earl however knew that Nicolson was in direct contact with Maclean. Lachlan Mor, who was concerned about his own security, was adamant that his dealings with the English were to be kept secret.[4]

*   *   *   *

Early in July 1595 Norris was sent into Ulster with an army. Its aim was to re-establish a garrison on the Blackwater and capture Dungannon, which was Tyrone's principal residence. As the English army advanced, Tyrone razed his castle to the ground. He also burnt all the country round about. This scorched earth policy had its effect.[5] Tyrone had however failed to demolish Armagh Cathedral.

This was a serious error as it could be converted into a fortress and gave the government a base to contest the earl's control of the eastern third of Tyrone.[6] It was thought in Dublin that Tyrone, who had gathered all his forces together, would stay on the defensive and 'stick to his bogs' until the Scots joined him.[7]

*   *   *   *

On 8 July Nicolson reported that Angus and Donald Gorm were ready to leave for Ireland. They were still endeavouring to persuade Argyll and Maclean to join them. The earl had sent his cousin the provost of Kilmun to Angus to persuade him not to depart and to have a conference with himself and Maclean at Carrick Castle on Loch Goil.

Angus however gave the provost 'ewill vordes', saying that he would never of his own free will agree to a meeting with Argyll and Maclean. Kilmun was so incensed that he challenged Angus to single combat with two-handed swords without armour[8] at Skipness before the whole Clan Donald and Clan Campbell. This somewhat bizarre contest did not take place[9] but it supports other evidence that the medieval attitude to warfare was still alive in the Gaeltachd.

Argyll was furious at Angus's truculence. He attempted to persuade Maclean to set upon the Macdonalds at sea whilst his own men attacked them by land. Lachlan Mor however had no intention of restarting his feud with the Macdonalds unless he was paid to do so and on 13 July John Cunningham reported to Bowes that 'Maclean has passed home to Mull', where he prepared to attempt to dissuade Donald Gorm and the two Macleods (i.e. of Harris and of Lewis) from going to Ireland.[10] Cunningham also sent a copy of Auchinross' letter to himself to Bowes which listed the gifts that Lachlan Mor desired for his work, including 'plate sleeves'. Auchinross himself, who was something of a scholar, wanted a 'tabill of the Kinges' beginning with King Fergus. He went on to say that as soon as the Macleods came to his bounds he would send word of their plans.[11]

On 15 July Nicolson reported to Bowes that Argyll was sick, 'decaying so fast without pain that some think he is bewitched'. He went on to say that Tyrone continued to try to bribe Maclean to join the rebels: 'He is mightily tempted with fair offers of money and gear ... but nothing will make him trust Angus MacConnell, or forgive Tyrone'.[12]

On 22 July Auchinross reported to Bowes from Dumbarton that on the 18th and 19th the Scots had passed to Ireland. Donald Gorm had 'vrakit' (ruined) his land in holding these forces to the number of 2,500 besides 500 furnished by Angus who joined them as they came south. Concentrating an army together was an administrative nightmare to all commanders at the time whether they were the Prince of Parma or leaders of a smaller concentration in Ulster and the Hebrides.

Angus had sent his eldest son with the expedition to Ulster 'so the conductors of this company are he, Donald Gorm MacConnell, Macleod Lewis and Macleod Harris'. Auchinross makes the point that when his master 'held but 600 men together' in garrison for three months at no expense to the queen 'none of them durst presume to pass to Ireland'.

Compelling them to turn back now would be more dangerous and more costly than preventing them from joining together. However, if Maclean were to be 'employed' he would make them return to Scotland. Not only that but he would 'make Tyrone beg mercy of her Majesty'. All he required in exchange was that the queen give him a present 'and advance him honourably'.

Auchinross claimed that the islanders had only gone to Ireland because 'their countrie could not support them any longer' and that if Bowes required his master's service they must meet and Bowes should produce a specific contract.

Lachlan Mor's diligent clerk wrote again to George Nicolson a week later underlining the points he had made before and in addition he stressed that whilst his master had his 600 men together the rebels not only did not dare proceed to Ireland as was planned but stayed at home together for three months eating up their country. But when Maclean dissolved his 'sober company' the others, seeing him prepare for quietness, immediately sailed to Ireland. They did so without powder or lead 'for my master "has convoyit" that from them'. He was in league with the lowland arms merchants and would not let them supply arms and ammunition unless they were first paid.

'If only Maclean were to be employed he would harry their lands. Then they will be forced "to seik for Scotland", every man to save his own house and dwelling. For all, or most, of the company are householders, who will respect little their profit in Ireland compared to their loss in Scotland. This must be dangerous to my master, yet I know he will not leave that which he has begun.'

'If he be employed', continued Auchinross, 'direct in all haste to Dowart a little ship, well appointed, with 50 or three-score men therein besides mariners. Let them have letters from Sir Robert [Cecil] and Mr Bowes to my master. At their arriving, wherever my master is I shall command the captain of Dowart to convoy their services and the writings to him ...' Auchinross adds that Bowes could trust his judgement as he had been Maclean's confidential clerk for sixteen years.

John Auchinross gives details of the movement of the northern rebels in yet another letter to Nicolson also written on 22 July. He states that 'On Friday 11 July, there came by sea by (i.e. past) our place of Duart, the number of 2,500 men, and in passing Macleod Lewis and the principal friends of Macleod Harris came on land and spoke [with] Maclean of Duart, to excuse themselves for their passing to Ireland with Donald Gorme MacConnell. The only cause thereof was their receipt of great gains which came to Scotland from Tyrone, and seeing the voyage was no way to hurt Maclean they thought good to take commodity and profit when offered, and answered Maclean that whenever he shall "haif to do so" against the Clan Donald that they shall be found ready in his service, as they have been before'.[13]

Rumours of Argyll's 'friendship with her Majesty of England' had reached the Islesmen. It was also reported that they had with them about thirty galleys 'lightly furnished with some smaller vessels'. Mr George Erskine suggested that the English should send their ships to the Isle of Rathlin to intercept this flotilla, 'as the ordnance of your ships shall so dismay them if once you enter in flight that without all doubt they will return'.[14]

On 23 July Queen Elizabeth herself wrote to Argyll praising him for his constancy to his sovereign. She went on to say, 'we understand that your cousin Maclean is much at your devotion, and one of power in those isles of the north, we desire that he may find by you how well you are disposed towards us, which we know will make direct his courses, and for which we will be most ready to requite him'.[15]

It was not to be long before both Argyll and Maclean were to have to do more than use powers of persuasion to distract the Islesmen from joining Tyrone. The islanders had not gone directly to Ireland. Instead they had journeyed around the Mull of Kintyre to Arran. Here they paused and held a conference. They had three courses open to them. Firstly to attack Argyll's country in order that they should not leave any enemies in their rear. Secondly to attack the Isle of Man.

Thirdly to go directly to Ireland and join Tyrone. After some deliberation they decided not to invade Argyll. Not only were the earl's forces potentially stronger than their own but they were 'able to abide longer together than theirs'. They believed it more sensible 'first to execute some other exploit and if that succeeded with supplies from Ireland to enter into war' with Argyll, whose friendship with Elizabeth was now common knowledge.

Notes

1. *CSP Ireland* v, 319.
2. *Irish Battles*, 100–101, 320–22, 326, 328.
3. Hayes-McCoy (1937), 242.
4. *CSP Scot.* xi, 518, 618, 620.
5. *Ibid*, 335.
6. Morgan, 186.
7. *CSP Ireland* v, 332.
8. *CSP Scot.* xi, 636.
9. Hayes-McCoy, 245.
10. *CSP Scot.* xi, 637.
11. *Ibid*, 638.
12. *Ibid*, 639.
13. *Ibid*, 647–650.
14. *Ibid*, 651.
15. *Ibid*, 652.

CHAPTER 15

Scotland and Ulster, 1595–1596

Macbeth. If we should fail?
Lady Macbeth. We fail:
But screw your courage to the sticking-place,
And we'll not fail.

Macbeth Act I, Scene vii

Lachlan Mor, having disbanded his forces before the Macleods visited him at Duart, had not been able to dissuade them from joining the rebels. He did not intend to be caught out again. As soon as the Macleods set sail he secretly assembled 300 of his best men. One hundred of them were his heavy infantry clothed 'in armour of coat and mail ... with two handed swords and iron head pieces'. Another hundred are described as 'fyirmen', presumably 'shot'. The final hundred were bowmen.[1] All were to remain with him in 'household and guard' which presumably means that they were accommodated at Aros or Duart.

Whilst he was in Arran, Angus sent letters to his allies, who had not yet arrived at the rendezvous, instructing them to join him for an assault on the Isle of Man. Among them was John Macian of Ardnamurchan, who had a following of 200 men. The bearer of his letter was intercepted by one of Maclean's followers. Lachlan Mor now knew what his adversaries were planning. He set a trap.

The latecomers were some 900 strong. They assembled north of Ardnamurchan Point and having been all day at sea arrived weary late one evening at the entrance to the Sound of Mull. They decided to spend the night at the little island of *Callow*, Calve Island, off the coast of Mull. It has a good anchorage called *Acairseid Mhor*, the big harbour.

As they had no reason to expect any threat, the Macdonalds failed to post sentries. It was a mistake. During the night the Macleans secretly landed on the island, seized their galleys and disarmed their sleeping adversaries. The captain of Clanranald, three of his father's brothers, the laird of Knoydart, the laird of Ardnamurchan, Donald Gorm's brother and many other gentlemen were imprisoned. They were held in Maclean's castles.

Those he 'lykit of' worst were held in irons 'to accustom them the better to take ease in patience'.[2] The remainder were ferried to the mainland nearest their homes. Their galleys, birlinns and boats 'which are of great value to my master are "stayit" ', wrote Auchinross to John Cunningham.

It was 'a pretty feat of war'. The story no doubt lost nothing in the telling. 'We know that Angus MacConnell and Donald Gorm will rage at this doing', wrote Auchinross, 'for all their number and force convened together these [prisoners] must rest where my master shall think good till he can be further advised.'[3]

Meanwhile Angus and the rest of the islanders were not having a very happy time. They had not arrived in Ireland as one body but in dribs and drabs. Their first landfall was in the Ards Peninsula. Here they probably made contact with emissaries from Tyrone. They then set sail again up the Bay of Carrickfergus, as Belfast Lough was then called, to Clandeboye where Tyrone's men were gathering cattle to feed them.

'I received yesterday', wrote Sir Geoffrey Fenton from Dublin on 30 July, 'advertisement of the landing of 1,600 Scots in the north, but I think they come not to abide but to return back again with the spoil of cows ... There is a bait laid to cut them off ... how it prevaileth, you shall hear by my next.'[4] Four days later, it was reported to Burghley that 4,000 Scots had landed in 'Great Ardes' and that Tyrone had offered wives to the bachelors amongst them. They would be chosen from the daughters of his gentlemen and freeholders in Tyrone, each man being allocated a wife whose degree was proportionate to his own.[5]

This bizarre bribe, which sounds like a tall story, was not the bait that was being laid for the islanders. It was set by Captain George Thornton of HMS *Popinjay* and Gregory Rigges of HMS *Charles,* who were cruising off the Ulster coast. They now sailed to close the entrance to the sea lough, trapping the islanders. On their way south, near Rathlin Island, they overtook half-a-dozen galleys. They sank two of them with a considerable loss of life. One man was captured and gave his captors the information that after spoiling Clandeboye the Islesmen had taken their prey to the Copeland islands.

The queen's ships followed the escaping galleys and fought an action off the islands, damaging more of their boats. The Islesmen were now trapped as men from the garrison at Carrickfergus joined in the action. Negotiations by letter between Thornton and the leading Hebrideans, who were not in the Copelands, now took place and in an extraordinary about-turn Angus and Donald Gorm offered to change sides.[6] A truce followed and Donald Gorm, writing from the Glens of Antrim, offered Queen Elizabeth his service in exchange for a salary and agreed to retire to Scotland until he received the lord deputy's reply.

Not all the islanders were prepared to change sides. Although Angus himself was, he sent his son Angus Og with 600 of his men to join Tyrone because he thought it unfair that 'materis are nocht keipit to the erle'.[7] Rory Mor, the formidable tutor of Harris, also remained in Ulster. He was attacked by some English horse and several of his men were killed. Driven back to his boats and furious with the Macdonalds,[8] he swore revenge on the English, set sail again and landed at Lough Foyle. He and 600 of his men were promptly hired by O Donnell[9] who marched his combined force of kern and Scots across the Erne into Connaught and on to Galway. They plundered 'and totally ravaged the country all around them, and carried off its flocks and herds, its wealth and riches, from all those they had met on their route ...'[10] Clare and Galway had previously been the only counties in Ireland free from revolt.

On 10 August 1595 George Nicolson reported to Bowes: 'On Tuesday last I rode to Glasgow, and on Wednesday night I came to Dunoon where Argyll and the most of his friends were in bed, but I was well received and made much of by such as were up. On Thursday, after his lordship's rising, I delivered her Majesty's letter, which he kindly received and also your own. After reading them he told me he was much indebted to you for showing his good will to her Majesty, and rested at her service, protesting that he would promise and perform whatsoever he could, showing me that the islesmen prepared to go had all gone to Ireland, but he heard nothing of them since their going, saving 700 or 800 whom Maclean had taken and stayed ...'[11] He went on to describe how when the Macleods had visited Duart, Maclean had tried to persuade Macleod of Lewis, 'sister's son of Maclean', to desert the other Islesmen and that they had become suspicious of Macleod 'and carried him captive with them so that he and his forces should not leave them ...'

Argyll also informed Nicolson that Tyrone had offered the Islesmen land in Ireland that he would capture from the English on which they might 'plant their friends'. He also said that Maclean had written to him to say that Donald Gorm had told the Islesmen 'that Tyrone had written to him that he was advertised by a friend with the Deputy that there was kindness between her Majesty and Argyll'. In other words, Tyrone had a spy in the Council in Dublin.

Dunoon had been fortified to resist any attacks by the Islesmen and 'all the country was under warning and watches kept'. After breakfast Argyll told Nicolson that a deserter from Tyrone had arrived at Dunoon. He had told the earl's servants that Tyrone would fight the English 'upon the coming of the islanders, for Tyrone says still he will not venture all on a day; for if they be overthrown and scattered once, God have mercy on them, he says, for they will never meet again ... For the Queen, he says, if she loses all can send as many more, but he cannot do so ...'[12] Tyrone, who was using classic guerrilla tactics, had no illusions as to his strength compared to that of Elizabeth.

Nicolson now reported that Auchinross reckoned that the only way to 'wrack' Tyrone 'is to pursue him in the north with a force of Scottish islesmen and that Maclean will undertake this on condition that he may have 500 or 600 good soldiers of her Majesty's within, and certain ships to keep his galleys that he may pursue Tyrone on one side and the Lord Deputy on the other side ...'[13] This outline plan was to be the basis of Lachlan Mor's proposals to the English which he was to elaborate over the next few months.

Auchinross claimed that the cost of hiring Maclean would be small. He reckoned that he would 'almost endure his own charge and find our men beef enough [in order] to have such a partie and doing against Tyrone ...' Auchinross also claimed that 'the Spaniards ... are daily looked for' by the rebels.[14]

Lachlan Mor, who had now joined Argyll, wrote to Bowes on 22 August from Garvie in Glendaruel in Argyll, where the earl had his base for hunting in the forest.[15] 'I have received your letter to which John Auchinross made answer in his letter ... Being desired by my cousin, Argyll, to repair to him at Dunoon, I appointed Auchinross to meet me there, and he had received from George Nicolson your letter of 24 July from Greenwich. For the honourable token that her Majesty has commanded should be sent to me I render my duty of humble service. John Cunningham 'shew' me that the token should be 1000 crowns. Let them be sent to George Nicolson ...'[16]

Maclean was surprised at the English conduct in the Copeland Islands. He continues: 'Your captains on the coast of Ireland could never have better advantage than they had of our Scotchmen after their 'heirschip' south of Carrickfergus and return to Coiplan Isles with the plunder. They might have broken all their galleys and made them all perish in that isle; yet they spared their lives and have received but four servants in pledge indeed they would have rendered principals if desired, such was their danger'.

Lachlan Mor went on to suggest that 'If my opinion be followed

Tyrone and O Donnell shall be pursued on both sides, to wit, by your Irish force on the one side, and by Argyll's and mine, with myself present, on this side. I wish you would move Argyll to furnish 2,000 men. I shall furnish other 2,000 and I would six or eight hundred of your "fyirmen" with hagbuts and 400 pikemen'.

He goes on to stress that it was essential that Bowes, who was still living at Berwick, came to Scotland. 'Your presence is most necessary that you must "speik" Argyll herein … Also I have two young boys, the sons of my cousins that were cruelly murdered by Tyrone, and if they of Ireland once know that I had landed there I 'tak opinioun' that sundry of them would leave him and assist me 'in his contrair'. I know that there are sundry gentlemen who follow him against their will.' Maclean was attempting to re-establish the old party of the sons of Sean.

He ends: 'I send my duty of humble service to her Majesty and commendations to Sir Robert Cecil. Let me know of anything in Scotland that may pleasure Sir Robert … I am here in Argyll at pastime and hunting with the Earl. I have respect to other kind of hunting than this present hunting of deer …'[17]

On 22 August John Archibald also wrote to Nicolson from Stirling that Angus had left Ireland 'with the loss of the most part of his best men'. The reason for his departure was not so much the losses he had sustained but because neither O Donnell nor O Neill had lived up to his promises.[18]

Rumours were everywhere. One was that 'the King of Spain has another fleet coming home with more treasure' and that he had ordered Huntly and Errol to return to Scotland.[19]

Lachlan Mor's imprisonment of Clanranald and the others had had its effect. They were now considered part of Maclean's following and were thought suitable recipients of Elizabeth's bounty.[20] The pro-English party now, according to Mr George Erskine, included Maclean, the Captain of Clanranald, Macneill of Barra, Macian of Ardnamurchan and 'Maclean of Lochbuy'. The latter, who had disappeared from the records for some time, was evidently not considered to be an automatic follower of Duart. Erskine went on to say that Maclean had sowed so much dissension between the confederates, 'which we foster daily', that it was unlikely they would return to Ireland.[21]

Lachlan Mor, it seemed, was now firmly back in royal favour. John Auchinross wrote to Bowes on 29 August that Maclean 'has been received by his majesty of Scotland on the previous day in the presence of Argyll and the earl of Mar with many other noblemen'. Elizabeth had still not decided to pay for the very real assistance she was getting in the Isles.

Lachlan Mor was to be encouraged and flattered but he was not yet 'employed'.

On 8 September one of his suggestions was acted on when it was noted by the lord deputy in a letter to Sir Robert Cecil that Captain Thornton was ready to sail to Maclean's castle. [22]

George Thornton, who must not be confused with the Irish Provost Marshal of the same name, had considerable experience of service in Irish waters. He probably came originally from Hull, where the Thorntons were a leading family of merchants. He first appears in the records in 1560 when he was arrested for piracy. He escaped the gallows and in August 1562 received a royal pardon in order that his talents as a seaman could be employed in the Le Havre campaign. His ties with the navy were strengthened in the late 1560s when his sister Elizabeth married Peter Pett the royal master shipwright.

Thornton first appears to have served in Ireland with the royal navy in 1566. He was to remain there for the rest of his service, often cruising from Carrickfergus to Lough Foyle to prevent the Scots crossing to Ireland.[23]

Thornton's journey to Duart in September 1595 was his first recorded visit to Hebridean waters. He was in the Sound of Mull by 9 September and sent messages to Maclean who was still with Argyll. Lachlan Mor hurried to Duart to find Thornton anchored below his house. They spent three days in discussions and on the 15th the *Popinjay* sailed for Ireland.

On 24 September Nicolson reported from Edinburgh to Bowes. Lachlan Mor had returned to Inveraray to 'my Lord Argyll'. Captain Thornton had left Duart and had taken with him letters from the earl and Maclean to Sir Robert Cecil, the lord deputy, the marshal and to Bowes himself. 'So far as I can see', wrote Nicolson, 'I find the earl of Argyll and Maclean (brother and sister children) in such natural love as the one will not be employed ... without the other.' [24]

Argyll had found in Maclean a councillor and a friend that he had failed to find amongst his Campbell kinsmen, to whom, since Cawdor's murder, he had been aloof and cold. Lachlan Mor had put behind him his quarrel with the sixth earl and had resumed the position his grandfather Hector Mor had had with the fourth earl.

Nicolson went on to argue the case for employing the cousins. 'Time', he wrote 'is precious.' They needed payment, 'for the token is too long delayed and Argyll too long unthanked, in so much as I heard it was said by some ... that England cares no further for any than the serving of their own turn'.[25]

Thornton had taken with him an offer of service from Maclean and Argyll, a copy of which was sent by the lord deputy Sir William Russell to Robert Bowes. Thornton's report repeated what had been said again and again: that Maclean would provide 2,000 men to fight against Tyrone in Ireland in exchange for a salary. He also stressed that both he and Argyll were determined to have their revenge on Tyrone for hanging their kinsman, Hugh Gavelagh O Neill. He also pointed out that the Scottish galleys with their oars were faster than her Majesty's pinnaces and that as Argyll was lord lieutenant of all the islands Maclean could not recruit without his consent.

Maclean had asked Thornton that his pinnace should protect his galleys in Ireland once they were beached. They were then at their most vulnerable.

The allowances to be paid the Scots were outlined. Every Scot who served with a long bow or halberd was to have 10 shillings a quarter. Every 'shot' with a piece was to have 20 shillings. All were to receive their victuals by the month, 'three madders of butter and six madders of oatmeal'.[26] If they did not get them they should be paid 10 shillings a month in lieu. The pay of those who were not 'shots' was to be 13 shillings and 4 pence for wages and victuals per month of 30 days. A 'shot' was to receive double.

In his covering letter to Bowes, with the offer of service, Russell says that he had written to Maclean to ask him how conveniently he could produce 2000 Scots to serve against the rebels in the spring. He needed them as many of his own men were sick and weak.

Whilst the government considered Lachlan Mor's offer, the confederates continued to press Argyll to join them. They stressed the ancient friendship between his ancestors and O Donnell and could not believe that the seventh earl would 'break friendship with them without occasion of some quarrel'. Nicolson mused that he supposed that Argyll's 'performance of his duty' to James VI, 'together with good occasion at her Majesty's hands', might be considered the cause of a quarrel.

George Erskine, who was Nicolson's source of this information, also reported that the confederates offered to pay this 'great tribute' to Argyll that had been paid to him by O Donnell in the past 'with the arrearages' due to him. The earl had however refused their offers. 'If the Queen was to give the earl some token of her friendship', commented Erskine, any further offers from O Donnell would be rebuffed.[27]

The 'token' Argyll required was hard cash. It was essential, Nicolson wrote to Bowes, that Maclean received the 'token of 1,000 crowns' which he had been promised by Sir Robert Cecil. Nicolson had heard that the confederates had received armour and gold from Spain and that Tyrone had increased the number of horsemen he employed. He was expected to use them to invade the south of Ireland. There was no alternative, Nicolson believed, but to employ Argyll and Maclean. Had they only been employed 'ere now', they would have broken the rebels' necks.[28]

Lachlan Mor was also becoming impatient. He evidently presumed that Thornton's recommendations had been accepted, for he wrote to Bowes on 5 October: 'Seeing I have entered in her Majesty's service', he would be grateful if Bowes would get the queen to write to the Scots king to get him to command Maclean to serve her. He was also wanting payment for his previous service in preventing Clanranald and the other Macdonalds from crossing to Ireland. 'Ere now', he wrote, 'I looked for the token ordained by her Majesty ... I marvel of the stay thereof ...'[29]

Lachlan Mor wanted more than gold and considered that he was due a favour. It so happened he had recently received a letter from George Cary, a gentleman living in Clovelly in Cornwall, desiring him to use his influence with the king of Scots and get him to write to Queen Elizabeth to obtain a pardon for one John Neill.

John Neill was in fact a Macneill who, when he was a young boy, had left Scotland in a ship belonging to a man named William Nycoll of the parish of Northam in Devon. Nothing had been heard of him for many years but apparently he had prospered. Unfortunately he had quarrelled with a captain who had challenged him to single combat. Whilst defending himself Macneill had the misfortune to kill his adversary. He was now in prison in Exeter.

Maclean asked Bowes to write to Sir Robert Cecil to persuade the queen to pardon John, who, Lachlan Mor writes, is 'a special kinsman to Macneill of Barra, who is my dependar [and] serves me in time of trouble with three hundred men'.

If John was pardoned and banished from England, Maclean would see he served the queen elsewhere. Bowes did evidently write to Cecil who in turn petitioned the queen. The latter however claimed that she had never in all her reign obtained the release of someone found guilty of murder. 'Yet because this is a stranger and that Maclean has so earnestly laboured for him her Majesty has commanded me [Cecil] to speak with her judges and to consider how possibly his life may be saved.'[30]

Although the correspondence dragged on for some time it is not clear what eventually happened to the unfortunate Macneill. The case does however illustrate that Maclean now believed he was in a position to

put pressure on the English authorities. It also shows that Maclean
looked after his dependants.

Lachlan Mor's failure to support O Neill was not popular with his
clan who were denied the opportunity of wages and plunder. His tenants
were also unhappy that their laird 'detains five hundred men daily'.
Presumably the tenants had to feed Maclean's men once they had been
called out for war. Feeding five hundred soldiers for any length of time
by the townships around Duart was not a joke. The soldiers themselves
were not happy. 'The young men tire and yet they must attend as he
commands', wrote Auchinross, pointing out to Bowes that Maclean
'holds no fewer under wages and retinue nor [than] he had in greatest
time of most trouble and wars.' Auchinross adds that his master found
it extraordinary that he had not received his 'token' which is 'dear
bought by him'.[31]

*   *   *   *

Lachlan Mor was still officially forfeit for his past misdemeanours. He
had still to settle with the comptroller for the crown's land held by him.
It was planned that he would visit Edinburgh in December 1595 to
settle both these matters. Such an expedition was expensive: Auchinross
considered it would cost between 16 and 18,000 merks. He pointed out
this fact to Bowes in a letter of 14 November 1595. In order to help
him out 'it would do him great pleasure' to receive the 'token' promised
by Elizabeth. 'I assure your lordship', wrote Auchinross, 'he has
spent mekle mair nor that token since March last in her Majesty's
service ...'[32]

In the same letter Auchinross informed Bowes of the doings of the
Macdonalds in Ulster. Angus had placed his second lawful son, also
named Angus, in his lands in the Glens. The latter was in league with
O Neill. Angus the elder who had thrown himself at Argyll's feet and
begged for mercy in September was now visiting the king at Linlithgow
where he sought to have the Rinns of Islay, which Lachlan Mor still
occupied as the 'kindly' tenant, granted to him in fee. The king ignored
his request and when Angus offered to invade the Isle of Man on the
king's behalf James told him not to 'meddle therewith, saying he would
have his service when time served'.[33]

In the meantime Lachlan Mor had been active on Argyll's behalf.
The earl's designs on Huntly's lands in Lochaber had been raised at
the time of the Battle of Glenlivet. He now wished to have his authority
there recognised by the local inhabitants. Lachlan Mor moved into

Lochaber by sea whilst 2,000 Campbells went by land. Lachlan carried out his assignment with such 'foresight and wisdom' that in the space of ten days he had obtained the eldest sons of two lairds in Lochaber as hostages. One, described as being Maclean's own cousin, was presumably Cameron of Locheil, the other being Glengarry. Maclean had carried out his coup 'without doing any harm in Lochaber'. 'Thus Maclean makes the earl more honoured and friended', wrote Nicolson.[34]

Angus continued to try and persuade Maclean to join the rebels and passed on messages from Ireland. Tyrone protested that he had never offended Maclean save only for the preservation of his own life which was threatened by Hugh Gavelagh, which was why Tyrone had 'schoitnit Hew O Neill's dayis'. He also reminded Lachlan Mor that his own forbears were 'of the realm of Ireland, wherefore [he] ought not to see them perish ...' Tyrone also promised to give land to Hugh Gavelagh and his brother Art's sons who were being cared for by Maclean. Tyrone also promised to provide pledges for his good behaviour towards Lachlan Mor. These pledges would be delivered to 'his place of Duart'. Maclean was tempted and is said to have agreed to think about Tyrone's proposal.[35]

Lachlan had still not given up hope of his 'token' but his patience was almost exhausted. On 20 December 1595 he wrote to Bowes 'to let me know if that promise is to be kept or not'.[36] After having deliberated, Sir Robert Cecil wrote to Bowes on 18 February 1595–6. Despite the time he himself had taken Cecil wanted an immediate answer to his questions.

'You shall understand', wrote Cecil, 'that her Majesty is now resolved to use the service of the Scots in Ireland, for which purpose you are now ... to consider how this may be done with her Majesty's least charge and best security.' He went on to say that the idea that they should be employed came first from Maclean, but now 'if it shall appear that the Queen newly seeks him', her bargaining power would be reduced. Bowes was to devise some method to make Maclean think that no decision had been made and that he should be persuaded to make an offer.

Bowes was to get him to propose what he would actually do, what number of men he would provide, what it would cost and whether or not he needed to be paid in advance. If he did, what guarantee would the queen have that he would do what he promised?

Cecil went on to say that the queen had been forced to make her decision as she 'finds these traitors to grow more insolent every hour (though I would have him think the contrary) ... The Queen hoped to hire between three and four thousand Scots'. She needed to know from Bowes whether she needed the king of Scots' permission and whether such permission would be more expensive. Cecil however believed that 'Argyll being dealt with, Maclean will not much stand upon the King's leave, who cannot in honour forbid it'.

Cecil had one other major worry: 'If the Queen for money can procure Scots, why shall not the rebels procure some also ...' If Lachlan Mor had obtained sight of this letter he would probably immediately have thrown in his lot with Tyrone. As it was, Bowes was out of contact with him. 'Since my return to Edinburgh', he wrote to Lord Burghley on 24 February, 'I have not heard from Maclean, whereof I marvel and pray your lordship to be directed how I shall proceed with him.'[37]

Bowes also replied that the king intended to 'draw the Isles of Scotland to his good obedience'. He proposed to use Argyll, Maclean and Mackenzie for this purpose and had given Maclean, who was still forfeit, permission 'to repair to his presence and to depart with safety'. Lachlan Mor's eldest son Hector had recently married Mackenzie's sister. As a result, 'they are of the greatest power and estimation in the Isles and Highlands', wrote Bowes to Burghley, 'and many of the greatest quality there seek for their friendship'. He continues, 'I am informed credibly that Tyrone and O Donnell have lately made means to call him and entertain many of the islands who are preparing to be ready to pass into Ireland in the end of March next'.[38] Elizabeth was running out of time.

Bowes reacted to Sir Robert Cecil's letter of 18 February by sending John Cunningham, an Edinburgh burgess whom he had used in the past, to Mull to find out more details of those islanders planning to go to Ireland.

Cecil was alarmed. On 4 March he wrote to Bowes: 'The Queen is wonderfully well satisfied with your manner of proceeding ... For Maclean I pray you hasten to bargain with him ...' Two days later Bowes wrote that the reason he had lost contact with Maclean was because he was 'presently in the Isle of Tiree beyond Mull and ten days journey from Edinburgh by the encumbrance and passage of many ferries'.[39]

Bowes had been speaking to Mackenzie, who had joined Maclean in pressing for the 1,000 crowns 'long expected'. Mackenzie reported that the new rebel force intended to leave for Ireland by the end of the month. Mackenzie promised to try and persuade Macleod of Harris, who had only just returned from Ireland, from returning 'thither with fresh power'. He and Cunningham both believed that Maclean would prevent the others from leaving provided he were paid.

Mackenzie would do his best to get Argyll to assist Maclean but the earl was so occupied in pursuit of John Campbell of Ardkinglas who was to be arraigned for the murder of Cawdor, that he could get no decision from him.[40] The Cawdor family had obtained 'Letters of Treason' against Ardkinglas and on 29 March 1595–6 a 'Commission of Justiciary' was authorised by the king to examine the case.[41]

Interest in London in the potential of the Hebrides, either as a friend or a foe, was rapidly increasing, and on 21 March 1595 Bowes's clerk in Edinburgh copied the anonymous report entitled 'The Isles of Scotland and the division thereof with the names of the Chieftanes'.[42]

* * * *

By 8 March John Cunningham had reached the west coast. He rested at Dunolly, where he had a conference with Maclean's ally Duncan Macdougall of Dunolly. The laird had already sent a boat with four of his special servants to Islay to find out what Angus was up to. Cunningham wrote to Bowes that day that Maclean was in Tiree. In fact Maclean was in Coll, presumably staying at Breacachadh, from where he wrote to Bowes on 18 March. His letter contained his detailed proposal to the English government. Angus and Donald Gorm were mending their galleys and their other vessels which were to transport their men to Ireland to renew the rebellion. He declared that once it was known that he was employed by the queen he could prevent them from leaving. All those living in the islands, he pointed out, were either his friends or his enemies. His friends would rally to his support and his enemies would not dare leave their dwellings.

He then proceeded to outline how he would crush the rebellion in Ireland. He himself would go with 2,000 of his own men and those of his dependents. He would also ask Argyll to provide a thousand men 'of my choosing'; 1,500 of his own men would be bowmen, 'who are very meet for that country'. These were his heavy infantry who wore 'armour of mail'. They would also be armed with two-handed swords, which would be useful if they had a pitched battle with the enemy. He would also provide 500 'fyermen'.

Maclean also suggested that the queen provide him with a further two thousand men. A thousand should be 'fyermen' and a thousand armed with pikes. If the queen could not spare two thousand, he required at least a thousand, two-thirds of whom should be 'fyermen' and a third pikemen. The commanders of the queen's men, he insisted, should not be 'those that are trained up in Ireland who crave the wars to continue'.

The queen's Irish were considered to have a vested interest in continuing the war. The opposite was the case with those who were veterans of the war in Flanders. Experienced officers who had served there believed there was nothing to be learned of warfare in Ireland, 'despising conflict with naked gallowglasses and kern, and begged to be employed in other countries'.[43]

As far as food was concerned, wrote Maclean, 'we that are Scottishmen shall furnish ourselves', whilst the queen's men should have their own supplies for the first six nights after they landed. Thereafter they would all live off the country, 'if fortune chance'.

Payment would be at a rate of 20 shillings sterling per man up to a limit of £2,000 sterling per month, which should be paid monthly from the day that his men embarked in their galleys until they returned home.

Lachlan Mor's plan was that his men should land in Lough Foyle and advance through O Neill's country until he made contact with the earl wherever he was to be found. At the same time the queen's forces, under the command of the marshal, should advance and join up with Maclean. Lachlan Mor evidently saw himself on an equal footing with Sir Hugh Bagenal. Once he had landed, Lachlan Mor believed that many of Tyrone's and O Donnell's men would desert 'and seek to me for making of intercession and mean with her Majesty for their peace'. He should also have liberty to pardon those who were not the ringleaders.

'It is to be remembered', he added, 'that this part of Ireland was never fully brought to her Grace's obedience nor of none afore her this many hundred years.' The rebels, he believed, would never be defeated unless 'they be persuaded on this side by Scottishmen. By the which with God's grace there is no doubt to compel them to render to her Grace's obedience and the Earl to beg mercy for his rebellion ...'[44]

In order for him to carry out his plan Lachlan Mor required that the queen sent him a hundred long bows and some gunpowder. He also would need munitions and presumably artillery, from the lord deputy, if the rebels defended 'any strengths'. He also insisted that the ships that brought the queen's men to Lough Foyle remained there during the expedition to protect his galleys.

Lachlan Mor also wanted a guarantee that if he reduced Tyrone's and O Donnell's countries to obedience he would obtain an annual pension for life. But 'in case God called me in her service', a pension should be paid to his eldest son during his lifetime. In exchange Hector should have 2,000 men at all times ready for the queen's service.

Finally Lachlan Mor did not forget his 'kyndly man' and servant John Macneill. It was essential that he be released and arrive at Duart fifteen days before the expedition set sail, as he, 'having our language', would be used as an interpreter.

This proposal is in John Auchinross' handwriting. He had evidently accompanied his master to Coll and was now to return with Cunningham to Edinburgh to continue the negotiations. Bowes was to deal with him as if Maclean were present.

*   *   *   *

Meanwhile Turlough Luineach had died. The first news of his death was reported to Burghley by Sir Hugh Bagenal from Newry on 9 September 1595. He also states 'the traitor [Tyrone] has gone to the 'Stone' to receive the name O Neill'.[45] The 'Stone' Bagenal is referring to was *Leac na Ri*, the king's stone.

It was claimed that *Leac na Ri* had been blessed by St. Patrick. By the sixteenth century it had been incorporated into a ceremonial stone chair, which stood on the hill of Tullaghoge, not far from Lough Neagh in the eastern part of the present Co. Tyrone.

The stone and the inauguration ceremony of the 'making' of an O Neill had a significance in 1595 for both the Irish and the English. The ceremony was in effect the coronation of a king. Irish lords, in particular the O Neills of Tyrone, claimed a local sovereignty which was incompatible with the sovereignty of Elizabeth as monarch of Ireland as well as England.

Hugh O Neill repeatedly asserted that he was a subject of the queen. His actions were at variance with his assertions. Certainly as earl of Tyrone he held a title which was the gift of the monarch, but his real source of power was not his earldom, but the name O Neill. The assumption of this title transformed the nature of the conflict in Ulster. It highlighted the issue of sovereignty.

Once Turlough Luineach was dead and Tyrone was installed at Tullaghoge, he was in effect 'Prince of Ulster'. Some were to claim that he had even greater ambitions. It was said by his followers during the earl's open struggle with the English that their aim was to win the island for themselves and to make O Neill 'Prince of Ireland'. It was even said that O Neill, as we must now call him, intended to be 'King of Ireland'.[46]

Tyrone was too astute a politician not to cover his back when he was made O Neill. He claimed that if he had not been installed someone else, either his brother Cormac MacBaron, or one of the sons of Sean would have been. Even greater conflict would have been the result.

Before Turlough Luineach's death Hugh had been sounding out the English for a reconciliation. 'I confess unto your Lordship', he wrote to Sir John Norris on 22 August, 'that I have offended Her majesty, and I am heartily sorry for it. I humbly beseech Her Highness' most gracious pardon and favour to be extended towards me and all inhabitants of Tyrone ...' A week earlier his men had tried to burn Newry and before the end of the month there had been serious fighting when the English re-supplied Armagh.[47] Many of the confederates, including Angus's men, fled.

It is difficult to assess how much the return home of the Scots affected O Neill's plans. Negotiations between the confederates and the government did take place and it is possible that this defection tipped the balance in a bid for peace. The crown was willing to make concessions but would only do so if it did not lose face. On the other hand the confederates needed a settlement that would guarantee their control of local issues. Looming behind both sets of negotiators was the threat of the Spanish intervention. Both sides appeared to want peace and by 18 October O Neill had made a contrite submission and even agreed to renounce the prohibited title of O Neill. The crown too moderated its position when it discovered how deeply the rebels were involved with Spain.

At the end of September 1595 a priest called Piers O Cullen was arrested at Drogheda en route to Spain. He was carrying letters from O Neill and O Donnell to Philip II in which it was claimed that the rebels were fighting to establish the Roman Catholic religion in Ireland. They offered the crown of Ireland to the Spanish king. As O Cullen's capture was the result of information supplied by Richard Egerton, one of O Neill's secretaries, it has been suggested that O Neill wanted the priest to be captured in order to frighten the government.[48]

Negotiations continued but as usual O Neill was playing for time and took advantage of the ceasefire to strengthen his position. The fort at Monaghan was betrayed to the confederates and O Donnell made a triumphant progress through Connaught.

By the beginning of January 1596 the crown's plans for an honourable peace were in ruins. The confederates demanded more and more concessions, including religious freedom.

They were in a strong position. They controlled the greater part of Ireland. They could expect to make good terms with the English. But would that be an end of the matter? Or would the English play a waiting game and renew their onslaught on the Gaelic lords and all they stood for once the time was right? O Neill's spies probably reported that the lord deputy had persuaded a majority in the Irish Council that the only solution lay in a renewed vigorous prosecution of the war. Such action would include the establishment of a garrison at Lough Foyle. It was estimated that such an operation would require 10,000 men. The risk and the cost would be considerable but many thought that a force in the enemy's rear in the heart of Ulster was the only way to defeat the rebels. But would Elizabeth make the funds and men available?

O Neill was equally aware of the strategic importance of Lough Foyle. He was in a dilemma. He could make peace or continue the war. If he did the latter he could only win the war if he drove the English out of Ireland once and for all time and kept them out. This meant driving them out of all their forts not just in Ulster but in the Pale. Could he hope to achieve this end without artillery? He also needed a larger army than he could hope to recruit in Ireland itself. He could only obtain the support he needed in Scotland or in Spain. Spain was the preferred option.

Swift 'patches' sailed backwards and forwards between Galicia and Ulster carrying urgent appeals for help from the chiefs. They took back with them blessings and vague promises from Philip and by March 1595 O Neill had begun to lose faith in help from Spain. As a last resort he sent his confessor with an ultimatum. Either help must be sent and sent in plenty, especially artillery, or he would make peace. Spanish influence in Ireland would be at an end.

Notes

1. *CSP Scot.* xi, 668.
2. *Ibid*, 667–8.
3. *Ibid.*
4. *CSP Ireland* v, 350.
5. *Ibid*, 358.
6. *Ibid*, 359, 370.
7. *CSP Scot.* xi, 684.
8. *Ibid*, 685.
9. *Annals of the Four Masters*, vi, 1975.
10. *Ibid; CSP Ireland* v, 371.
11. *CSP Scot.* xi, 676.
12. *Ibid.*
13. *Ibid*, 678.
14. *Ibid.*

15. I am grateful to Alastair Campbell of Airds for this information.

16. *CSP Scot.* xi, 684.

17. *Ibid.*

18. *Ibid,* 686.

19. *Ibid.*

20. *Ibid,* 688.

21. *Ibid.*

22. *CSP Ireland* v, 313.

23. Tom Glasgow, Jr, 'The Elizabethan Navy in Ireland (1558–1603)', *Irish Sword* vii, Winter 1966 No. 21.

24. *CSP Scot.* xii, 23.

25. *Ibid,* 24.

26. A madder was a measure in Ulster, varying acording to locality between 1½ and (more usually) 2 gallons. I am indebted to Kenneth Nicholls for this information.

27. *CSP Scot.* xii, 31.

28. *Ibid.*

29. *Ibid,* 36.

30. *Ibid,* 35–37, 145.

31. *Ibid,* 42.

32. *Ibid,* 57.

33. *Ibid,* 58.

34. *Ibid,* 50, 58.

35. *Ibid,* 103.

36. *Ibid,* 94.

37. *Ibid,* 144.

38. *Ibid,* 149.

39. *Ibid,* 156.

40. *Ibid,* 157.

41. *HP* i, 152–6, 157–9.

42. *CSP Scot.* xii, 172.

43. *CSP Ireland,* vi, 382.

44. *Ibid,* 171.

45. *Ibid,* 386.

46. G. A Hayes-McCoy, 'The making of an O Neill', *Ulster Journal of Archaeology* Vol. 33, 89–94.

47. *CSP Ireland* v, 374, 384.

48. Morgan, 194.

CHAPTER 16

Spymasters and their Spies

Porter. Knock, Knock! Who's there,
I'th' other devil's name? Faith, here's an equivo-
cator that could swear in both the scales against
either scale; who committed treason enough for
God's sake, yet could not equivocate to heaven:
O, come in equivocator.

Macbeth Act II, Scene iii

During the months that followed O Neill's ultimatum to Philip II everyone involved in the struggle for Ireland sought information and made their assessments. In Spain the king, now a sick and bitter old man, insisted on controlling everything from his cell in the Escorial. Philip's mania for minutiae had doomed the Armada and would ultimately do the same for all his plans.

The king was almost alone in realising that Spain was in no position to attack England with another Armada. He had probably given up any hopes he once had of conquering England. O Neill's ultimatum however aroused Philip sufficiently to send Captain Alanso Cobos to Ulster to report on the military situation there.[1]

Cobos arrived just in time to prevent the confederates from making peace with the English. 'I arrived', he wrote from Leffer at the head of Lough Foyle on 15 May 1596, 'at the time when the Irish chiefs had almost concluded peace with the Queen on terms satisfactory to them-selves.' He went on to say that he persuaded them to change their minds, 'solely on conscientious grounds and out of affection for his Majesty'.

Philip responded by sending two more captains, both experienced military advisers, to Tyrone. They were issued with a list of specific questions to answer. Firstly they were to ask precisely what the chiefs required from Spain. Their answer was that they needed arms for 10,000 men: 'Corselets, pikes, morrions, harquebusses and muskets, powder balls, cord &c'. They also insisted that these munitions were accompanied by 1,000 Spanish soldiers.

The second question was also of crucial importance: whether or not
unity existed among the chiefs and if they would obey Tyrone? Did the
latter 'command by authority or prayers?' The answer was that both
O Neill and O Donnell 'are like one man, and the rest respect them'.

The next question was particularly dear to the king's heart. 'Was the
uprising', he wanted to know, 'a Catholic league for the support of the
faith, or was it for their private ends?' The confederates' religious zeal
had not initially been apparent, but they were able to persuade the
emissaries that they were making war sincerely in defence of the Catholic
faith and that they would not seek help from heretics.

The king also wished to know how many men the confederates could
put into the field and how they were supplied. The answer was that
they had 6,000 foot and 1,200 horse. They carried sufficient food with
them for the time they expected to be away from home, and although
the land was 'desolated by war', there was sufficient for their own needs.
It would be necessary to build new mills to provide food for any incomers.

The king wished to know if there were waggons for guns. He also
wanted to know the state of the passes, fords and bridges. The answer
was that river crossings were difficult. Most were fordable and others
were crossed by boat or had bridges. He also enquired if there were
any roads 'to the territories and ports that they wished to conquer',
which were suitable for artillery. The reply was no and that as the
ground was 'very marshy' it would be impossible to move artillery to
any port which the Spanish fleet might wish to occupy.

The quality of the ports held by the queen was also of interest to
the king who particularly wished to know which of them was capable
of receiving 'a great fleet to attack the Catholics'. The reply was the
most detailed answer yet: 'The ports possessed by the Queen are the
town of Drogheda, with an ancient wall, the city of Dublin, also an
ancient fortress, and the residence of the Viceroy. The munitions &c,
are kept there and a small garrison. Rosse is an old fortress. Waterford
has a tower with a little ordnance and a port capable of receiving a
good fleet. Wexford an old fortress and Dungarvan a harbour with a
castle and a few English. Youghal is an ancient walled port. Cork an
ancient port. Limerick an ancient walled city, capable of harbouring a
great fleet. Galway the same. These are all the ports held by the Queen'.

The spies did not know if the confederates used carts and horses to
transport their forces, or what shipping would be required for the
expedition. They were more forthcoming concerning cavalry. When
asked, could the Irish do without cavalry or if not, how many they
required, they answered that 'a thousand lancers and two or three

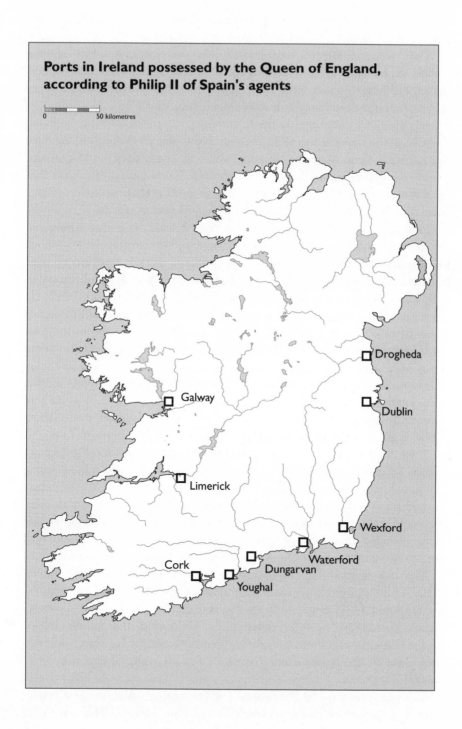

Ports in Ireland possessed by the Queen of England, according to Philip II of Spain's agents

0   50 kilometres

Drogheda

Galway

Dublin

Limerick

Wexford

Waterford

Cork   Dungarvan

Youghal

hundred mounted harquebussiers' were required. Horses could be purchased in Ireland.

They were unable to answer the question of which fortresses the
rebels expected to seize. Pioneers could be recruited locally but 'spades,
picks, hatchetts' would have to be sent plus a full company of pioneers
to instruct the local people in building fortifications.

Surprisingly the captains made no reply to the request to provide
details of the queen's forces in Ireland. How many? Which places were
garrisoned? How were they resupplied? Nor could they give details of
English shipping in Irish ports. They were however able to state that
if 'a strong force were to be sent ... It is certain that, as soon as they
saw our fleet many of the inhabitants would declare for us'.

Philip also wished to know whether John Norris, who was considered
by the Spanish the best soldier in England, was commander-in-chief.
The reply was that the viceroy was William Russell and Norris was
commander-in-chief. Finally it was pointed out: 'You are well aware of
the difficulty there was in finding the pilots'. Those who had taken them
to Ireland had no experience of the coast north of Galway. The emissaries
were therefore instructed when they entered Donegal, or any other port,
to let the pilots examine it thoroughly. They were also to let the pilots
go ashore and reconnoitre the coast as far north as Cape Teelin. They
were to pay particular attention to examining Sligo, Donegal, 'Easky'
and Teelin and to ask Tyrone for a couple of pilots 'if there were any
who know the coast well. Take four if you can get them, and offer them
good wages on his Majesty's fleet'.

That was all. It was an extraordinarily inadequate intelligence on
which to risk an expeditionary force and win a kingdom. It is also a
damning indictment of how little the Spanish knew about the situation
in Ireland, a country whose leaders were being encouraged to risk their
lives and fortunes on behalf of Spain. Philip was a cold-blooded statesman
who regarded men, however great, as simple pawns in a game he played
for the greater glory of the Roman Catholic Church and Spain.

The two Spanish captains were back in Lisbon at the beginning of
June. They brought with them more letters from the chiefs begging for
aid, at least 1,000 men, 'to keep the war alive until the army comes'.
Count Portallegre, who debriefed them, wrote that 'the people seemed
to the captains very fond of fighting and very apt for it. They can raise
and place in the field as many men as may be wanted, and they offer
40,000 ...'

Two ensigns who had accompanied the captains also made a report
that in a number of instances contradicted their seniors. There were no

bridges or boats by which to cross rivers. 'We have reason to know this', they wrote, 'as we travelled 37 leagues with these chiefs. There is not a tree nor a bit of timber in the north with which to make bridges.' The people they thought were well disposed but it was impossible to travel on the land 'as you sink up to the knee ...'

They agreed that the Irish had 'enough victuals for themselves ...', but they took with them on the march only 'butter and milk for drink. This with herbs and a little oat bread suffices for them'. Milk was not purchased as 'such is not their custom; and if people go from one part of the country to another, they receive butter and milk for their sustenance from the natives of the country they go to ...'

They also gave details of the strength of the confederate army, which they claimed totalled 5,900 foot and 1,080 horse, who were now spread about on the different estates. They also commented on their weapons. 'They have darts, bows and arrows, shields, like ours (i.e. round) and like Hungarian bucklers. They have no muskets and few harquebusses.' It is probable that they had only seen O Donnell's men.

These reports, and the constant flow of emissaries from the Irish chiefs to him, convinced Philip that he could establish a firm foothold in Ireland at comparatively little cost. Captain Cobos was accordingly sent back to Ireland in September 1596 with letters to all the principal Irish chiefs ordering them to congregate at the monastery of Donegal in October. The chiefs were assured in the king's name that Spanish aid would soon be arriving.

They recommended somewhere on the north-west coast such as Galway for landing troops. Although there had been an English garrison there for the last three months, the town was close to the lands of a confederate. Once the Spanish fleet came into sight they believed the town would surrender. If however contrary winds blew the fleet into St. George's Channel they thought it should head for Carlingford Lough. There they would be able to make contact with O Neill's people. As Newry, the main English base in Ulster, was at the head of the Lough the rebels were evidently confident of dominating the countryside outside the town.

Cobos then gave details of the location of the English troops in Ireland. The whole force, he claimed, amounted to only 4,000 infantry in fortresses and 400 English lancers. He went on to say that he gave one of the king's letters to O Dogherty (O Docherty) and one to 'James Oge Mc Sorley boy, a Scotsman, who holds some ports on this coast opposite Scotland. He is a good soldier and very brave. He was neutral when I arrived previously, but he is now great friends with the Catholic chiefs'. Cobos thought it would be a good idea if the king wrote to him as he would be greatly flattered.

*   *   *   *

The English authorities also had the use of undercover agents. Intelligence in Ireland was the responsibility of Sir Geoffrey Fenton, the long-serving secretary to the council in Dublin. In March 1596 he had reported that 'powder, calivers and muskets had been brought to Lough Foyle from Scotland for Tyrone and O Donnell'.[2] He now kept London informed of the progress of Cobos' mission to O Neill and even had a spy who was present at the meeting between the earl and Cobos at Killibeggs in May.

Fenton's reports went either to Lord Burghley, the Lord Treasurer, or to Sir Robert Cecil, particularly the latter after April 1596 when he was appointed Elizabeth's Principal Secretary of State. Cecil, the highly intelligent, hunchbacked second son of Burghley, was to prove as efficient, unscrupulous and ruthless a spymaster as the old fox his father.

Cecil had a network of spies throughout Europe. Several were based in trading centres. Some, such as the Frenchman, Chateaumartin, who was the English consul in La Rochelle, turned out to be double agents. Philip II thought so highly of Chateaumartin that he paid him a retainer of 100 escudos per month, even though he knew he was also paid by the English.[3]

Intelligence in Scotland was provided by both the official English representative there such as Robert Bowes and from covert agents. Many were pretty unsavoury characters, such as Thomas Douglas. Douglas, a brother of the laird of Whittinghame, was trained in Rome by the Jesuits, 'whose intelligences and politics and treacheries are known to him'.[4] His brother was employed in the offices of James VI's secretary Elphinstone (to whom he was related by marriage) and was in an ideal position to obtain secret intelligence. Douglas was an unscrupulous adventurer whose activities were not limited to reporting news. He was to claim to have organised the poisoning of James Og McSorley and to have narrowly failed in a similar attempt on the life of O Neill. Cecil appreciated his value and characteristically retained him in his service and paid him well. Equally characteristically when his usefulness had ended, after the Union of the Crowns, Cecil did not lift a finger to save him from execution for forgery in 1609.[5]

Perhaps the most typical of Cecil's agents were the Mowbray cousins, Francis and Philip, a younger son and a cadet respectively of the family of Barnbogle, whose great-grandfather had been Treasurer of Scotland. They were Roman Catholics and the religious wars had ruined their family. Francis's sister was in the service of Mary Queen of Scots, had married her secretary and was living in exile in the Spanish Netherlands. She provided the cousins with an ideal entrée to the Roman Catholic expatriates and to their plots.

Like Douglas, the Mowbrays did not limit themselves to gathering intelligence. Both were desperate men who were prepared to undertake any deed, including murder, and to serve any master in Ireland and the Low Countries as well as Scotland. They were also adept at political intrigue. Philip attempted to arrange an *entente* between Huntly and Cecil to the latter's embarrassment. Francis became involved, possibly as a double agent, in the correspondence between Cecil and a number of the Archduke's staff. When he finally incurred James VI's enmity Cecil let him go to his execution and made no effort to save him.

Cecil and his spies made use of ciphers, which the secretary usually deciphered in person. It was his principle that 'never one intelligencer know of another for you know that they will cut one another's throat'.[6] Nor did he hesitate to misinform his own agents if it was politic to do so.

Once an agent was employed, steps were taken to disguise his relationship with Cecil. Sometimes agents were covered by bogus arrests, or by Cecil's supposed displeasure. Once they were unmasked they were no longer useful. When an agent was detected Nicolson considered it a point of honour to protect him. Cecil was less scrupulous. First and last he was preoccupied with the success of the queen's government and incidentally with his own personal ambitions.

Although the situation in Ireland demanded urgent action, and the queen had given her permission to hire the Scots, Cecil was not yet ready to proceed. 'I think it very good to remember you', he wrote to Bowes on 18 February 1595–6, 'that some good wise Scot that knows both the North of Scotland and Ireland is sent to me that I may speak with him.'

Cecil wanted an independent assessment of Maclean's suitability. The agent had to be a man whom Maclean would trust. He must also 'not be any man of great note for then he will look for some great reward'.[7] Bowes selected Mr Denis or Dioness Campbell, dean of Limerick, an illegitimate son of the fifth earl of Argyll and Lachlan Mor's first cousin. They had known each other since 1570 and had probably been brought up together at Inveraray.

The dean evidently satisfied Cecil, for on 2 April Bowes wrote to him from Edinburgh to say he had that day received Sir Robert's letter of 8 March 'at the hands of Mr Dioness Campbell'.

The dean had had a brief meeting with his chief on his arrival in Edinburgh, but 'had so small leisure to confer' with Argyll that the latter had 'appointed him to repair to him' at Stirling. In the same letter Bowes reported that John Cunningham and John Auchinross had returned to Edinburgh from Maclean with the latter's proposals. Auchinross was now to travel south to discuss them with Cecil himself. However, before he left Edinburgh he had to present a petition from his master to the king.

Auchinross had also asked that Bowes's servant George Nicolson should accompany him to London. Bowes agreed to this request. He gave Nicolson written instructions as to what it was intended to achieve by the mission. Bowes makes the point that he had not 'acquainted the King, Argyll or the dean of my proceedings with Maclean', nor did he intend to do so before he learned whether or not the queen had accepted Maclean's proposal.

The dean knew that it was intended to employ Scots in Ulster and had recommended that his eldest brother, the provost of Kilmun, should have command of the expedition. At the very least he should have command of Argyll's people. Bowes made the point to him that it was essential to have 'one able and sufficient person to be chosen general of all the regiments'. He said that he had offered Argyll the command himself, but had made it clear that he favoured Maclean and that the provost should be colonel of Argyll's companies. Both the dean and his brother were said to be pleased with this solution.

Bowes further instructed Nicolson to see that Auchinross delivered Maclean's written proposal to Cecil and his authority for his servant to negotiate terms. If Maclean was to be employed, it was essential that the pay his companies were to receive was first agreed. Auchinross and John Cunningham must also receive payment for their work.

If on the other hand it was decided not to employ Maclean, Nicolson was to find out how he was to deal with him concerning the 'token' Maclean expected for his previous work. Bowes reminded him somewhat unnecessarily that Maclean was expecting 1,000 French crowns. Excuses 'will not I think content him'. Bowes had no desire to have an irate Lachlan Mor turning up in Edinburgh.

Bowes made the point that O Donnell 'by writ and other ways has sought to agree Maclean with Tyrone, making fair offers and that Maclean had returned writ to O Donnell that he likes and will follow his counsel and will give them aid'. Maclean, Bowes pointed out, was playing a double game 'to learn the state of things and the earl's mind ...'[8]

In the meantime Calais had fallen to the Spaniards. As a result it was being said in Edinburgh that the Irish rebels had broken off negotiations with the English as it was thought the 'Spaniards will speedily send succours into Ireland to Tyrone ...'[9]

By the end of the month it was reported that Maclean was to be with Argyll at Stirling or Castle Campbell on 5 or 6 May. Bowes was urgently awaiting the return of Auchinross and Cunningham and a decision as whether or not the queen was to employ Maclean.

The dean succeeded in persuading Argyll to raise his men to serve in Ireland, provided the king agreed. Leading Campbells offered their service to the queen and believed that they would be especially valuable, 'in regard that few of the Isles in Scotland or on the frontiers in Ireland towards Argyll will fight and draw blood against the Campbells'.[10]

Late in April the dean produced his report. Unlike the report Cecil had received in March 1595, it deals in personalities, particularly with that of Lachlan Mor. It begins with comments on the background to affairs in the Western Isles and continues with his recommendations concerning the employment of Maclean.

The report is one of the most important intelligence assessments Cecil received concerning the pros and cons of employing Hebrideans in Ulster. In it the dean however makes some curious assertions. Firstly he states that the Macdonalds were upstarts descending from a family of that name in Fermanagh who were now vassals of Maguire. They had however 'grown to greatness ...' which was 'no less dishonourable than prejudicial to the State and dignity of the Princes of Scotland. Their lords did assume as well the name of Macdonald as the title of highest dignity after the manner of their Irish ancestors, their captains doing the like over their families in their several possessions as McIlaine [Maclean], Macleod Lewis, Macleod Harris ...'

He goes on to say that they had presumed to give battle to the king, particularly at Harlaw, 'wherin the King's forces were overthrown ...' As a result the name and dignity of Macdonald was abolished and 'the earls of Argyll, by means of their loyalty, valour, faithfulness and good fortune ... obtained from their Prince large territories, high honours and offices by inheritance, [such] as to be Lord High Stewards of Scotland, Lord Justice General, Lords Lieutenants of the Isles ... Whilst several were chosen Lord Chancellor of Scotland'.

To summarise: the Macdonalds had always been 'most hateful' to the Princes of Scotland, as usurpers of the patrimony of the crown. They were also 'very odious' to the house of Argyll, whose rising grew by their ruin. This somewhat simplified history of the West Highlands, which might be called the 'authorised' Campbell version of history, continues with an account of the Dunyvaig family who had in turn 'usurped the name and dignity of the MacDonald'.

The dean goes on to call Maclean's grandfather 'old Laughlen MGillaine' when his name was Hector. That he also calls Lachlan Mor's father 'Laughlen Oge McIllaine' when his name was also Hector is, to say the least, curious. He explains the background to the quarrels between Lachlan Mor and Angus and the feuds between the other families in the Isles. He also states that in these feuds Maclean 'most commonlie had the upper hand', as his faction 'was thought muche stronger by reason of his consanguinity with the principal lords of the islands'. He was also unsure whether or not some of them would now follow Maclean. Cameron of Locheil, for instance, who was Maclean's first cousin, was at loggerheads with Macintosh and this 'sept being very treacherous amongst themselves, and their country troublesome and remote, what supplie Maclean can have of them, I know not. They be verie strong valiant and comelie persons, well skilled in archery and in the use of the two handed sword ...'

It is worth studying the dean's report in some detail. To get the flavour of his thinking it is necessary to quote it in its original language.

After having commented on the background he goes on to say, 'As towchinge the employinge of the illanders in Ulster against Tyroen, although I must and doe honor and affecte McIllaine amongest my derest kinsemen, beinge my cosen germaen, the rather for the good partes which I have always noted in him by sixe and twentye yeres acquaintance; yet, in regard of my dutyfull devotion towards the furtherance of Her Majestys service, prefferringe the same before the private commoditye of eny, I am of oppinion that Mcillaine with his owne forces, is not hable to undertake the waight of this service, or compas this action, for the reasons and considerations followinge:

> First: McIllaine and those out ilanders, in eny greate nombers, have not come to Ireland, to my knowledge or remembrance and hereinge, theis 30 yeres. At leaste they had no contynuance there, neither did eny notable exploytes, that I cold learne.
>
> Secondlie: The ilanders have byn noted better men at home, then in strange countreys.
>
> Thirdlie: The ilanders [are] more experte and vallerous at sea in gallies, then upon the land.

The dean is probably correct in saying that the Macleans as a clan had no recent experience in Ireland. Their brief descent on Lough Swilly in 1584 had hardly been glorious or of any length. There is also no evidence that Lachlan Mor himself was even present in this engagement.

The comment that the islanders were reputed to be better men at home than abroad is less easy to justify. It may have been the received wisdom in mainland Argyll, but there is no other evidence that this was the case. Certainly Rory Mor Macleod of Harris' expedition into Connaught in 1595 disproved the dean's statement.

That the islanders were more expert at sea than on land is again unproven. They were undoubtedly expert in the use of their galleys and Mr Denis says that the Macneills of Barra, who followed Maclean, were reputed to be the best seafaring warriors in the islands. They were however no match for the royal navy in open water as Captain Thornton's defeat of some of Angus's galleys off Rathlin in 1595 amply illustrates. The great virtue of the Hebridean galleys was their mobility and ability to operate in shallow waters. They could strike virtually anywhere on the Irish coast, in places where Thornton would not dare to venture. Hebridean galleys were at their most vulnerable when they were beached, a fact that was fully appreciated by Lachlan Mor.

The dean goes on to remark:

> All which notwithstanding, McIllaine, if he hath made any offers, may be well excused in theis respectes:

> McIllaine, hapelie not knowinge that Tyrone did trayne his men and order the warr by marshiall dissipline, by reason of his experience and education amongst th'Englishe, but rather that he wolde followe the ancient course and manner of the Irishe, was in good hope to have suppressed him.

Although Mr Denis did not believe that Lachlan Mor was 'able to undertake' the service that he proposed to the English, he thought his cousin had acted in good faith. As we have seen, Tyrone's training programme did not really get underway until 1594 and it is possible that reports of the earl's actions had not reached Mull by the summer of 1595.

*   *   *   *

The claim that Maclean would not be able to defeat Tyrone needs further comment. As the Battle of Glenlivet is the only occasion when we have first-hand evidence of Lachlan Mor's skill as a leader and details of the weapons his men used, it is worth re-examining the battle in some detail.

There is nothing in the accounts of Glenlivet to suggest that Lachlan Mor was modernising his force or carrying out a similar exercise to Tyrone. In fact the opposite is more likely. The evidence from Glenlivet suggests that Maclean himself was fighting in the 'ancient course and manner', when individual skills and courage were more important than the ability to follow orders and repeat routine drills.

One account of the battle states that the van of Argyll's host, which Lachlan commanded, was made up exclusively of islanders.[11] It consisted of '3000 brave men, well accustomed to war. Of these, 2000 had firearms, the rest bows, Lochaber axes and swords; the latter were all protected by coats of mail ...'[12]

Lachlan Mor himself wore '*ane habershoune,*' a sleeveless coat of mail, over a *jacke*, a quilted leather jacket and a *murrion*, a steel helmet. He was armed with an axe which could be grasped with both hands to add weight to a blow. It was the weapon of the islanders' Viking ancestors and as terrible in a mêlée on land as on board ship in a sea fight. He used it to devastating effect.

It is worth emphasising that a third of the van consisted of heavy infantry. The 1574 Act of Parliament laid down that one third of the 'rising out' of the Hebrides should be accoutred as Maclean. This third was made up of professional soldiers, gentlemen 'quilk dois na labour', heavy infantry the equivalent of the galloglas in Ireland. However, unlike their Irish opposite numbers, who had discarded their axes and were now described as being armed as 'shot and pikemen',[13] the native Hebridean heavy infantryman clung to his traditional weapons.

In addition to bows, Lochaber axes and swords, another account states that this third of the vanguard at Glenlivet had 'darts and targets'.[14] Darts had been the favourite Irish weapon. They are described as casting spears or javelins.[15] They were attached to the thrower by a string that enabled him to retrieve his missile. At close quarters they were extremely effective and at Glenlivet many of Errol's men were wounded by Maclean's darts. It is however doubtful if they were a match for muskets and other improved matchlocks.

Targets, or targes, were circular shields. They were to be one of the most versatile weapons used by the Highlanders and were in use well into the eighteenth century. They were probably made of leather, wood and brass and at least the later versions had a screw-hole in the centre in which a bayonet could be fixed. At the Battle of Glenlivet it is specifically stated that they were part of the weaponry of the heavy infantry.[16] In Ireland c. 1600 they were carried by the *Kern*.

The Hebridean heavy infantry had at one time been equipped with bows and arrows. However, by Glenlivet, archers were described as having no armour, for lightness. Unlike the Irish, who were never noted as archers, Hebrideans were renowned for their skill with the bow and arrows. Good bowmen could hit an enemy accurately at 150 to 200 yards.

The 'new Scots' in Ireland preferred the original claymore, *claidheamh-mor*, the great two-handed sword of the Highlander, with which the Camerons are said by Mr Denis Campbell to be particularly skilled. These formidable 'slaughter-swords' were becoming obsolete in Ireland but they were used effectively at Glenlivet by the vanguard to prevent Errol's horse from breaking their line. Well-armed and armoured infantry could still be used effectively against horse who had little infantry support and it appears that, apart from his cannon, Huntly's force was as antiquated in its weaponry and tactics as Maclean's. This would not have been the case if the Macleans had fought Tyrone.

The Hebridean vanguard was not without modern weaponry. The greater part, 200, were equipped with firearms. They were however the old fashioned 'hagbut' or arquebus, the earliest form of matchlock. Maclean's men were said to have 'discharged their shott so thick and strongly' that it looked at one stage 'that the victory must have been theirs'.[17] The early matchlocks however were quite incapable by themselves of stopping a cavalry attack that was pressed home. They also created so much smoke that it could itself affect the rest of the battle. At Glenlivet the wind changed at a crucial moment, blowing into the eyes of Maclean's van, blinding his shot and playing no little part in the outcome of the battle.

Curiously it is nowhere mentioned in any of the accounts of the battle that Maclean's men were armed with pikes, which, as we have seen, revolutionised continental warfare a century earlier. It is however worth noting that in his letter to Bowes of 22 August 1595, Lachlan Mor offered to provide 400 pikemen. It is therefore probable that the eye-witness accounts of the battle failed to mention them. It is unlikely that Maclean had been converted to their use since Glenlivet. It is also difficult to see how he could have fended off Errol's cavalry without them.

Tyrone certainly used pikes and they were now used by the galloglas, 300 of whom in 1600 were described as 'the best furnished men for the war and the best apparelled that we have seen in the kingdom'. They were well trained, drawn up in order 'as close as they might, everyone trailing his pike and holding the check of the same in his left hand ready to push'.[18]

Mr Denis was undoubtedly correct in thinking that Lachlan Mor was going to have a more difficult task in defeating Tyrone than he thought: 'McIllaine, having made this offer in sommer last, as I conjecture, did not forecast th'encrease of Tyrones forces by the rebellious confederacie of the most of Conought, and of the Reylies; neithe then was happelie certefied of the nomber of the ennemyes. Yet consyderinge that the pride and insolencie of Tyrone and his complices, standinge upon most presumptious and undutyfull demands, semeth to arise of this conceyte partlie, that the soilders prest here hence to serve there, by reason of cold, wett, hunger, waterishe and fresh beofe and want of lodginge, besides greate toyle which of necessitye they must abide, not agreable, ye rather contrary, to this clymett, and the deinty tender fare of theire native country, bredinge suche sudden and dangerous alteration in theire boddyes, as they are sene for the most part to shrinke in the service: in regard whereof, for abatinge the ennemyes pryde aforesaid, I think it no il policie to enterteigne McIllaine, whose people for abidinge all hardines of toyles are not enferrior to those of Ulster.

'Further, those of Ulster, and especiallye there footemen, have byn reputed, by the oppinion of men of experience in Scotland, to be base mynded and tymerrous, so that three hundrothe of Scotts wold never shrinke to assault six hundrothe of them. Besides, the hope of the ennemy in the streingthe of theire parts may be taken away by the ilanders service in this, that the army marchinge throwe the same, theire light men may be guided by good guydes throughe bogges and woods to assaulte them behind theire backs with swords and arrowes, so as the army may securlie goe throwe.

'Moreover, they may be lustie curragious and forward in theire manner of fight and weapon, if they have a good leader; for forredging and lose skirmishinge, theire bowmen are verie fitt and skilfull; for feats, assaults and handy blowes, there swordmen shall serve to verie good use, for that generallie, they may be men of strong bodyes.

'McIllaine himself, from tyme to tyme, hath proved valiant, wise, trustie, fortunate, and of reasonable good experience accordinge to his yeres; tale and of a feare complexion; feared and yet honored and well obeyed of his kinsemen and followers; so as in regard of his person authoritye and direction, Her Majestys service doubtles shalbe well furtherred. For, after th'Irishe sayinge, the sufficiencie of a leader is equivalent with two parts of his reigne. For which respects, I hold McIllaine to be used as a chefe, thoughe not a sole intrusted, to accomplishe the action; wherein the Earle of Argeile his speciall care and furtherance, is principallie required, for divers consyderations. In settinge down of which, thoughe I may hapelie feare to be accounted to be too affectionate towards my name, yet having a care and zeale to advance the service to my uttermost, I am forced to unfold my conceite; for the better tryall whereof your honor may crave the lord imbassadors res-olution in the same. The reasons be theis.

'First: The Earl is lord lieutenant of the ilands, more feared universalie, then the Kinge obeyed, by those ilanders.

'Secondlie: Yt is to be doubted leaste Tyroen shold deale with the McDonells to invade McIllaines countrey in his absence; which practise if Argeile wold seme to favor, th'other must have byn forced to retorn for his defence, and Her Majesty made to presse more supplies out of England. In which tyme, the season shold be muche spent, and the service greatlie interrupted.

'Thirdlie: Yt is probable that yonger brothers and lose men of Argeile and the countreys about, will receive the Earle and O Donells offers, if they be not spedelie sollicited from hence; and in dede McIllaine wold be loathe to serve upon them for feare of further displeasure by efusion of blood, the McConell by all liklihod will prosecute with all hostilitye, if they doe ayd th'enemy.

'Fowrthlie: The working of Argeiles affection and enterteyninge of the Campbells with McIllaine, thereby leavinge to Tyrone onlie the McDonells, will greatlie abate his curradge, the rather for that that sept wilbe loathe to serve upon the Campbells for the cawses aforesaid.

'Fiftlie: There have no principall septe to my knowledge theis 30 yeres ben experienced in the service of Ulster, or throwlie acquainted with the state of that countrey, saive the Campbells and McConells of Kentyre, with theire followers, the first beinge commonlie enterteigned by O Neale, the last by O Donell.

'Sixtlie: The better sorte of the Campbells are of an honorable disposition, favorers of religion, trusti, valiant and civilie inclined.

'For procuringe the greater nombers out of Argeile and the confins, who in dede are best acquainted with the services of Ulster, yt were verie requisit that some one chefe man of hability and creditt in that countrey (the nerer the Erle in blood, the better disposed) shold be secretlie sollicited with all expedition, and very good enterteignement allowed him and his under captens, the soildiors havinge the allowance of the ilanders.

'Yt were also necessarye that a motion were made, that, whensoever they shold be destituted of victualls, being left to forredge and pray upon th'enemye by waters or tempest or otherwayes, so as they doe not slacke the opportunity of the service, they may be provided for those tymes with the garrizons, paying a rate for the same proportionable to theire enterteignement, leaste the lacke of foode sholde hinder or linger the service.

'To take away all conceyte of jelousie and discontentment from McIllaine (in that I wishe some chefe man of the Cambells to be joyned with him in the action), the imbassedors wold be moved to certifie McIllaine of the power, nomber and order of th'enemy, wishinge him with all care, as well to deale of himself, and also to advise the lord imbassedor, which chefe man of the Cambells were fittest to be dealt withall.

'James Cambell, the yonge lard of Laers, of no great experience or depe judgment to be a chefe commander, yet valiant and forward for himself, whereof he made some good profe in the trobles betwixt his uncle and others; his creditt and acquaintance, thoughe he be a Cambell, is not great in Arguyle, for his fathers inheritance is somewhat remote from thence.

'McIllaine also, with all expedition, is to be moved to lay down and certifie what nomber of men he will undertake to bringe with him, what weapon they shall use, what nomber of every sorte, what day he wilbe in arreadines, that some pinnace or freegat may be sent to conducte him to his landinge place in Ireland, which must be appointed by the Lord Deputy and councell in Ireland; a caveat to be geven him that he bringe of his native followers and trustiest frends, leaste if he drawe strangers of all sortes unto him, bearinge him neither love nor honor but onlie regardinge theire pray, Tyrone, as he is pollitick, may work a devision perhaps or treachierye amongest his companyes, to the great lettinge of Her Majestys service and the frustratinge of his honorable meaninge.

'Yt were good that the Cambells were in a redines to come about this same tyme to the place prefixed; the Lord Deputy, Lord Generall, and all other commanders, to use them with great courtesie and kindenes, I meane the better sorte in theire degrees; for thereby theire affections are naturallie moved to all good offirs: no disdaine, no contempte, no hard speches to be offered by eny soildiors, upon great penalties, for preventinge of discontentments and mutonyes, wherein cases towchinge theire credytt or reputation may readelie fall out; in all controversies, the governors inclyninge to favor the stranger, by all meanes endeavoringe to enter-teigne love and ametye betwixt the soildiors and them.

'Three principall garrizons is necessarie to be placed in Ulster; th'one at the Black Water, nere Ardmagh; th'other at the Ford of the Leffer, nere Strabane, upon the border of Tyreconnell; the third about Coolerain, or thereabouts.

'Yt were not amys that McIllaine and the Cambells were devided in severall garrizons, to be commanded and directed by the Generall in severall partes for service. This syperation shall brede an emulation betwene them, stryvinge for honor and creditt, and earnest desire to gaine and benefitt themselves upon the enemy.'[19]

*   *   *   *

What is one to make of this assessment? It is a remarkable document, especially as it was written by a clergyman and not a soldier. It is also a far more valuable report than any that Philip II received from his military agents. It also underlines the fact that the dean was a practical politician who accepted the facts of the situation. He knew before he wrote it that Bowes favoured Maclean as commander of the Scots to be sent to Ulster. To a Campbell, particularly one as closely related to Argyll as Mr Denis was, it was essential that it was the earl himself who was given command of the Scots to serve in Ulster. The Campbells were already dangerously divided by the prosecution of Ardkinglas and the slights offered to the earl by the king. The earl was suffering a crisis of confidence; he thought 'that Huntly finds over great favour in England and that Argyll is little regarded thereby', Bowes wrote to Burghley on 30 April.[20]

Mr Denis however appears to accept that there was little likelihood that his chief would be appointed. Argyll 'standeth as yet I suppose indifferent', added the dean to his report, particularly as he was much solicited 'by yonge O Donnell, who offereth him that yerely tribut out of Tyreconnell', which his grandfather had received in perpetuity from O Donnell.

One inducement to make Argyll move against Tyrone, Mr Denis suggested, would be to inform him of the 'entercourse and practyses between Tyrone and Huntlie with his conferate papists'. Huntly was Argyll's greatest enemy and if he was told that some of Tyrone's horsemen had fought in Huntly's ranks at the Battle of Glenlivet it might be enough to get him off the fence.[21]

There is no comment in the English State Papers to show what Cecil thought of Mr Denis's report. It is however possible to get some idea of what was agreed from Bowes's letter to Cecil of 7 May. Writing from Edinburgh, Bowes says that he had paid both Auchinross and

Cunningham the rewards Sir Robert had recommended. Auchinross received £30 and Cunningham £20. Bowes goes on to say, 'I am right glad that you have given such good contentments as well for Maclean ... Her Majesty's service in Ireland or elsewhere in the Isles and Highlands of Scotland shall at all times ... be greatly advanced thereby ...' Maclean received £150 sterling. Auchinross writes that his master accepted the queen's 'liberality showed to him in a very thankful manner ... acknowledging and protesting his devotion to her ...' [22] Lachlan Mor himself wrote to Cecil on 8 June to thank him for his 'great favour and goodwill offered to me'. It therefore seems certain that Cecil had verbally agreed to employ Maclean but had not committed the agreement to paper.

Cecil still dithered. Lachlan Mor's major proposal, which promised him both glory and English gold, continued to be discussed. Sir John Norris was in favour of employing Scots at Lough Foyle provided that 1,000 English foot and 100 horse were there. The queen might then be served 'by the Scots without danger'; without an English garrison 'the drawing in the Scots may be more hurtful than profitable, for they encroach fast upon the country'. He quotes the example of the Macdonalds' recent takeover of the Route, 'whence they will not be easily dislodged'.[23] For 'it is known to all men that they be no welcome guests ...' as 'they run about the country making no difference to spoil whom they can'.

The lord deputy was more supportive when replying to Cecil's inquiry concerning the wisdom of employing Scots. He considered that '3,000 Scots, well led by a man affected to Her Majesty, would do more service upon the Ulster rebels than double that number of English'.

Despite the need to do something and despite all the evidence that a decision had been made to employ Maclean, the executive order for him to move to Ulster was not given. It is probable that it was thought that a lull in the fighting in Ireland at this time made a decision unnecessary. Lachlan Mor, however, continued to keep some of his men together at his own expense. The queen's 'liberality' was not sufficient to solve Maclean's increasing financial problems. On 18 February 1595–6 John Cunningham had arranged a loan for him.[24] In July 1596 Cunningham was again involved in another short-term loan of six thousand merks jointly borrowed by Maclean and Kenneth Mackenzie of Kintail from Edward Johnston the Edinburgh merchant burgess.[25] It was a debt that was to haunt the family of Duart for many years to come.

Notes

1. *CSP Spain* iv, 619.
2. *Ibid*, 489.
3. Alan Haynes, *Invisible Power. The Elizabethan Secret Service, 1570–1603* (1992), 137.
4. *HMC Cecil* x, 460.
5. *CSP Scot.* xiii (part 1), xxx.
6. *HMC Cecil* xi, 22.
7. *CSP Scot.* xii, 145.
8. *Ibid*, 201.
9. *Ibid*, 194.
10. *Ibid*, 198.
11. *Spottiswoode Miscellany* i, 264.
12. Sir J. G. Dalyell (ed), *Scottish Poems of the Sixteenth Century* (London, 1801), Vol. II, 145.
13. PRO SP 63/180. No. 40 (1)
14. *Spottiswoode Miscellany* i, 264.
15. *Irish Battles*, 19.
16. *Spottiswoode Miscellany* i, 264.
17. Dalyell i, 148.
18. *Irish Battles*, 111.
19. PRO SP. Eliz. Scotland LVIII, 72, 57.
20. *Ibid*, 198.
21. *Ibid*, 72, 57.
22. *CSP Scot.* xii, 220.
23. *CSP Ireland* vi, 52.
24. SRO RD1/57 H 66 r & v.
25. *Ibid* /63 H 285v–287v.

CHAPTER 17

'To Defend Religion'

Malcolm. Come, go we to the king; our power is ready;
Our lack is nothing but our leave: Macbeth is ripe for shaking,
and the powers above. Put on their instruments. Receive what
cheer you may; The night is long that never finds the day.
Macbeth Act IV, Scene iii

The earl of Argyll's star was in decline. In June 1596 it was reported that he was resolved 'to travel in foreign nations'. He asked for a safe conduct on the coast of England and requested that his cousin the dean Mr Denis Campbell, who was an English subject, should accompany him.[1] Then to his fury the earl learned that Colonel Sir William Stewart of Houston had been chosen by the king as Lieutenant of the Isles for the forthcoming expedition to the Hebrides.

He had good reason to be furious. Stewart had served for some time as a soldier of fortune under the Prince of Orange. He then returned home and entered King James's service. In 1583 he was made commendator of Pittenweem and in 1590 had commanded the fleet that took James to Denmark to collect his bride. His origins were less illustrious. One version is that he commenced life as 'a cloutter (i.e. repairer) of shoes'. Another is that he was a son of Thomas Stewart of Galston.[2] Both stories could be true. James was not averse to employing men from humble backgrounds. To Argyll, Stewart's preferment was an insult.

Argyll, the new earl of Athol, Mackenzie and Maclean were all ordered to attend the Lieutenant at Dumbarton. Instead of doing so Argyll remained at home and 'excused himself by sickness'. The king, who was evidently irritated by the earl's refusal to attend the rendezvous, commanded Argyll 'to repair to him' immediately. Some observers believed that the king's actions would drive the earl into the rebel camp.[3]

Throughout 1596 the earl's and the Cawdor family's prosecution of Ardkinglas had dragged on. The trial itself was twice postponed and when it finally took place on 22 September, 'nane of the Kingis advocatis compeirit to persew him'.[4] When the whole matter was dropped it was yet another example of the earl's increasing isolation.

One reason why he was unpopular with the king was that he was identified with the 'Protestant' party of which the murdered earl of Moray had been a leading member. The king on the other hand was believed to favour 'Roman Catholics' led by Huntly. James's leniency to the northern earls had made him unpopular with the urban populace, led by the ministers whose sympathies were with Moray.

In fact James was a far less partisan supporter of Huntly's religion than his 'Protestant' critics alleged. During his absence in Norway and Denmark Mr Robert Bruce, the minister of Edinburgh, had exercised considerable authority, with full royal approval; he had also officiated at the queen's coronation, whilst Mr Andrew Melville had recited a Latin poem. At this stage of his reign James had been out of humour with the English church and delighted Presbyterians by extolling the perfection of the Church of Scotland. He had also given protection to refugees from the anti-puritan campaign in England. He had allowed the gradual increase in the authority of presbyteries, at the expense of that of the bishops, and in May 1592 parliament had at last authorised Presbyterianism. This was a concession which was probably designed as a bargain to wean the ministers from their political opposition.

James needed support from the ministers at least until he had broken the back of the political threat from the Roman Catholic earls. Once the northern earls had been excommunicated by the General Assembly and forfeited by parliament, the king had marched against them accompanied by Andrew Melville and other ministers. The earls declined to face the king and fled. In March 1595 Huntly and Errol went into exile abroad. The ultra-Protestant party was triumphant.

It now overreached itself. It had been recognised for some time that the leading ministers did not accept any limit to their authority. In 1592 the Kirk had tried to prevent Scottish ships from undertaking charters for French 'Roman Catholic' merchants; in 1593 the General Assembly persuaded the convention of royal burghs to suspend trade with Spain. An attempt was also made to forbid the Monday market in Edinburgh on the grounds that preparations for it defiled the Sabbath. The clergy had even tried to interfere with English affairs.

Neither the authorisation of Presbyterianism in 1592, nor the exile of Huntly and Errol in 1595, had convinced the minister of the religious soundness of the government. They even began to attack the personal habits of the king and queen. In March 1596 James was rebuked for swearing and the queen was condemned for 'not repairing to the word and sacraments', attending balls and of 'spending of all time in vanity'. In September 1596 Andrew Melville had his famous interview with the

king at Falkland, when he lectured 'God's silly vassal' on his subordi-
nation to the church. At about the same time the minister of St Andrews
preached that 'all Kings are devil's children', and accused Queen Elizabeth
of being an atheist. In these circumstances James can be forgiven for
having lost his patience with the Kirk and its political supporters.

To counter the power of the ultra-Presbyterians the king agreed that
the earls of Huntly and Errol should be allowed to return to Scotland.
They returned home secretly in June 1596 and came to terms first with
a convention in August which agreed that they might remain in Scotland
provided they satisfied the king and the church. This course was bitterly
opposed by Mr Robert Bruce, who had previously been a great favourite
with the king. If the king decided to go ahead, he would have to choose
between Huntly and Bruce, 'for us both you cannot keep'. The king
broke with Bruce once and for all.

Steps were also taken to end the feud between Huntly and Argyll.
Argyll however refused to meet his adversary, claiming that as Huntly
was excommunicated, he could not have any dealings with him.[5]

As the earl of Argyll's influence plummeted, so Maclean's increased.
On 18 March 1595–6 Lachlan Mor, who was still officially forfeit,
had written from Coll to John Lindsay, Lord Menmuir, James's secretary of state, professing his loyalty to the king.[6] Menmuir, who had
married Cawdor's widow, was one of the group of eight advisers to the
king known as the Octavians. They had originally joined together to
organise the queen's finances. They had been so successful that James
had taken them into his own service. The Octavians, who were suspected
of being sympathetic to Roman Catholicism, were anathema to the
ministers.

In June, having satisfied the Lords Auditors of the Exchequer 'anent
all thingis quhilkis wer layed to his charge', Maclean appeared before
the king at Holyrood House. His forfeiture was cancelled. He was restored to all his lands and honours. It was also agreed that a proclamation
should be made charging the king's 'lieges not "to sklander, murmour,
reproche and bak byte" the said Lachlan for any cause or crime bygone'.[7]
King James also knighted Lachlan, possibly at the request of Queen
Elizabeth to whom he had appealed for 'advancement' when he proposed
to lead his expedition to Ulster. Ulster was now quieter: Tyrone was
restraining his forces whilst he bargained with the English and waited
for help from Spain.

Sir Lachlan, as we must now call him, continued to acknowledge
Queen Elizabeth's goodness to him and to offer her his services in
Ireland. On 14 December 1596 it was reported that some companies of

Spaniards had arrived in Ireland. It was a rumour which, Bowes claimed, Maclean believed was without substance.[8]

An incident now occurs which shows Sir Lachlan in a new light. On 17 December 1596 the king was holding a meeting with the Octavians in the Tolbooth of Edinburgh, whilst a service was being held in St Giles' church. Amongst the congregation were lords Lindsay and Forbes, Sir Lachlan, Macdougall, Kennedy of Bargany and several other gentlemen who supported the ministers.

The sermon that day was preached by Mr Walter Balcanquill, who spoke of the present troubles of the church. Then, turning to the noblemen present, he upbraided them for their lack of zeal for the Kirk and compared them unfavourably with their predecessors. After the service he invited them to meet to discuss what could be done about these problems.[9]

Many others joined him and the meeting room was so congested that the ministers could hardly obtain entry. Mr Robert Bruce, however, having pushed his way through the crowd to the noblemen, barons and burgesses, addressed the assembled company. He outlined the danger to the Kirk from the return of the northern earls and from their supporters on the council. He asked the audience to raise their hands and promise 'to maintain the religion presently prefessed in Scotland', and present a petition to the king requesting him to dismiss the popish earls.

The evidence as to what happened next is contradictory. Spottiswoode says lords Lindsay and Forbes, with the lairds of Bargany and Blairquhan, Mr Robert Bruce and another minister were chosen to present the petition which they immediately took to the king, who said they were talking nonsense. 'Lord Lindsay in a passion replied ..."that they would not suffer religion to be overthrown"'. A considerable number of people were now 'thronging unmannerly into the room', and the king went out to join the Octavians, commanding that the doors be shut.[10]

Sir Robert Gordon of Gordonstoun however claims that before leaving church a number of those present decided to kill the Octavians and ran headlong from the church shouting 'the sword of Gideon, the sword of Gideon'. Their cries were overheard by some of the king's train who were listening at a secret door which led from the church to the Tolbooth. When they heard of the plan to murder the Octavians they barred the door. This, Gordonstoun claims, deterred lord Lindsay and Maclean and their associates whose 'courage failed; and so being astonished they vanished and parted asunder, not knowing whether to goe or what course to tak as men usuallie doe in such popular tumults, whereby they ar led by the multitude ...'[11]

Sir Robert Gordon, who was no lover of Maclean, is insistent that Sir Lachlan was one of the plotters against the Octavians. Robert Bowes, who was one of Maclean's supporters, claims that Sir Lachlan had held up his hand with the rest and agreed 'to the utmost of his power ... he would maintain the religion presently professed in Scotland'. But then, hearing the tumult in the street, 'he sought access to the king for defence of his person, which he could not attain. There upon he rode in great haste to the earl of Argyll', who was then in Stirling.[12] Roger Aston, a gentleman of the bedchamber to James and an English spy, says that after the petitioners made their request to the king to dismiss several of the Octavians, as they were 'enemies to the religion and greatness of the state', the king said he would think about it. Mr Robert Bruce, however, when he returned from the meeting, declared that there was 'nothing to be looked for but extremity'. It was now that Bruce asked those present 'to hold up their hands in defence of the good cause' and that some went outside crying 'arm, arm'. Some cried 'God and the Kirk', others 'God and the King'.[13]

Aston says that the ministers sent a letter to Lord Hamilton to join them and that 'they also directed a secret messenger to the earl of Argyll'. This messenger, although he is not mentioned by name, was presumably Sir Lachlan.

Despite the tumult the king was able to leave the Tolbooth with the council unmolested and returned to Holyrood. The next day he travelled to Linlithgow. On his way there he met Argyll and Maclean who were hurrying to Edinburgh. James, who had now received details of what had happened in the church, rebuked Maclean 'for his posting to Argyll and for holding up his hand among the noblemen and barons for defence of religion'. Sir Lachlan however was unrepentant and replied 'that when the King honoured him the other day with knighthood he then avowed to defend the religion, the King's person and estate, which was why he had held up his hand as this vow he protested to keep during his life'.[14]

Bowes says that the king was pleased with this reply 'and received him into his favour and good entertainment'. Another source said later that when the king rebuked Sir Lachlan he was extremely angry with him and that when Maclean protested he would die for his religion, 'the King scorned and said that Highland men had not that religion'.[15]

What is the truth? It would seem probable that Sir Lachlan was sincere in his protestations. He had been brought up in the heady atmosphere of Calvinism which prevailed at the court of the fifth earl of Argyll. It was also untrue to say 'that Highland men had not that religion'. Lachlan Mor's friend and ally Duncan Macdougall of Dunollie in a letter dated 11 September 1595 to Robert Bowes asks him to give 'my hearty commendations ... to your bedfellow with whom I have made my acquaintance in St. Giles's Church'. He continues: 'The zeal and fervency that I know to be in your Excellency concerning God's religion which we profess move me above all to do what lies in my power for you',[16] which sounds like the protestation of a zealous Protestant. On another occasion, when he wrote to John Cunningham the Edinburgh burgess, Macdougall says: 'I pray you command me hartlie to the ministers'.[17] Highlanders were no less sincere Presbyterians than their Lowland brethren. They were just different.

For example in 1624 when lowland ministers were carrying out a visitation of the presbytery of Inverness they were shocked at the sight of ministers dressed in plaids and bonnets. To lowland eyes they must have looked like barbarians who did not belong to the Kirk. Although the Gaelic-speaking clergy may have looked completely alien to their lowland counterparts, they were merely wearing the normal dress of a Highlander. As Jane Dawson has recently pointed out: 'These ministers were good Calvinists but they were also good Gaels. They had evolved a distinctly Gaelic form of Calvinism by taking the ideas and institutions of the Kirk and fitting them into a Highland context'.[18] James VI was wrong when he asserted that his Gaelic-speaking subjects were 'wild savageis voide of Godis feare and our obedience'.[19]

Notes

1. SRO RD1/63 H 246.
2. *HP* iii, 72.
3. *Ibid*, 311–2.
4. *Ibid*, i, 150.
5. *CSP Scot.* xii, 389.
6. NLS. Adv. MS. 29–2–6.
7. *RPC* v, 295.
8. *CSP Scot.* xii, 392.
9. Spottiswoode iii, 27.
10. *Ibid*, 28.
11. Gordonstoun, 234.
12. *CSP Scot.* xii, 403.
13. Gordonstoun, 234.
14. *CSP Scot.* xii.
15. *CSP Scot.* xiii, 260.
16. *CSP Scot.* xii, 12.
17. *CSP Scot.* xi, 606.

18. Jane Dawson 'Calvinism and the Gaelheadtachd in Scotland', in A. Pettegree, A. Duke and G. Lewis (eds), *Calvinism in Europe 1540–1620* (Cambridge, 1994), 231–2.
19. *Collectanea*, 115.

CHAPTER 18

The Nadir of Angus Macdonald

Macbeth. They have tied me to a stake; I cannot fly,
But bear-like, I must fight the course.
Macbeth Act V, Scene vii

Lachlan Mor's great rival, Angus Macdonald of Dunyvaig and the Glens, was probably born in 1550. He was therefore not ten years older than his brother-in-law. He can only have been 46 in 1596. However, he was beginning to lose his grip on events. He did so at a disastrous time for his family, for the king, forever strapped for cash, now began to look on the Isles as a source of increased royal revenue. The island chiefs were summoned to Edinburgh to settle their outstanding dues for crown lands they held with the Lords of the Exchequer. In May 1596, to make it clear that he was serious, a royal proclamation was made to the freeholders with a yearly rent of 300 merks to assemble at Dumbarton well armed and with forty days' provisions to join the king for an expedition to the Isles.

Maclean hurried to Edinburgh and with the 'help of his friends' settled his debts. Donald Gorm and the Macleods of Harris and Lewis agreed to do the same. Angus did not. 'MacConnell is like to be committed if he shall appear', wrote Robert Bowes to Lord Burghley on 14 June 1596.[1]

Angus had no intention of appearing. On 13 June he was reported to have arrived in Ulster. No-one there was quite sure what he was about. On 16 June Tyrone wrote to Norris in Dublin that Angus had arrived in the Route with 400 men, 'but knows not of yet what he intends to do'. On the same day the earl wrote in Gaelic to O Donnell that he 'would have gone without fail', to meet the commitment to end the troubles in Ulster, 'but that Angus M'James is coming with a great freight of Scots into Ireland. His son Gilleisboigg has arrived already with a great many'. Tyrone believed he could not 'give his back to them for fear they should spoil his country'.[2] A copy of this letter was sent by the earl to Dublin. Angus's presence was one more device O Neill was using in the cat and mouse game he was playing to make time before the Spanish arrived.

Captain Charles Egerton at Carrickfergus had also heard of Angus's arrival and reported to the lord deputy on 26 June that after he had landed with a few Scots Angus had gone straight to Tyrone at Castleroe, a fort inside O Cathan's territory where O Neill received his share of the Bann fishery. 'Some say', Egerton writes, 'the earl sent for him in great haste, others that Angus came over to seek help of the earl against M'Lanna, who has lately attempted his country of Ile'. [3]

O Neill admitted that Angus had visited him. On 22 June he wrote again to Norris that he 'had this day taken order with Angus M'Connell for his immediate return to Scotland'.

In Scotland it was believed that Angus had, with the aid of O Donnell, recruited 3,000 Irishmen who were to 'withstand Colonel Stewart and especially invade Maclean and his possessions'. Apparently Lachlan Mor had recently slain twelve of Angus's men in revenge for their killing of one of his servants in Inveraray. Bowes now asked Lord Burghley to send Captain Thornton and the *Popinjay* to prevent the Irish from landing in Scotland. [4]

Angus's visit to Ulster was to have disastrous consequences for his lands there. Word evidently got out that he was desperate. In August 1596 James son of Sorley Boy lord of the Route, Angus's cousin, invaded the Glens.

There was little love between the cousins. In February 1593–4 Angus had informed Dublin that James MacSorley was responsible for recruiting Scots to serve in Ulster. In April 1596 James repaid Angus in kind when he informed Dublin that his cousin was coming out of Scotland with 1,500 Scots to aid O Donnell. Some in Ireland believed that the quarrel between the cousins had been fomented by O Neill. [5]

James MacSorley had been late in committing himself to the rebellion. Once he had seized the Glens, he seems to have come off the fence. He raided Lecale, the district around Downpatrick, 'with all his savages', wrote an English officer. 'Lecale is all wasted and spoiled, and not left worth anything.'

Angus fled to Scotland. In an attempt to make amends he came to the king at Linlithgow 'suiting for his favour and grant in many things touching his possessions and liberties claimed, which are not like to be granted to him as he requires', Bowes wrote to Burghley. [6]

Meanwhile preparations for the expedition to the Isles continued. The commendator of Pittenweem was authorised to levy a thousand men and appoint officers to command them. Argyll was ordered to send two hundred men under the command of his kinsman Campbell of Auchinbrek. The Islemen were ordered to remain quiet at home. James MacSorley however was invited to provide assistance.

Preparations dragged on through the autumn, as the government endeavoured to find sufficient money to pay for the expedition. A reconnaissance party was sent to Kintyre to discover whether or not Angus would oppose the expedition.

Another character now enters the story: James, Angus's eldest legitimate son, whom we last met astride his uncle Lachlan Mor's shoulders, at Mulindry in Islay. James had since 1592 been held in Edinburgh as a pledge for his father's good behaviour and was in the service of Lord John Hamilton. Early in 1596 he had petitioned the king that his father might enjoy the crown's possessions in the Isles which his ancestors had held. He offered to pay a yearly rental of a thousand merks Scots. It was however pointed out that Cawdor had offered ten times that figure, on Angus's behalf, five years earlier. James was given a license to proceed to the Isles to persuade his father to submit and probably to get him to make an increased offer for the rent of his crown lands.

In October James returned from the Isles and on the 5th appeared before the Privy Council at Holyrood House, bringing with him a letter from his father. In it Angus gave James his authority to negotiate and agreed to 'abyde firmelie' by anything his son agreed to. He also renounced to his son all his lands and any he might receive 'of his Prince's favour'.

It was to prove to be an inept arrangement and could only mean that Angus did not know his son. Nor did he appreciate how bitterly his people resented his failure to hold on to his lands in Ulster. They were now to have even greater cause for resentment. At the Council the king's decision was that:

1. James should remain at court and not depart without the king's permission.

2. Angus should, as soon as convenient, remove himself, his family and his dependants and all those who were not actual 'tenants and possessors' of the ground from Kintyre and Gigha.

3. That Angus should keep good order in Islay, Colonsay and Jura and not allow any 'Sorning' there to anyone to whom the king had 'granted title to any part thereof'.

4. By 25 December he should appear before the king with his eldest son James and with his natural son Archibald, 'Gillespic Dubh'. He should also deliver up his castle of Dunyvaig to the Lieutenant.[7]

Once these actions had been completed the king would decide what to do about the lands that Angus and his kinsmen possessed. It was a body blow to the Macdonalds. By removing Angus and his dependants from Kintyre and Gigha he had destroyed their economic base. By not allowing 'Sorners' i.e. 'gentlemen that labour not', he had done the same to Angus's ability both to defend his property and provide mercenaries for Ireland. It was a situation which no chief could accept.

At the end of October the expedition at last sailed and on 1 November Pittenweem held his court at Kilkerran in Kintyre as Campbeltown was then called. Chiefs such as Farquhar Mackay, John Maceachern and Hector Macneill were allowed to hold their properties once they had promised to be answerable 'to his Hienes lawis, and to observe, hope and fulfill the samin'. They had also to provide pledges for their good behaviour.[8]

Angus had been present at Kilkerran on 1 November. Five days earlier his last hope of resisting the Lieutenant had failed when James MacSorley had written to the king to tell him that Angus had offered him great reward if he helped him expel the royal troops from Kintyre. That Angus should have appealed to his rival who had taken over his lands in Ulster underlines the fact that Angus was no longer living in the real world.

Early in 1597 Angus himself came to court to hear the king's verdict on his future. Two plans were discussed. One was to get Angus to resign all his possessions in Islay and to retain those in Kintyre. The other was the one the king had already agreed to, i.e. to deprive him of his lands in Kintyre and confine him and his dependants to his land in Islay. He was however to give up any rights he believed he had to the Rinns of Islay.

In order to test his sincerity Angus was to find security for the arrears of his rents due to the crown and to remove his clan from Kintyre and the Rinns. He was also to hand over Dunyvaig Castle by 20 May. Angus agreed to these conditions and returned to the Isles to put them into effect. Meanwhile his son James, who had recently been knighted, remained at court as a pledge for his father's good behaviour.

Soon after Angus left for the Isles the king received a letter from James MacSorley flattering the king and magnifying his own service to him. In it he claimed that Angus was illegitimate and that he, James MacSorley, was the rightful owner of the Macdonalds' lands in Islay and Kintyre. The king replied encouragingly and invited James to visit the court in Edinburgh.

James MacSorley was a subject of Queen Elizabeth. The king's encouragement of him needs some explanation. His own Gaelic-speaking subjects may have been anathema to him, yet he was encouraging a man who spoke no English and was as great a Gael as any. Several contemporary Scottish writers of the period speak of the lord of Dunluce as 'a man of handsome appearance and dignified manners'. Yet despite James VI's enthusiasm for handsome young men it can hardly have been for this reason alone that he showered favours on MacSorley. The key probably lies in James VI's obsession with inheriting the English throne. If his claim was disputed physically he was going to need all the allies he could muster. The evidence, if it ever existed, has been destroyed but it would seem likely that James was endeavouring to build up a party of his supporters in Ulster. He flirted with Tyrone but he was a rebel. James MacSorley, undecided and with his dual nationality, could have been a useful link with the confederates.

Whatever the reasons, James MacSorley arrived at court where he became a great favourite. He was knighted by James, given crown lands in Islay[9] and was rumoured to be engaged to the queen's favourite, the sister of the earl of Gowrie, despite the fact that he was already betrothed to Tyrone's nine-year-old daughter, whom he eventually married.[10]

Dunluce's claim that Angus was illegitimate was turned down. A decision in his favour would have destroyed the legitimacy of most Gaels who inherited their estates and been born when Celtic secular marriage was the custom. He did however leave Edinburgh with a salute from the guns of the castle.[11]

Notes

1. *CSP Scot.* xii, 244.
2. *CSP Ireland* vi, 9.
3. *Ibid,* 30.
4. *CSP Scot.* xii, 311.
5. *CSP Ireland* v, 216–17, 514; vi, 72.
6. *CSP Scot.* xii, 326.
7. *RPC* v, 321.
8. *HP* iii, 73–79.
9. *CSP Scot.* xii, 543.
10. *CSP Ireland* vi, 448.
11. Gregory, 274.

CHAPTER 19

The Isle of Coll, 1596–1597

Siward. The time approaches
That will with due decision make us know
What we shall say we have, and what we owe.
Thoughts speculative their unsure hopes relate
But certain issue strokes must arbitrate ...

Macbeth, Act V, Scene iv

The Rev. Alexander Maclean Sinclair, the author of *Clan Gillean*, thought that Neil Mor was killed in the latter part of 1596 or the beginning of 1597.[1] It is not entirely clear why he thought that this was so. He had received copies of papers in the Coll charter chest, which had been transcribed by my great-uncle H. A. C. Maclean. They show that on 4 March 1593 Lachlan Maclean of Coll petitioned for an inquisition as to his title to the estates of which his father and grandfather had died 'seized' within the sheriffdom of Tarbert.

Hector Maclean of Coll, *an cleireach beag*, was dead by 25 April 1583, when Colin earl of Argyll obtained the gift of 'the ward of the heritage of Hector Maclean of Coill from his decease until the entry of the heir; with the relief of the same, and the marriage of John McClain, "nevoy" and apparent heir of the said Hector, his "guidschir", or of other heir succeeding'.[2] Three months later the earl sold this gift to Lachlan Mor, when he settled the latter's outstanding debts to him for 5000 merks.

Although the clerk of the Register of the Privy Seal stated that the name of the heir was 'John', it is clear from the entry in the Register of Deeds that this is a clerical error and that it is Lachlan that is meant. Lachlan Mor now had the right to all the profits from the Coll estate, including Lachlan Maclean of Coll's marriage.

As Lachlan of Coll's mother, Marion daughter of Hector Og and Lady Janet Campbell, could not have been born before 1558 it is unlikely that Lachlan of Coll could have been born before 1573. He appears to have been an only child. According to Coll tradition recorded by Allan Maclean of Crossapol, Lachlan was four years old when his father died. As there appears to have been only one Hector Maclean of Coll in April

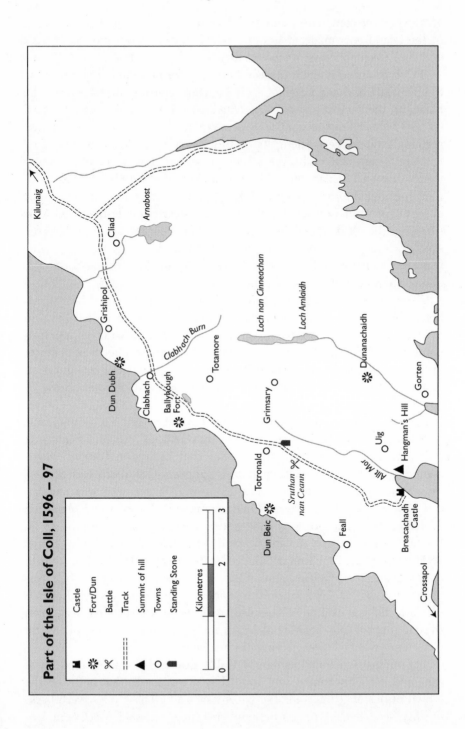

Part of the Isle of Coll, 1596 – 97

1579 when the complaint to the Privy Council concerning Duart's seizure of the island was made, it is quite likely that Coll tradition is correct and that Lachlan's father Hector Roy was dead by 1577.

If Coll tradition is again correct, Lachlan Mor pre-empted his purchase of the ward and marriage of Coll by endeavouring to take over the island on the very day *an cleireach beag* died. This incursion was defeated by Neil Mor at *Sruthan nàn Ceann*. Crossapol, who unlike most traditional accounts states precise lengths of time, says that Neil Mor managed the Coll estate for eight years and preserved it against all attempts made on it by Lachlan Mor. As Lachlan Mor was legally entitled to all the profits of the estate from 6 July 1583, it is unlikely that he did not obtain control of Coll until 1591. It is however possible that Neil Mor managed the estate from the death of his nephew Hector Roy. If Crossapol's timing is to be taken seriously it is possible that Neil Mor managed Coll for eight years from 1577, during his brother's old age and for a couple of years after his death.

Crossapol states that Lachlan of Coll was brought up in Macintosh's household. As the chief of that clan at this time was also called Lachlan Mor, it is possible that Macintosh has been confused with his Maclean namesake. If this is the case it would seem that Lachlan was brought up by his uncle at Duart. Evidently he did not have as good an education as his uncle received at Inveraray and Lachlan of Coll was unable to write, at least in Scots.

Further evidence that Lachlan of Coll was brought up by his uncle is obtained from Lachlan Mor's letter in Gaelic to Malcolm Beaton. It mentions 'the laird of Coll' and implies that he was in Lachlan Mor's company when it was written. It also suggests that there was no animosity between Lachlan Mor and his sister Marion, who was Lachlan of Coll's mother. In the letter Duart commands his personal physician Malcolm Beaton to go 'to the daughter of Argyll's daughter and to do her all the good that you can'. Marion was evidently referred to in this style in contemporary literary Gaelic.[3] After Hector Roy's death Marion married Charles Maclean, son of Allan Maclean of Ardgour. She was probably living at Ardgour on the shores of Loch Linnhe when Lachlan Mor's letter was written as he also requests Beaton to visit his cousin the daughter of John Stewart of Appin and Katherine, countess of Argyll. Her home was in Appin, across the water from Ardgour.

The inquisition into Lachlan of Coll's title to his estates took some time and it was not until July 1596 that it was found that he owed the crown duties of £1,440 for the barony of Coll.[4] These dues were presumably accepted for on 20 September 1596 Archibald MacConnell of

Largie and *Iain dow Mcrannald McAllaster of Kilchamak* became cautioners for Lachlan when he agreed to make payment to the earl of Argyll, in his capacity as sheriff of Tarbert, for 'all bygone duties of the lands of Coll etc owed by the young laird to the king'.[5] It is surely significant that these two Macdonalds were amongst Angus Macdonald of Dunyveg and the Glens' staunchest allies.[6] As we have seen, Lachlan of Coll had probably been brought up by his uncle at Duart. The fact that he was unable to sign his name in Scots[7] hardly suggests that Lachlan Mor took much interest in his education. That Coll should now turn to his uncle's enemies for help underlines the breakdown in relations that had occurred between the two Macleans.

The duties were presumably paid for Lachlan obtained a precept of sasine, which stated that it had been found by inquisition that Hector Maclean of Coll, Lachlan's father, had died seized of the barony of Coll, whose lands were enumerated, and that Lachlan was the lawful and next heir of his father. Although Lachlan's father had died before his own father *an cleireach beag*, he had legally been the owner of the Coll estate since 1558, when Hector senior resigned the estate in his favour. On 24 October 1596 Lachlan's attorney handed this precept of sasine to the notary public and received the symbolic earth and stone in return.

It was one thing to obtain sasine. It was another to get possession of the land. Sir Lachlan Mor was in Coll in March 1595–6, which had perhaps been under his control since he purchased Lachlan of Coll's ward, relief and marriage in July 1583. There were advantages to Lachlan Mor in holding on to Coll: he obtained the rent paid by the tenants occupying the land, including the *cudeigh*, a night's entertainment. What was probably more important to Duart at the time was that he controlled the rising out of the fencible men of the barony of Coll which was 140 men in the island itself plus 50 from his lands in Mull and more from Morvern. As a result he refused to hand over the estate. Lachlan of Coll sued his uncle. Both uncle and nephew appeared before the council at Linlithgow on 23 December 1596. Coll complained that although he had been served and retoured, i.e. formally declared to be the heir of his father, infeft and seized in the estate of Coll, which had belonged to his predecessors and held directly from the crown 'past memory of man', he was now 'maist havelie molestit, troublit and opprest' in the possession of his lands by Lachlan Maclean of Duart and his deputy Rory Beg Maclean.[8]

The latter not only refused to hand over the estate, but intended to demolish 'the complenaris place and castell of Bretach'. Lachlan of Coll had by chance chosen his timing well. The king was sitting with the council and was in no humour to pander to Sir Lachlan. Duart was ordered, on 24 hours' notice, to deliver Breacachadh to Sir William Stewart of Houston, Lieutenant of the Isles. He was also instructed to give Coll possession of his estate within 30 days and allow him and his tenants to 'peaceablie brouke, labour and menure' the same on pain of a fine of 10,000 merks.

Uncle and nephew went on to settle what was probably the major bone of contention between the two families, ownership of the former church land in Coll. This property known as the 'two ends of Coll' had been obtained by Lachlan's grandfather at the time of the Reformation. It was valuable property. The west end of Coll in particular is some of the most productive land in the islands.

Mr Thomas Craig, advocate, the erudite author of *Jus Feudale* who had appeared for Lachlan's grandfather almost twenty years earlier, once again appeared before the Lords as procurator for Maclean of Coll. He handed in an obligation to be registered in the Books of Council and Session. In it Lachlan of Coll agreed to assign 'all richt title … clame of richt kyndness and possession that I, my predecessors and successors have to … the Kirklandis lyane in the two endis of the yle of Coll …', always providing that Maclean of Coll and his heirs and assignees had the 'service and manreid [manrent] of the possessors, tennentis and occupeairs of the said Kirk landes in all time cuming'.[9]

Sir Lachlan Maclean became landlord, Lachlan Maclean of Coll became chief. It was the very situation that the crown was trying to put a stop to. In future the occupiers of land in the two ends of Coll would pay rent to Maclean of Duart, but they would pay their calps, death duties, to Maclean of Coll, who in return would provide them with personal protection.

Lachlan of Coll was in possession of his estate by 23 March when Aula Macaulay of Ardincaple became a surety in 2,000 merks that he would 'deliver the house of Bretach for the advancement of the King's service upon six days notice'.[10]

As he was prepared to stand up to his uncle, it is not improbable that one of Lachlan's first acts on becoming laird was to exercise his judicial rights as a baron and avenge his great-uncle Neil Mor's murder. Maclean Sinclair tells the story that four of the murderers were seized when they were playing shinty on the beach at Calgary in Mull. They were taken to Coll, imprisoned for some time and then executed at *Cnoc a Chrochaire*, the hangman's hill.[11]

Hangman's Hill is half a mile across the machair from Breacachadh Castle. It was probably the traditional place where criminals were executed on the island. In 1994 the skeleton of a woman was found at the foot of the hill close to the burn known as *Allt Mor.* It is possible that she had been executed there by drowning. Women were executed by drowning, men by hanging, unless they were of superior rank when they were beheaded. In 1896 when Stewart removed the summit to make a tee there for his golf course, four skeletons were unearthed. Some locals said that they were the murderers of Neil Mor.[12]

Coll is described in 1595 as being very fertile 'alsweill of corns as of all kind of catell. Thair is sum little birkin (i.e. birch) woodis within the said ile. Ilk merk land payis yeirlie

5 bolls beir
8 bollis meill
20 stone cheese
4 stones of buttir
4 mairtis
8 wedderis
2 merk of silver
2 dozen of pultrie.'

The amount of cheese and butter included in this rental plus the 'mairtis', i.e. an ox or cow fattened for slaughter, shows how important cattle rearing was to the community of Coll at the end of the sixteenth century. This fact is underlined by the silver rent, which could only be obtained by the selling of cattle on the mainland.[13]

What is surprising is the amount of arable land that must have been present to be described as being 'very fertile alsweill of corns', beir, i.e. four or six-row barley (which is hardier and coarser than ordinary two-row barley) and meill, i.e. oatmeal.

The short growing season, strong winds and heavy rain and the large areas of the acid soil, which make up two thirds of the island, do not make Coll ideal for growing crops. It is however also true today that local gardeners can produce excellent crops in small areas of ground – once they have a windbreak.

It has recently been argued that the joint-occupation open-field system, *runrig*, whereby each landholder or tenant had several strips of land which were not contiguous, was not a very ancient method of working the land in the Hebrides. It is now suggested that this system was preceded by a method of land use where single tenants had small walled fields, presumably for a considerable length of time. That such a system existed in Coll is suggested by the number of surviving walls and small fields in farms such as Totronald, Grimsary and Totamore.[14]

It was obviously essential that the island produced as much 'victuals' as possible with the minimum amount of labour if it was to support the 140 fighting men Coll is said to have raised. The anonymous author of the 'Description of the Isles of Scotland' tells us that in the Hebrides 'na labourers of the ground are permittit to steir furth of the cuntrie quhateir thair maister have ado, except gentlemen quhilk labouris not, that the labour belonging to the teiling of the ground and wynning of thair corns may not be left undone'.[15]

The 'gentlemen quhilk labouris not' might be away from home 'watching thair enemies' for a year. The occupiers of the land however were not 'molestit' nor were they 'permittit to gang furth of thair awin cuntrie and Ile quhair they dwell'. In other words they were tied to the soil. How many such 'churls' lived in Coll in the late 1590s is not known. It was the mobilisation of this class in Ulster by Sean O Neill that had revolutionised warfare there. It was to be another half-century before such a revolution took place in the Hebrides.

Most 'farms' in Coll were valued at 20/-. Others such as the laird's own demesne at Breacachadh and nearby Feall were valued at 3 merks each, whilst the east end of Coll was valued at 6 merks.[16] It would therefore seem probable that the farms valued at 20/- are each one merkland and that each merkland supported four fighting men. Who were these men?

They certainly would have included younger sons of Macleans on the island who were members of the Coll family (see Table 2). It would also seem certain that the Mackinnons on the island, who were said to have been 'real Mackinnons' out of the chief's own family, were included.[17] Amongst them was Donald Mugach who fought at *Sruthan nan Ceann*. His uncle *Alister Mor* was also remembered as a renowned warrior.

It is probable that the sons *Jon bane Mcdonelour*, who made their bond of manrent to Hector Maclean of Coll on 25 February 1568–9, were included amongst these fighting men a generation later.

At this time younger sons of chiefly families were given land in liferent. Thus Neil Mor obtained Quinish in Mull and Lachlan of Coll's uncles Allan and John, *An cleireach beag's* sons by his second wife a Macalister of Loup (a Kintyre family renowned for its mercenary activities in Ulster), were respectively given Coll's farms of Auchnasaul in Mull and Grishipol in Coll. The younger sons formed the basis of the managerial class of lease holders or tacksmen, *fir-tacsa*, responsible for the land that was worked by the *nativi*, the churls tied to the ground. They were also the subordinate commanders of the clan in times of

war. Thus Neil Mor led the Coll men at *Sruthan nan Ceann* and Allan
Auchnasaul led his nephew's men at *Traigh Ghruinneart.*

The fecundity of the Macleans' women, added to the casual nature
of Celtic secular marriage, had enabled the clan to take over vast areas
of land in the great days of its expansion. Now that new land was not
available in Scotland there was not enough to go round and younger
sons of younger sons with no landed responsibilities to assume and
inherit were spared social demotion by joining the ranks of the fighting
'swordsmen', or *buannachan.*[18] That Coll could support 140 (almost today's total population) is a remarkable testimony to its fertility and to
the success of the manner in which it was farmed. It is possible that
this high productivity was achieved by the pre-runrig methods that are
only now being identified.

Coll's castle of Breacachadh is described, in the 'Description of the
Western Isles', as 'ane great strenth be reason of the situation thairof
verie neir the sea, quhilk defendis the half thairof and has three walls
about the rest of the castell ane thairof biggit with lyme and stane, with
sundrie gude devises for defending of the tower ...' These 'sundrie gude
devises' comprise a parapet with obliquely aligned loops suitable for
firearms. Above each doorway on the east and south side of the tower
is box machicolation, a device for dropping stones etc. on assailants.
Evidence from excavations and a field survey suggest that these 'gude
devises' were installed in the late sixteenth century.[19] They involved
raising the original curtain wall more than three feet in places. The
excavations also suggest that at the same time as these improvements
were made the tower itself was remodelled. Its original entrance was
blocked up or restricted in size and a new door inserted above it, level
with the new parapet's walkway. At the same time a turnpike stair was
inserted in the south-east corner of the tower replacing an earlier mural
stair which was either blocked up or in one place converted into a prison
cell. The turnpike stair has a lintel of sandstone dogtooth moulding at
its entrance in the lower hall. It terminates in a cap house which gave
access to the parapet walk around the top of the tower.

The original flanking tower had a series of three canted machicolations
at the level of the flat-topped roof which covered the entrances through
the curtain wall. They could have been used either with a bow and
arrow or later with firearms and it was probably unnecessary to alter
them when the remodelling of the defences was carried out in the late
sixteenth century.

Who was responsible for these defences? The evidence of the 'Description' would suggest that it was written after the 'sundrie gude

devises' were installed. There is evidence in the 'Description' that it was written in 1595, this being the date when John Stewart of Appin, who was apparently living in March 1592–3, is on record as having died. The 'Description' refers to him as though he were alive.[20]

Turner and Dunbar suggest that the remodelling was virtually complete by 1593. They believed that Hector Maclean of Coll died in that year. The 'Decription' and subsequent evidence in Argyll Transcripts show that he was dead by 1583 at the latest. It would therefore now seem probable that the reconstruction of Coll's castle was the work of Lachlan Mor, who probably thought he would never have to hand the island back to the Macleans of Coll. The threat to demolish the castle was probably made in a fit of pique when he realised that he had spent a considerable sum of money on a castle which was to be of no benefit to him.

An alternative scenario would be that these improvements were carried out before Lachlan Mor obtained Lachlan of Coll's ward relief and marriage in 1583, or at least before Lachlan Mor seized the Coll estate from Neil Mor sometime in the 1580s. Both scenarios would suggest that the castle was badly damaged when Duart's men captured it and beheaded Hector Allansoun in 1578. Dennis Turner however points out to me that there was a fashion at this time to do away with narrow mural stairs in tower houses and replace them with more convenient turnpike stairs. He cites the example of Kinlochaline Castle in Morvern which was also owned by Lachlan Mor.

The discovery of a Spanish vessel used for carrying water, several sherds from which were found at the foot of the south-east corner of the tower house, suggests that the reconstruction dates from the very late 1580s. Numerous examples of such vessels are found in ports in the South of England and South Wales. It is very unusual to find one in the Hebrides, the probability being that it came off the Armada galleon in Tobermory. If, as seems likely, the 'sundrie gude devises' at Breacachadh were the work of Sir Lachlan Mor, it is perhaps another example of his intention to invade Ulster. He could do so with a clearer conscience once he had left his lands well protected against a counter-attack by O Neill's Scots allies.

The 'Description' goes on to state there was 'ane uther wall about that (i.e. the curtain wall of the castle) within the quhilk schippis and boittis are drawin and salvit. And the third and the uttermost wall of timber and earth, within the quhilk the haill gudes of the cuntrie are keipit in tyme of troublis or weiris'.

Breacachadh was probably not the only fortification on Coll at the time. There were several crannogs, artificial man-made lake dwellings, on the island. There is one in Loch Cinneachan, one in nearby Loch Amlaidh and perhaps one in the drained loch at Ballyhough. Tyrone is said to have used his crannogs as store-houses and places of retreat after he demolished his castle of Dungannon to prevent the English from having an object at which to strike.[21] There are also several forts and duns on the island. It is impossible to say how recently they have been occupied. It is however unlikely that their useful defensive position would not have been used at least as observation points during the unsettled days of the late sixteenth century.

Farms on the north coast of Coll from Feall to Cliad and in the centre from Grimsary to Uig, which were probably the homes to the majority of the people, all had their forts, duns or crannogs. Dun Dubh, which is Grishipol's fort, is a formidable defensive site with precipitous drops on three sides. It overlooks the approaches to the north coast of Coll from the Outer Isles from where the Macdonalds of Sleat or Clanranald were likely to attack. It is also the northernmost of these fortified positions which might be used to co-ordinate the defence of this part of the island. It is probably significant that Grishipol was given to his uncle by Lachlan Maclean of Coll.

It is perhaps even more significant that Allan, the elder uncle, was given Auchnasaul in Quinish, Maclean of Coll's estate in the north-west of Mull. Allan was to lead Coll's men at the battle of *Traigh Ghruinneart* in 1598. He was probably the leading warrior of his day in the Maclean of Coll family. Quinish was vulnerable to attack by land up the old drove road from Aros on the Sound of Mull and it was probably no coincidence that Allan succeeded his uncle Neil Mor as custodian of this valuable property.

Quinish does not appear to have had a castle or other defensible site, which is perhaps why Neil Mor hid out in the hills. Coll's estate at the north-west corner of Morvern, Drimnin, did. Drimnin Castle occupied a level summit area overlooking the Sound of Mull. It was a small rectangular building on an east-west axis, with a small projection, perhaps a stair turret, at the east end of the south wall. It was no more than 13 m. in width. Its captain was Neil Mor's son Allan who also possessed Coll's estate in Morvern,[22] perhaps in liferent.

Notes

1. *Clan Gillean*, (1899) 387.
2. *RSS* viii, 1282.

3. *SGS* xiii Pt i, 56–65.
4. *ER* (1595–1600), 382.
5. AT vii, 281.
6. *RPC* v, 321.
7. SRO RD1/55 f 364.
8. *RPC* v, 354.
9. SRO RD1/ 55 H 364 R & V.
10. *RPC* v, 678.
11. *Clan Gillean,* 387.
12. *Ibid.*
13. *Celtic Scotland* iii, 437.
14. Robert A Dodgshon, 'West Highland and Hebridean landscapes: have they a history without runrig?', *Journal of Historical Geography* (1993), 383–98.
15. *Celtic Scotland* iii, 139–40.
16. AT 28 June 1558.
17. Breacachadh Castle Papers (BCP), Crossapol Manuscript.
18. Allan I. Macinnes, 'Crown, Class and Fine: The 'Civilizing' of Scottish Gaeldon, 1587–1638', *Scottish Studies.*
19. D. J. Turner and J. G. Dunbar, 'Breacachadh Castle, Coll: Excavations and Field Survey, 1965–8'. *Proceedings of the Society of Antiquaries of Scotland (PSAS)*, Vol. 102. Session 1969–70, 154–87. This report states that I purchased the Castle in 1965. In fact I did so in 1961.
20. W. Munro, 'Roll Call of the Isles', *West Highland Notes & Queries* Series 2 No. 1, March 1988, 5.
21. *Irish Battles,* 112.
22. BCP Crossapol MS, 41.

CHAPTER 20

1597

Malcolm. This murderous shaft that's shot
Hath not yet lighted; and our safest way
Is to avoid the aim. Therefore, to horse;
And let us not be dainty of leave-taking,
But shift away: there's warrant in that theft
Which steals itself, when there's no mercy left.

Macbeth, Act II, Scene iii

The uneasy truce in Ireland lasted throughout the winter of 1596–7. O Neill protested his loyalty to Elizabeth whilst he waited for Cobos's mission to bear fruit. On the English side discussion dragged on as to the advisability of hiring Scots in general and Sir Lachlan in particular.

George Nicolson continued to worry about the situation in Ulster and think how he could best persuade the queen to employ Maclean. On one occasion in January 1596–7, on hearing discussion of Ireland, he was unable to sleep at night. He began to wonder how he could best be of service. The next morning he wrote down his thoughts which he sent on to Lord Burghley.

His thoughts are in the form of a paper entitled 'A discovery of the advantages the Irish rebels in the North have against the English'. 'It is to be noted', he writes, 'and held for a truth and woeful experience has taught that the English (how good soldiers so ever) are not able to endure the hardness that the Irish of those parts live in, but by cold and hard diet more by thousands have died than by the hand of the rebel.

'It is also certain that the bogs, mosses and woods (which are in those parts huge and many) are strengths and sanctuaries for the Irish and their relief at all occasions against the English and the English man's impediment against the Irish.

'Likewise it holds in general that the Irish being better footmen than the English come and go to and from the English at their pleasure and advantages, thereby annoying the English and flying their own harms.

'By men of like kind and bringing up in cold and hard diet the rebels may best be encountered and overthrown in their advantages aforesaid ... the Scottish Irish are of like kind and bringing up in hardness etc, and the worthiest of them in no kindness, bond or mind but in deadly feud with Tyrone and in such friendship with some in that rebellion as being employed in service against Tyrone, would not only by their forces, with the assistance of some of her Majesty's, faithfully and ably in the rebels' own advantages serve her Majesty in regard of her pay and especially of their hatred to and to be revenged on Tyrone, but also upon their landing in Ireland draw their friends from Tyrone and so weaken him as he shall soon be overthrown, and thereby the Spaniards afraid of coming thither, who will not venture to land but under the protection of some party to receive them in arms; and the Irish seeing her Majesty to have the services of the Scots who were want to be their aid and refuge (as yet some of them are) will be ever thereafter afraid to rebel or offend again. By which her Majesty shall have the honour and victory with great profit hereafter and that in short time by this means of "backsett and foresett" of the rebels and drawing their friends from them.

'If her Majesty like this course the King of Scotland must be moved herein and no doubt will willingly agree there unto. For his Majesty ever seemed to me more than two years ago and divers times since at my dealings with him to be most willing to pleasure her Majesty against these rebels and every way else. Thereon the earl of Argyll and Maclean may be dealt with for forces and Maclean drawn to go in person to lead and govern the Scottish forces, which he can do most gallantly and will do faithfully, and agreements must be made in these behalfs.' [1]

It was Nicolson's most eloquent appeal to Burghley to employ the Scots in general and Maclean in particular. There is no mention of any reply to Nicolson's paper in the State Papers. It is possible that Sir Geoffrey Fenton saw it, for in the following February he argues against the proposal to allow 3,000 Scots to enter Ulster at Lough Foyle. One of his reasons was that once they were established in Ulster, would the English ever get them to leave? They are, he wrote, 'a needy beggarly people and not easily expelled out of the country where they have taken a footing'. The recent example of the Macdonalds' occupation of the Route was often quoted as an example. They were also expensive. It was unlikely that Fenton thought that the Irish rebels could be defeated by the Scots of Kintyre or the islands. They were too like their fellow Gaels in Ireland. 'Dogs will not eat dog's flesh', he argued.[2]

The most telling point to Burghley was perhaps that it had always been the policy of the government of Ireland to keep the Scots out of the north of Ireland.[3] Sir Robert Cecil was even against the Scots trading with pro-English Irishmen.

Reports of the movements of the rebels and their friends continued to pour into the Cecils. Not all concerned the Irish. On 10 January Henry Knowlis wrote from an unidentified Kilmacthomes Castle that 'three or four weeks since there came to this house, from the north, Mr Fawkener, the priest who brought with him an English gentlewoman, named Ann Wilmar, sister to the Wilmar that married the widow of Francis Throgmorton, who was executed'.[4] The Throckmortons were an ancient Worcestershire Roman Catholic family. Francis had acted as the link between Mary Queen of Scots and the Spanish ambassador Mendoza. He had been seized by Walsingham's agents, tortured and executed. Any connection of his in Ulster was a worry to Cecil especially as Ann Wilmar had been a lady-in-waiting to the countess of Tyrone for four or five years and now intended to travel to England.[5]

Meanwhile Tyrone waited for a reply to his letters to Philip II with increasing impatience. Eventually in March 1597 two small Spanish ships with some money and gunpowder arrived in Killybegs. This insignificant assistance infuriated the Irish who were beginning to murmur 'that they loved the worst Englishman better than the best Spaniard'. O Neill himself told the officer who brought this meagre help that the Spanish were a deceitful nation, who 'had cozened the Irish'.[6]

Rumours of the cargo on these Spanish ships rapidly reached Scotland. On 11 April Robert Bowes wrote to Cecil that 'Sir James MacConnell has informed me and others that two Spanish ships with 500 soldiers, armour, weapons and money were arrived in Ireland and come to aid of O Donnell with promise that he should be shortly furnished with greater forces by the King of Spain'.[7]

He also reported that the earl of Argyll had sent for Maclean and other friends to receive their advice for his journey into foreign parts and for other weighty affairs.[8]

The following month Bowes wrote to Burghley that he had 'been advised that the troubles in Ireland are like to be kindled again'. He enclosed a letter from Maclean's agent John Auchinross which was full of foreboding. 'Without doubt', he wrote, 'the earl of Tyrone has of late received great quantity of armour and gold from Spain and O Donnell has of new directed some gentlemen to my master desiring earnestly his assistance accompanied with two thousand men, to whom offer is made of gold, silver and other furnishing. This "meckle" my master has willed me to let your lordship know with diligence seeing they are new come to him and that you make her Majesty and Council acquainted herewith, so that if they esteem not of his service he must license his men to go over to Ireland, whom he has stayed to this present giving them sustenation, accorded to them use of his land, and by whom he has stayed others of mind to go over.'

Meanwhile the Roman Catholic earls were keeping a low profile. On 18 June it was reported that Huntly had come with one man to the court at Falkland 'at two of the clock after midnight', that he had a conference with the king and duke (i.e. Lennox his brother-in-law) and others and departed within four hours.[9] A week later both Huntly and Errol were 'at the sermon in Aberdeen'. In other words they were conforming to their agreement made the previous year to satisfy the king and the church. This they had done and they were absolved from their excommunication. It was however noted that Huntly's uncle, the Jesuit Mr James Gordon, had been sent to Ulster for discussions with Tyrone.[10]

Tyrone continued to fume at the lack of effective aid from Spain. What neither he nor the English realised was the chaos and utter state of demoralisation that existed in Spain. English spies might report the great naval preparations being made by the Adelantado of Castile, but after five months of intermittent activity at the ports nothing was ready. At the beginning of July the Adelantado's secretary, Pedro Lopez de Soto, wrote to the Council of War to complain that: 'Everything is in confusion; uniforms for the men are lacking and the cavalry is unfit for service. There is no money to provide anything, no meat, no wine, no siege artillery, hardly any guns for the ships themselves'.

Correspondence between Tyrone and the English authorities continued with the usual courtesies, but when Lord Burgh succeeded Sir William Russell as lord deputy at the end of May the tone changed. The new lord deputy's letters to his chief antagonist were now couched in the bluntest manner and his methods were no less aggressive. Attempts were made to eliminate O Neill himself. In June 1597 he was nearly taken. Captain Symes wrote directly to Cecil from Dundalk that he and his party had 'come so suddenly upon him [Tyrone] that they nearly took the earl and his wife; but a villain spy ran and gave him warning'. The earl was so hotly pursued that he and his wife had no time to mount their horses but fled to the woods on foot. The raid was not without its value for as Symes wrote, 'we killed divers of his men, and brought away three thousand cows, and, had we come one hour sooner, we had got ten thousand'.

Lord Burgh now mounted a surprise relief of Armagh. At the same

time Sir Conyers Clifford, the governor of Connaught, marched towards
Lough Foyle. The offensive was initially a success. Lord Burgh successfully crossed the Blackwater himself leading the vanguard. O Neill,
surprised, failed to gather all his troops who obtained no help 'from
Tyrone's camp in the woods'.[11]

The offensive however soon ran out of steam. Burgh withdrew and
Clifford, hearing the news, also decided to retire. O Donnell thought
that he would try to escape under cover of darkness, but 'God forbid',
wrote Sir Conyers, that the enemy should be given 'any such cause of
pride'. Although the passages over the Erne were watched by his adversaries, there was to be no secrecy in Clifford's withdrawal. Morale
was high and he ferried his way across the Erne with drums beating
and ensigns flying. The column was attached along its length with
furious assaults by the rebels. The attacks were uniformly repulsed. It
took the column six hours to get to Bunduff, by which time their
ammunition was exhausted and Clifford's men had only their pikes to
defend them. Sir Conyers himself fought on foot with his soldiers. At
Bunduff the enemy foot gave up the struggle but the cavalry continued
to harass the column until at last it reached the safety of Athlone. It
was a gallantly fought action, but it was still a defeat for the government.

O Neill was by now an expert at guerrilla warfare. He used the
country with a skill that more recent guerilla commanders would envy.
He was an elusive opponent, as Lord Burgh wrote to Cecil: 'For, as he
is the dishonestest rebel of the world so he is the most cowardly, never
making good any fight, but bagging with his shot, and flying from bush
to bush'.[12]

Burgh had attempted to capture him at night at his camp in the
woods. 'But it is impossible', he writes, 'for he lodgeth dispersed in the
thicks, and holds no firm guards, but throws himself and all his into
sundry groves, lurking scattered like wolves or foxes, fitter to hunt
with dogs than to find with men; and so jealous and mistrustful he is,
as he parts, in the evening from his men, not suffering any to know his
cabin, saving one or two to wait on him, and in the morning they meet
upon some appointed place cut out of the woods, and if they have an
alarm night or day, they advise whither to fly beforehand.'

It had been some time since Robert Bowes had been in contact with
Maclean. In mid-August 1597 the English ambassador wrote to Cecil
to say that he had spoken to John Auchinross. 'I have excused my long
silence towards Maclean and seeking to understand ... his present disposition and estate for services in Ireland for her Majesty against the
rebels ...' Bowes also sought to know what monthly rate might be paid

to the company serving under him and pointed out that the rates the rebels were offering would be much lower than those demanded by Auchinross. O Neill had written again to Maclean, wrote Bowes. Tyrone was also writing to inferior commanders above the heads of their chiefs to persuade them to serve him against the English.

Auchinross argued that the Irish offer if it was 'converted in silver ... would exceed' the sum Lachlan Mor was asking from the English, i.e. 20/- for each soldier per month. Auchinross goes on to say that Maclean continued to prevent his men from going over to Ireland 'and has hindered Tyrone (against whom his hatred yet "incistis") from the aid of all others in the Isles to the great discomfort of Tyrone'.

Lachlan Mor had also refused 'great offers made to him by O Donnell both to himself and to Argyll and all yet in vain'. He went on underlying the fact that he was not getting paid.

At the beginning of September James MacSorley was writing to the king for advice, asking whether he should serve 'her Majesty or take part with the earl of Tyrone'. The king had replied that he should serve the queen.

On 27 September the dramatic news reached Edinburgh that Argyll had reconciled Angus and Maclean. The king was not pleased and wrote to Sir Lachlan to tell him so. O Donnell was still imploring Maclean to come to his aid. Lachlan however continued to resist his overtures. Peace was evidently in the air for on 7 October it was learned that Huntly was at long last 'to be quiet of that quarrel of Moray's slaughter and would refer it to the arbitration of any four Stewarts of account' as long as they agreed that neither his life nor his lands should be forfeit. Huntly offered 'lands and marriage' to help confound the matter, 'which will breed troubles again [in a] few years', wrote Robert Bowes.

In November Lachlan Mor himself wrote to Bowes from Duart to remind him 'how far her Majesty is disappointed of her affairs in Ireland' and again offering his services or he would be forced 'to license my men to serve where they may ...'

This was his last letter to Bowes, who died on 16 November 1597. He was replaced by George Nicolson, who on 9 December wrote to Cecil that Huntly was still trying to end his feud 'with Argyll and so many of Moray's friends as can be'. He had also found among Bowes's papers a letter from Maclean saying he was surprised to have heard nothing 'of the pension spoken on by your honour to his servant [Auchinross]'. Many islanders were preparing to cross over to Ireland to serve Tyrone, 'a matter worth looking into in regard of the especial and good service that may be done by Maclean and of the evil that may come by the passing of the Scottish to the earl', wrote the indefatigable Nicolson.[13]

On 12 December Huntly, Angus and Errol arrived at court at Holyrood House.[14] At the Parliament that followed they were formally restored. The ceremony was carried out with considerable formality. Argyll, Mar and their friends were conspicuous by their absence. On the 17th one John Macartney wrote that 'the three earls are come into Parliament with their forces for two causes. One is to let Huntly's enemies understand how great he is and of what power; for their came with him the earl of Sutherland, the earl of Caithness, the earl Marischal and the earl of Buchan with all the gentlemen of the Isles and all their forces that they could procure'. The gentlemen of the Isles are not listed but they can hardly have included Maclean despite his new rapprochement with Angus. Argyll, although 'desired by the King and the Council to subscribe a letter of truce', firmly stayed at home. 'This is interpreted for a beginning of disobedience', wrote Macartney, 'but neither King nor Council can devise a way how to be revenged on him'.[15] Argyll safe in his country could still defy the government when he chose to.

The Parliament held in Edinburgh passed an act which was to have unfortunate results for the Macleans. It was entitled 'The inhabitants of the Isles and Hielandis suld schow thair haldings'. In the preamble it was stated that the inhabitants of the Highlands and Islands had neglected to pay their annual rents and to perform the services due to the crown. They had also, through their 'barbarous inhumanity', made the region which was naturally fertile 'altogether unprofitable either to themselves or to their fellow country men'.[16] As a first step to remedy this situation it was ordered that all landlords, chiefs of clans and other proprietors of lands and fisheries in the Highlands and Islands should appear in Edinburgh before 15 May 1598 and produce the title to their property.[17]

The record of the proceedings of the Exchequer which followed this act has not survived. Dr Hector Maclean however has a story which is probably associated with the event but which he places some fifteen years later. His story is that when the chiefs had to show their titles to their estates they had to answer to their names or forfeit a certain share of their estates. While Maclean was changing his clothes his name was called, 'which he not answering to was adjudged to the forfeiture of the twenty pound land of Garvyavich in Lochaber, of which Huntly took a gift and all the friends and interest Maclean could make, could never get the sentence recalled'.[18] This was Huntly's revenge for Lachlan Mor's insult to him at the Battle of Glenlivet.

On 17 December Sir James MacSorley arrived in Edinburgh again. Early the previous month he had fought a pitched battle with Sir John Chichester, governor of Carrickfergus. Chichester had sent for Dunluce to explain his actions in raiding the Island of Macgee. Instead of having a peaceful discussion Chichester ordered his men to charge the Scots. He was however heavily defeated. Sir John himself was killed, two officers were captured and several wounded. There was a danger that Carrickfergus itself might fall.

Sir James came to Edinburgh at the king's request and when the Treasurer, the earl of Mar, protested that the king should not see him, James replied that he had invited him before he had killed Chichester. He was however too occupied to see him the evening he arrived. But MacSorley had vowed to see the king before he took off his boots; he therefore slept in them.[19] 'He is here very well entertained both with the King and Queen', wrote Roger Ashton to Cecil.

During the winter of 1597–8 James was misled into believing that Elizabeth meant to deny him the English succession. Chichester's defeat had been greeted with applause in Edinburgh and James used intemperate language about England in Parliament. Elizabeth was furious and on 4 January wrote the king a threatening letter reminding him that he dealt 'with such a King as will bear no wrongs and indure [no] infamy'.[20]

MacSorley remained in Edinburgh for several weeks. During this time rumour of a Spanish invasion were rife, whipped up by one of Tyrone's men who had accompanied MacSorley and brought with him a letter from O Neill which Huntly delivered to the king and which Ashton saw. In it Tyrone excused his rebellion, making the old excuse that he was not fighting against the queen but against her deputies.[21]

Nicolson was alarmed. In February he reported to Cecil that the king had written to Maclean 'to be with him at Edinburgh next month pretending it is to have his advice for bringing of the islands to his better obedience, but what other business he has with him I know not. The king has sent him without warrant for his safe return'.

MacSorley may have been acting for Tyrone but he was also looking after his own interests. He asked the king to grant him Dunyvaig Castle in Islay, 'for what purpose may be doubtful', wrote Nicolson.[22] Dunyvaig had been garrisoned by the king's servants since the commendator of Pittenweem's expedition the previous year. Angus now recaptured it.

Angus failed to keep to the promises he had made and his son Sir James was once again permitted to visit Kintyre to persuade his father to keep his word. Angus however seems to have repented of his offer to strip himself of his possessions in favour of Sir James. The Macdonalds were completely disillusioned with Angus's leadership, and once Sir James arrived in the Isles he was persuaded to take matters into his own hands.

A quarrel between Gorrie Macalister, the young laird of Loup, and his tutor was the excuse for a revolution amongst the Macdonalds. Young Loup killed the tutor whose sons took refuge with Angus. It was to be stated at Sir James's trial some eleven years later that the laird of Loup 'was verrie desyrous to have thair lyves'.

Sir James sided with the young laird and, learning that the tutor's sons were with his father at Askomull in Kintyre, Sir James, in the words of the 'dittay' (statement of the charges), 'accumpaneid with your brother, Angus Oig, and the said Laird of Loupe, with tua or thre hundreth barbarus, wikked and bludie Hieland-men, soirneris, and avowed maliefactouris, all bodin in feir of weir, with hagbutis, pistoleltis and utheris forbidden wappones, upone the [thirteenth?] day of Januar (fyftene dayis or thairby eftir yule) in the yeir of God 1597/8 come in the nycht to the said hous of Askomell, quhair the said Tutour of Loupis sones war takand the nychtis rest, lipsing for no trubill, danger or invasioune to haif bene maid be any man aganis thame; and invironed the samyn, in all sydis, with grit numberis of your armet men; and about the brek of day, calling in to theas who war within, to rander the hous and thame selffis to you, thay, for feir of thair lyves and of the mercieles crewaltie of you and your bludie assisteris, refuiseing to rander; albeit ye knew that Angus Mcconeill, your father, was within the house, with whome ye had privat and friendlie meiting and conference that same nycht, and had pairtit from him in sic professioun of love and naturall deutie and reverence, as ye had presentit and gevin to him ane pair of pistolettis: Nevertheles, casting of all bandis and respectis of conscience, honestie, and of nature, to your father, and to your mother Fynwall Nikclane, quhome ye knew to be also within the said hous, ye godleslie, barbaruslie, uiprouslie and tressonabillie, be your self and your complices, in your name, of your causing, command, assistance and ratihabitioun, set fyre in all the four coirnerris of the said hous; quairby your saidis parentis, and haill remanent persones being within the said hous, being brocht at the verrie instant to extreme danger of thair lyves, and your mother crying out to you, 'Theif! Will thow burne thy mother?' Ye nawayis causit stay or slokin [slaked] the fyre, bot sufferit the samyn to rage, quhill [until] the ruif of the hous began to fall; and your father haifing sufferit most crewall extremitie, and being brunt in thre or four pairtis of his body with that fyre, was forcet to rusch to the dur, quhair

ye had prepairit ane number of grit treyis to be laid croce the dur, ather
to stay his furth cuming, to the effect he micht be brunt within the
hous, or micht be so hinderit in his furthcuming, as he sould indoutitlie
fall in your mercieles handis: accoirding to the quhilk proiect, he, falling
amangis the said treyis, was pudillit in ane myre [dragged through a
miry puddle] be your servandis, in your sicht, and thaireftir transportit,
in his sark [shirt], to Smerbie, tuo myles distant from Askomell, quhair
ye tetherit him in irnes, with ane uther of your prissoneris, and detenit
him in that most unnaturall, mercieles and miserabill estait, be the space
of ane quarter of ane yeir'.[23]

Sir James was to claim that he had the king's authority for seizing
his parents. At his trial he produced a retrospective warrant authorising
'the taking of his father Angus McConeill, the manner, forme and circumstances done thairin ...' It was signed by the king at Falkland and
dated 8 August 1598.

Nicolson reported to Cecil that Angus had been planning to seize Sir
James before the heir turned the tables on him. The latter now refused
to hand his father over to the king 'but keeps him in perpetual captivity'.[24]

Sir James's actions seem to have been modelled on his uncle Lachlan
Mor's coup d'état twenty years earlier. 'Now', Nicolson continues, 'Maclean and Sir James, who is Maclean's sister's son, are like to agree to
run a course together, which surely Maclean upon good conditions for
him and the King's direction may be drawn for the Queen's service, and
it were but to recover the Glens which McSorley keeps from Angus
and his son'.

Nicolson could not resist using any factor to persuade Cecil to employ
his protégé. In March he returned to the old topic of Maclean's payment
when he wrote to Lord Burghley. 'Indeed it is true', he writes, 'that Mr
Secretary (i.e. Cecil) about this time two years ago at Greenwich said
to John Auchinross that her Majesty would entertain and make Maclean
her pensioner, and in hope thereof Auchinross held himself satisfied for
his master and indeed contented him with the 150 lib. then given him,
although he alleged that 1,000 crowns were promised; which in some
sort was so indeed, and that then he looked for that sum. Since which
time Maclean expected accordingly a yearly pension and divers times
moved my master (i.e. Bowes) to that effect. Now, as the matter stands
some 200 lib. would both satisfy him and (I think and dare say) bind
him to her Majesty's service. And I would not doubt thereafter but to
draw him for a small consideration to do a great service, to make an
incursion with 3,000 men into the rebels' country of Ireland where her
Majesty should appoint, to take great spoils on them and some of their

houses for her, so as they might have some 500 of her Majesty's trained soldiers with them and artillery, munitions and other necessaries for helping to win the houses with, as also to stay a good time there ... And in this service, if her Majesty should like it, I would desire to serve, such hope have I in Maclean and in the good success. This 200 Lib if your lordship please to give order to Mr Lynforth or Mr Craven in Watling Street to pay here to me ...'

Nicolson goes on to point out that Sir Lachlan 'is very like to rule Angus MacConnell's people now that Angus is in captivity ...' He passes on the news that Argyll had taken leave of the king and was about to set off on his travels. He also makes the extraordinary statement in view of what had happened in the past that the earl was 'to leave all his friends and living in order and to the charge of Glenorchy'. Nicolson metaphorically shook his head when he wrote, 'I suspect he [Argyll] grows strange because he was no way regarded'.

The earl must have lost all hope of preferment at King James's hands to leave Scotland at this time. For Nicolson encloses in his letter a copy of a proclamation issued by the king forbidding his subjects in the Highlands and Islands to travel to Ireland to assist Tyrone and O Donnell and take part with them 'in all their seditious conspiracies against the Queen, his dearest sister, their sovereign'. The inhabitants of the west-coast lowlands were also forbidden to furnish the rebels with 'victual, powder, bullet, armour and all other munitions for the war'.[25] James had at last come off the fence. The queen's furious letter and Nicolson's nagging had achieved their aim.

Ten days later Nicolson wrote again to Lord Burghley, enclosing a note written from Duart on 15 March from John Auchinross who had 'gone to his master and is not yet returned'. Auchinross had taken with him an offer from Burghley, which does not appear to have survived but which evidently included an offer to Maclean along the lines of Nicolson's previous letter.

Auchinross's note answered Nicolson's request for information about the Isles. As he suspected, MacSorley was not England's man but Tyrone's. 'Ye shall understand', he wrote, 'that Sir James McSorley at his being last at Court with his Majesty did send letters direct from the earl of Tyrone and himself to Macleod and Donald Gorme MacConnell desiring their aid this summer, as also to travail with Maclean my master to pak up the quarrel betwixt the earl and him'.

Maclean had stated that he had not decided what course to follow but that he would make up his mind by 1 April. 'It is of truth', Auchinross continued, 'that Macleod is to be at him again within ten or twelve days to what effect I know not. I understand that there is further commission directed from the earl now of new since the passing here of Sir James MacSorley.'

The suggestion that Lachlan was considering assassinating O Neill should have convinced London that his hatred of the earl was greater than his desire for 'entertainment'. For once Tyrone was dead there would be no need for his men. The rebellion would collapse. Maclean's desire for revenge for his cousin's execution at Tyrone's hands was an obsession as great as Nicolson's to employ him.

Auchinross goes on to the detail of establishing a 'strength' at Lough Foyle, 'which may be done with little help seeing the ground of good strengths is there. And we think that our being there a month with some of yours with us having [pioneers] ... this strength may be good. So we understand having a ship and a little pinnace and their ordnance with us this strength may be made and in the meantime our men to run forays to trouble the country'. He goes on to repeat Sir Lachlan's earlier plan to have a joint offensive co-ordinated with an advance by the English from the Pale.

Once the firm base was established at Lough Foyle, it would need only 2–300 men to hold it. The remainder with the use of 'a pinnace' and their galleys would have the necessary mobility 'to direct of their number sometimes to land on one port, sometimes on another port on the sides of Lough Foyle as vantages and occasions may be had, this form would touch the earl to the heart and trouble him so that by our opinion a mean or other would be had to make you quit of him'.

Nicolson had asked Burghley to make certain that no word of the agreement with Maclean reached George Archibald. George was the brother and messenger of Mr John Archibald, Glenorchy's private secretary. Glenorchy, who was now to Nicolson's surprise in control of the Campbells, had been in communication with Bowes. He is 'a very honest and honourable gentleman of great wealth, credit and power', wrote Nicolson to Burghley on 16 March. Black Duncan was a consummate intriguer. He had been described as 'a cultivated barbarian of colossal energy'. He planted innumerable trees on his vast estate, both for timber and ornament. He built the castles of Finlanrig, Achallader and Barcaldine, remodelled Kilchurn Castle on Loch Awe and built substantial houses at Lochdochart and Benderloch. He bred horses, was a keen falconer, wrote poetry and in addition to his native Gaelic and Scots spoke French and Italian. He sired seventeen children by his two wives and also had several bastards. This remarkable man was now Nicolson's agent and Sir Lachlan's rival in producing mercenaries to serve Elizabeth.

On 29 March George Nicolson wrote to Lord Burghley 'that the islanders come not in, neither give their obedience, looking for trouble between her Majesty and the King and for changes in the Court here to occupy the King so as he cannot attend them'. He goes on to say that 'Argyll is not gone yet but may possibly be stayed to help these matters'.

One of those who was watching to see which way the wind would blow was Donald Gorm of Sleat, who was writing to the queen for recognition as lord of the Isles and 'for renewing the old bond he has ... between her Majesty's predecessors and his'. If Elizabeth and James did not come to any agreement Donald Gorm believed he was safe to pursue his own ends without interference from Edinburgh. He was also at war with Mackenzie. The latter, whose sister had married Maclean's eldest son, had recently executed the latter's cousin Torquil Dubh Macleod of Lewis. The Northern Isles were in an uproar. It was against this background that Rory Mor Macleod of Harris was negotiating with Maclean to persuade him to join Tyrone. By mid-April Auchinross was back in Edinburgh and was demanding, in Maclean's name, to know whether he would be employed or not.

Auchinross had received Nicolson's most recent letter after he had left Duart. As a result he turned back to discuss its contents with Maclean, who sent his 'most humble thanks to her Majesty for remembering him' and asked that his pension might be sent to him in whatever 'quantity her Highness likes'. Once the pension arrived Sir Lachlan had instructed Auchinross to be 'easy in his other pay, seeing his own particular against Tyrone will move him to be ready in his pursuit'. He goes on in veiled speech to discuss 'that service that I wrote to you last'. There can be little doubt that he is talking of the plan to assassinate Tyrone. In that too he had given Auchinross 'full commission to deal with you in the special and in the particular of that service, wherein her Majesty will find great ease ...'[26]

Nicolson's letter to Burghley also enclosed an offer of service from Donald Gorm describing himself as 'Lord of the Isles of Scotland and Chief of the whole Clandonell Irishmen, wheresoever, whom the whole chiefs and captains of the clans undermentioned are faithfully bound, obliged and sworn to follow, serve, obey and assist with all their powers and forces in whatever his attempts and enterprises, that is to say:

the Captain of the whole Clanranald
the laird of Glengarry,
the laird MacRanald in Lochaber.
the Captain of Clan Cameron

the laird Macian of Ardnamurchan,
the laird Mackinnon of Strathardle.
Neil Macleod, Tutor of Lewis and brother german to the deceased
Torquil dow Macleod of Lewis, lately betrayed and murdered
by the craft and mean of Mackenzie of Kintail.

With to which Donald Gorme also are faithfully bonded and confederate
the laird Macleod of Dunvegan and Harris, brother-in-law to said Donald
and Sir James MacDonnell, elder son lawful of Angus MacDonnell of
Dunnyveg and Glens, now through his unnatural behaviour towards his
said son detained captive to the said son'.

This extraordinary communication contained an offer of service to
the queen including making 'defections from his Majesty's obedience
and laws'. He offered to stir up rebellion and trouble throughout Scotland
against James and to serve Elizabeth in Ireland. He was, he claims,
'privy to the earl of Tyrone's late secret course and practises here with
his Majesty of Scotland, in whose favour the earl of huntly dealt very
earnestly and secretly with his Majesty to have Tyrone's suit granted ...'

He also claimed to be able to discover the dealings and intentions of
the three late restored earls Huntly, Angus and Errol, 'who have got
themselves (by his Majesty's special care and politic industry) received
again in the bosom of the Church in Scotland, meaning nothing less in
their hearts than that which they have outwardly in the eyes of the
world accomplished ...' He also was able 'to learn some of the Spanish
special and privy practises and intentions against her Majesty ... through
the very special credit, entire friendship and familiarity I have with Mr
James Gordon, Jesuit ... and with divers the Scots papists, Jesuits and
seminary priests, whose diabolical, pestiferous and anti-Christian courses,
practises and intentions I hate now with all my heart and soul, I protest
now before God and his angels': a statement that must have raised a
puritan Cecil eyebrow.

The whole offer sounds as though it was dictated during one of
Donald Gorm's celebrated visits to one of his tenants. His delusions of
potency were soon to be thwarted when he sent home his wife to her
brother Rory Macleod of Harris. According to tradition she had only
one eye. With what sounds like alcoholic bravado Donald Gorm sent
her home riding on a one-eyed horse, attended by a one-eyed man and
a one-eyed dog. Rory Mor is said to have sent back a message to Donald
Gorm, saying that when his sister had married him they had forgotten
to have a wedding bonfire. He would see that a blaze would mark its
dissolution. He then called out his men and raided Trotternish. In
reprisal Donald Gorm raided Harris, where he carried off a large booty

of cattle. In turn Rory Mor raided Uist, even taking goods out of the precinct of the church at Carinish which the people considered a sanctuary.[27] Donald Gorm was a dangerous lunatic and had stirred up a hornets' nest.

On 16 April 1598 Nicolson was sent a questionnaire to answer from London. He must have wondered if anyone ever read his reports when he had to answer such questions as:

Questions to be answered for the Isles of Scotland

First, what part of the same belongs to the earl of Argyll?
Item. Who rules the people in them under him?
Item. Who is the owner and commander of the Isle of Bute and what fort and castle is in the same?
Who has the rule and possession of Kintyre and what castles or strength is in the same?
In what island Maclean's possessions are and with whom is he married and what children he has?
In what place does Angus MacConnel inhabit and with whom is he married and what children has he?
Where has James MacConnel any lands in the Islands?
What kin is Sorley Buy to James MacConnell?
How are the Lords of the Islands in concord and discord among themselves and how are they divided into factions?
Who is that claims to be Lord of the whole Isles?
Who has the rule of Islay and who has the rule of Mull?
To whom does the castle of Dunaverty belong in Kintyre?
What Scottishmen inhabit Rathlin?
Where does the lord of Glenorchy dwell?
How long have the 2 Campbells been conversant with the earl of Tyrone?
What call you the laird's son that shall come into England?
Where does John Archibald dwell in Ireland?

On 27 April Sir Robert Cecil, who had evidently read Donald Gorm's offer, wrote to Nicolson: 'I have of late received divers letters from you containing offers made to her Majesty of great service to be done by Maclean and others of the islands of Scotland against Tyrone and other the rebels there which require some further consultation for acceptance thereof then at this present I can give you but with in a few days I hope to give you some good answer thereto ...' Nicolson must have groaned but at least he would have been pleased to read further when Cecil writes 'I have paid to one Craven, as you may perceive by his own letter herewith sent 150 lib. of your entertainment ...'[28]

*   *   *   *

On 2 May George Nicolson at last was able to write that the 'earl of Argyll is passed through this town ...' He adds that he 'may be acknowledged in court with favour and thanked for his good will shown her Majesty anent her Irish causes ...' He might also be interrogated about the 'ambassadors, as they were termed in Argyle [who] were lately with his lordship from her Majesty's rebels of Ireland, O Donnell and others, that his lordship may be courteously moved to discover for her Majesty's service their negotiations with him and his answer to them'.

The dean of Limerick had been with Argyll when he met O Donnell's 'ambassadors'. He told Nicolson that the earl's reply 'was wise and honest'. It had been planned that the dean should accompany Argyll on his travels. This had not happened, perhaps through the influence of the countess of Argyll who loathed Denis Campbell.

On 11 May Cecil again wrote to Nicolson to say he had heard from Glenorchy. He was to be told that 'her Majesty accepts his good offer'. Cecil had written three or four lines to the laird himself. His offer to send someone into Ireland 'to discover secrets' was not however acceptable as this was the specific responsibility of the lord deputy.

Some time later John Archibald, Glenorchy's man of business, announced that his master had 'made publish in the whole counties of Argyll, Lorn and all the remaining Highlands that none ... pass into Ireland under pain of death'. Glenorchy was already exercising his new powers.

Communication between the rebels and James VI continued to excite Nicolson's concern. On 9 June he reported that 'a Scotsman came out of Ireland from MacSorley with letters, to what effect I know not. But I hear the King read the letters in his bed that night and was very glad, saying he should have answer the next day'. In fact he did not do so but did instruct his secretary to write to the rebels to have nothing to do with Angus's bastard son Archibald (Gillespic Dubh). Nicolson also reported that Maclean might be persuaded to help Angus's son James against MacSorley. He went on to say he had but one life 'and that if her Majesty employ Maclean I will peril [it] in the service, for I know the party (i.e. Maclean) to be of power and fortunate and wonderful constant and honest. And sure it could not be an especial policy and service for her Majesty to have the islanders once in blood with the rebels'.

Angus had at last been delivered up by his son Sir James and was, by 12 June, imprisoned in Dumbarton Castle. 'I have been dealt with by this young man that delivered his father', wrote Roger Aston to Cecil, 'not only to be his friend here but also to be a mean to her Majesty for him that by her favour and assistance he may attain too those lands in Ireland which his father had before called the Glens now possessed by MacSorley, her Majesty's rebel. So soon as that young man had settled his turns he means to make all the force he may against McSorley. I entertain this by all means I may. By this her Majesty loses nothing.'

Sir James himself wrote to the king in June that his bastard brother who held Dunyvaig for their father 'is gone to McSorley and that McSorley, O Donnell and O Neill agree to assist him'. The king was extremely irritated but heard later that McSorley would do nothing without the king's authority.

John Auchinross was giving up hope of the English honouring their pledges. On 17 June he wrote to George Nicolson: 'Ye know what affection my master felt for her Majesty's service against Tyrone, what was promised and of his receipt and how I made him content with Sir Robert's promise. Ye also know what commission ye had to travail with him for attending and waiting on service which he according thereto has ever stayit his own men and others of the Isles from the aid of Tyrone ... Now he craves with diligence of you to let him know what succeeds and follows the former promise of Sir Robert ... If her Majesty craves service of him against Tyrone her Highness may have the same. If not, he understands that Sir Robert's promise and your warrant should be acknowledged accordingly, whereof he craves to be resolved shortly since with his charges he has done his duty'.

Things in Ireland were moving to a climax. On 25 July Nicolson reported 'there are such speeches of Irish matters as grieve to hear. McSorley is the earl's lieutenant, that they have great musters of the field, that they triumph and either are lying about Carrickfergus and will be to besiege it ... and think in short time now to put out the English from that country'.

Nicolson wrote one last desperate appeal to Cecil to employ Maclean. On 31 July he wrote, 'he is the one man of this nation without exception of any (save the King who must command him if he do anything) that will do the best service if he be employed. If he have no answer, he will account himself free of his offers. He has a thousand men presently ready'. Some of the Scots Council had asked Nicolson if Maclean was going to Ireland in the queen's service. 'I say plainly not that I know of.'

On 2 August he wrote again. 'Yesterday I received your Honour's letter of the 25th of the last understanding thereby *that the resolution anent Maclean is deferred* and Irish courses also for any great prosecution till the next spring. Indeed the year is far spent yet the party being ready with great forces which were judged here to be for her majesty's service may have gud time yet for incursions against the earl, both to trouble and harm the traitors to the drawing of them together by the ears and to give her Majesty a trial what Maclean may do and what his service is worth ... what he will now do I know not. But I judge that except he be satisfied anent that which he looked [for] ... he will not deal I suspect but run other courses, it being said here that O Donnell has sent him 19 horses and other things of worth ...'

Nicolson played his last card when he wrote without using veiled speech that 'Maclean, if he be used I know hopes to stir some of the best about to Tyrone to assault his life'. Cecil's clerk noted that: 'Maclean ready with great forces 200 lib. to be sent to Maclean and 100 crowns to Auchinross. He desires his suit to be remembered. This to be answered before the 20th'. Cecil himself probably underlined certain passages in the letter which was in fact answered by 10 August. It was too late. By nightfall on 5 August 1598 Sir Lachlan Mor Maclean, 'Great Maclean of Duart', was dead.

A week later at the Battle of the Yellow Ford, near Armagh, the English army suffered the worst defeat it was ever to experience in Ireland. Nicolson might have been excused if he had said I told you so.

Notes

1. *CSP Scot.* xii, 436–38.
2. *CSP Ireland* vi, 232.
3. *Ibid,* 227.
4. *Ibid,* 199.
5. *Ibid,* 200.
6. *CSP Spain* 1587–1603, ix.
7. *CSP Scot.* xii, 507.
8. *Ibid.*
9. *Ibid* xiii, 21.
10. *Ibid,* 48.
11. *CSP Ireland* vi, 310, 343.
12. *Ibid,* 364.
13. *CSP Scot.* xiii, 73, 75, 88, 95, 120, 126, 127.
14. *RPC* v, 427.
15. *CSP Scot.* xiii, 135, 136, 138.
16. Gregory, 275–6.

17. *RPC* v, Ixxvi
18. NLS. MS. Acc. 7609.
19. *CSP Scot.* xiii, 138.
20. *Ibid*, 148–9.
21. *Ibid*, 138.
22. *Ibid*, 165, 168.
23. Robert Pitcairn, *Criminal Trials in Scotland from 1488 to 1624* (1833), 6–7.
24. *CSP Scot.* xiii, 168.
25. *Ibid*, 172.
26. *Ibid*, 196.
27. I. F. Grant, *The Macleods* (1959), 196–97.
28. *CSP Scot.* xiii, 198.

CHAPTER 21

The Battle of *Tràigh Ghruinneart,* 5 August 1598

Sergeant ... The merciless Macdonwald -
Worthy to be a rebel, for, to that,
The multiplying villanies of nature
Do swarm upon him – from the western Isles
Of kerns and gallowglasses is supplied;
And fortune, on his damned quarrel smiling,
Show'd like a rebel's whore.

Macbeth Act I, Scene ii

On 5 August Sir Lachlan Mor landed on the beach at the head of Loch Gruinart in Islay. He came to have a meeting with his nephew Sir James Macdonald of Knockrinsay, Angus's son. A fight took place. Maclean was killed. These are the bare facts of an incident of which every Gael in Islay still knows something, even today. Nothing else about it is certain. Within a week of the battle contradictory reports of what had happened were circulating throughout Scotland.

No eye-witness account of the battle has survived. In order to attempt to unravel what happened it is necessary to examine all the evidence, including traditional stories about the battle which were passed on by word of mouth to their descendants by those in Islay who had taken part. One recent *seanachaidh* in Islay was the late Gilbert .Clark, Port Charlotte, who helped field workers from Edinburgh University's School of Scottish Studies who visited the island. He heard his stories from many different people and remembered details from each of them. His version of the battle of *Tràigh Ghruinneart* was recorded in Gaelic by Ian A Fraser in 1968 and translated by D. A. MacDonald and Alan Bruford. It was printed in *Tocher* in 1992.

Clark starts by telling of events in Islay during the earlier stages of the Maclean-Macdonald feud. He goes on to say that after that the dispute got even worse. 'Lachainn Mór gathered the host and the ships of Mull to take Islay by force. The MacDonalds in Islay did as best

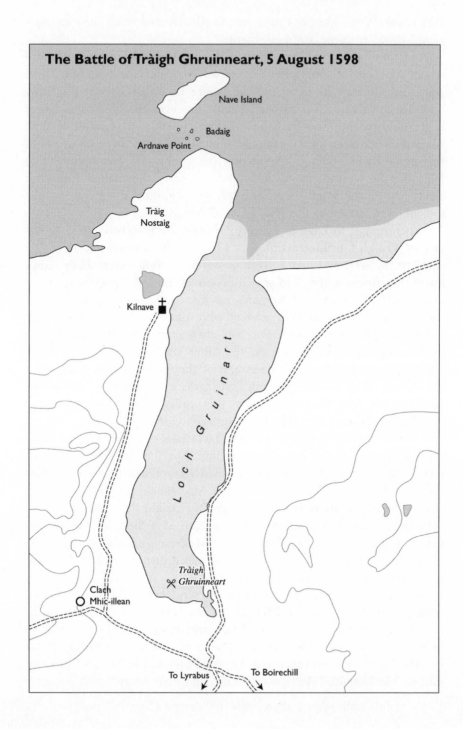

The Battle of Tràigh Ghruinneart, 5 August 1598

Nave Island

Badaig

Ardnave Point

Tràig Nostaig

Kilnave

Loch Gruinart

Tràigh Ghruinneart

Clach Mhic-illean

To Lyrabus   To Boirechill

they could. Word went out to Arran, to Kintyre and to all their kinsfolk round about to come and help them.

'And there was a witch – they called her the Doideag Mhuileach – whom Maclean of Duart kept as an adviser, and she told him there were three things he must not do, before he sailed against the Islay men. He must not ... or rather he must go three times sunwise round a green knoll that was in front of Duart Castle, but instead of that, Maclean went clean against the old woman and went three times round this mound widdershins. The second thing: she told him if he got to Islay that he was not to put into land at a place they called *Nòstaig*, a sandy bay on the North-West of Islay. And the third thing, not to take a drink of water from the *Well of Niall Neònach*.

'When he got to Islay he put into *Nòstaig*. He marched across to the side of Traigh Ghruinneart: it was a hot day in autumn and they just came to the well and had a drink of water ... well water. They didn't know that this was the *Well of Niall Neònach*. But all three things were done contrary to the old woman's advice. And there was a fourth. I don't know if it was the old woman who told him this or who it was: not to raise his standard on *Cnoc nan Aighean*, and he did that too.

'Anyway, the MacDonalds on the other side were gathering every man they could. They had MacAoidh of the Rinns, a man famous for his skill at arms; and the Ollamh Ìleach was a famous physician to the MacDonalds. And there was a man they called Mac a Phrior: he was well-known as a soothsayer, like Coinneach Odhar [the 'Brahan Seer'] and men of that sort. And he said to MacDonald – he told him he could tell him how the day would go for him, but that he would have to promise him a piece of land that they called Seann Fheòirlinn – *Sunderland* we call it today – and *Coul*, as a reward. MacDonald promised faithfully that if the day went well for him they [sic] could have that.

'Well, the battle was joined and it seemed as if the Islay men would have the worst of the day, because the Mull men were above them on high ground. But as the battle went on more men arrived to help the Islay men.

'And there was a little man there – a wretched little man who had come across from Jura, and he offered his services to Lachainn Mór. And Lachainn Mór turned round and said that he could not bear to look at such a miserable creature among his men. This enraged this wretched little man so much that he went over to the MacDonalds and said to MacDonald, "Will you take me into your army?"

"I certainly will, even if there were a thousand like you".'

"Well", Dubh-Sìdh said ... that was what they called this little man, Dubh-Sìdh – a Shaw from Jura and Dubh-Sìdh said to MacDonald: "If you take care of all the rest of the Mull men, I'll look after Lachainn Mór myself".

And I'll tell you later how this happened.

'The battle began. As I've said ... the Mull men were up on the high ground and the Islay men were down below. Anyway the Arran men arrived to help them, and this is what they did because they were late: they came to land at Portnahaven ... and they marched up by the side of the loch and up by a place they called *Boirechill,* this side of Traigh Ghruinneart: and what should they come upon but a party of the Mull men down below them, away from the battlefield. I don't know what the Mull men were doing there, about two miles away from the battle-field. But the Arran men came upon them unawares and killed every single one of them. And to this day they call that place *Torr na Muileach* [the Mull Men's Mound], at the back of Lyrabus.

'Well, when Lachainn Mór and his men saw this band approaching, they thought there was a great host there and their courage began to fail them and they moved down to a place they call *Sliabh a Chath* [the Battle Brae] and the Islay men got a better chance to get a footing up on firm ground.

'And there were trees, patches of woodland there at the time, and this Dubh-Sìdh climbed up into one of the trees – and the day was hot. Maclean of Duart took off the steel armour that was protecting ... his breast, and he bent down over the well to have a drink of water. As he stood up Dubh-Sìdh planted an arrow in his breast and killed him.

'And the army, his army, panicked now and they fled, and they came to a church with the Islay men in pursuit – they came to the old church of *Kilnave,* a few miles down beyond Sliabh a Chath. They went in there thinking they would be in sanctuary but the Islay men had gone berserk so that they set fire to the church, and every man who was in there was burnt to death except for one who managed to escape. And the Islay men were after him, but he must have been pretty fast: he managed to keep ahead of them. He swam out to sea near Nave Island – and there's an islet there – with an arrow in his thigh. He swam out till he reached this islet they call *Badaig* and he stayed there, at the back of the islet, till the Islay men had gone away. And he came ashore then and he stayed on in Islay ever after, and we still have people whom they call to this day Clann Mhuirich na Badaig ... the Curries of Badaig.

'But I've got ahead of my story. I should have told you about ... how the Arran men got on.

'When Lachainn Mór fell and the battle was over, one of the Arran men came along, Angus MacDonald, a near kinsman to MacDonald of Islay. He saw a fine ring on Lachainn Mór's finger. He bent down to pull his ring off but the ring was so tight that he couldn't get it off. He cut off the finger. And one of the Mull men was lying near him. This man was still alive and this infuriated him so much that it gave him a burst of strength, the Mull man, and he reared up and planted an arrow in Angus MacDonald and killed him. They carried off the body of Angus MacDonald ...

'Well, in those days it was the custom among the Gaels – the Highland clans – that their closest female relatives were by them on the battlefield. And so it was with Lachainn Mór: he had his foster-mother and her son with him when he came ... The day after the battle, when things had settled down, his foster-mother and her son Duncan brought a slype and a horse to take Lachainn to *Kilchoman* and bury him in the High Church of Kilchoman. Now the man was so big and massive that his feet were sticking out at the front of the slype and his head was jolting from side to side at the other end. Duncan began to make sport of it – laughing. His mother asked him what he was on about. He said:

What a come-down for Lachainn Mór – lying there on his back nodding to and fro like that!

This made his mother so furious that she drew a knife and killed her own son. That's the place they call *Carn Dhonnchaidh* [Duncan's Cairn] to this day, a little settlement where there were a lot of crofters at the time.

'Anyway his foster-mother went on with the few men she had with her and Lachainn Mór was buried at the west end of the High Church of Kilchoman. But tradition says that at that time the Church was different and that it was inside the Church that Lachainn was buried, though today the building being different, he lies outside the Church. And to this day they speak of the tombstone of Lachainn Mór of the Two Hearts. There's a great stone slab there. I'm sure that it's an hour-glass that's on it, though the people believed that it was two hearts that were carved on this slab.

'And when everything had settled down the Ollamh Ìleach was given a great reward and MacAoidh of the Rinns was rewarded for his services, and this Mac a Phrior, he got the estate of ... Coul and Sunderland and these two pieces of land were held separately from the rest ... of this part of the island till a few years ago. That piece of land had a separate proprietor.

'And, as I've said before, the Arran men, instead of going back to Portnahaven and taking the boats they had left there back to Arran, they crossed the moors and got boats on the other side of the island to take them across to the mainland, and from there they could get over to Arran.'

It should be pointed out that all these stories have appeared elsewhere either in print or in manuscript collections. For instance, Sir Robert Gordon of Gordonstoun has the stories concerning the witch's warnings in his account written in 1639 and published in 1813. A. Maclean Sinclair has the story of Dubh Sìth the marksman from Jura.[1] Whilst the story of the simple young man who mocked Lachlan Mor's corpse appears in Donald Macdonald's unpublished manuscript of 1826.[2] They could therefore be based on literary accounts rather than genuine oral tradition. Much of the detail of the battle however could only come from local people.

Dr Hector Maclean's version of events is slightly different to the Islay story. He claims that after Angus had executed Lachlan Mor's uncle John Dubh, the king gave him a commission of fire and sword against Macdonald. He also ordered Macleod and Locheil to assist him and together they burnt the whole of Islay. Angus locked himself up in Dunyvaig and resolved to buy peace by giving Maclean half the island.

He goes on to say: 'The best harbour in the island of Islay is called Port Ascaig, this place Maclean would have with his division of the island, as being the most convenient harbour for landing from any part of his estate, it was also the most convenient for the other parts of Macdonald's property, who would not upon that account give it away, so disagreeing upon the matter, they appointed to meet sometime thereafter to adjust the difference in a friendly manner; accordingly Lauchlan Mor went to Islay again on the day appointed, with his eldest son and his whole clan, landing in an island called Island Niave, where he left his son and men except some seven score who accompanied him to Gruinart being the place appointed, from whence he sent his proposals to Macdonald.

'Macdonald sent back some of his gentlemen with an answer and ordered them at the same time to observe how Maclean was guarded, they seeing his men few in number and observing the boats of those upon the island ebbed beyond the possibility of being launched, owing to the length of the shore, the depth of the sands and the bulk of the galleys, returned to Macdonald telling him that now or never was his time to be up sides with Lauchlan Mor, upon which he attacked him with all his Islay men, those of Kintyre being not yet come up.

'Maclean made a brave resistance and obliged the Macdonalds to give ground three different times, at last the Kintyre men coming up, over-powered Maclean and his small party, he himself being shot in the belly through his steel targe, the greatest number of his men were cut to pieces around him, chusing rather to die bravely than survive their beloved chief and master, the few that survived could not launch their boats and go to the island, but were obliged to fly to other places from whence they could not get safe passage home.

'Thus in the year 1598 fell the brave Lauchlan Mor, the scourge of the Macdonalds, much lamented by his neighbours ...'[3] This account concertinas the events that led up to the battle and is obviously wrong. The actual details of the battle itself do not really contradict anything in the Islay account.

The core of both stories is the generally accepted one that the cause of the dispute concerned land in Islay. Sir Robert Gordon says that it was caused by Maclean's 'covetous ambition'. As a Gordon, Gordonstoun had no love for Maclean, who he says 'haveing some credit at Court ...' had purchased 'the inheritance of the whole Ile of Ila ... being alwyse hitherto the possession and inheritance of the Clandonald; all which MacKlain did now think to bring easalie to passe, Sir James Mackdonald (the just inheritor thereof) being young and his father Angus Mackdonald being aged. So MacKlain assembleth his whole tryb, and their assisters, and in a warlyke maner invadeth Ila ...'[4]

Gregory accepts the statement that Sir Lachlan had procured a grant from the king of part of Islay, forfeited by his old rival Angus Macdonald. This opinion is supported by an entry in a letter from Robert Bowes to Lord Burghley dated 26 March 1596. He reports that Angus's son Sir James had 'made a suit to the King that his father might have ... such possessions of the King's in the Isles as MacConnell's ancestors before held and occupied'. Maclean however was also interested 'and composition directed to be before the King and Council the 15th of May next. The King favours Maclean and others seek his contentment. There-fore MacConnell's suit has not prevailed ...'[5] Angus had not given up. On 8 June Bowes reported that Maclean was 'hindered in his suit to the King and Council by means of Lord John Hamilton labouring in the favour of MacConnells against Maclean'.[6] Maclean therefore levied his vassals, proceeded to Islay to expel the Macdonalds 'and put himself in possession of his new acquisitions in the island'.[7] Unfortunately details of the land granted to Lachlan Mor have not survived.

On the face of it this scenario appears to be quite acceptable. The Macleans had been trying to obtain the Rinns of Islay for at least fifty years. There is however other contemporary evidence which makes the generally accepted version suspect and puts events in a more sinister light.

✻   ✻   ✻   ✻

News of Lachlan Mor's death quickly reached Edinburgh. On 7 August the English agent known as 'Pater' wrote to Nicolson. He says on the previous day: 'I received advertisement from a friend declaring that Maclean being in Islay ... at a tryst appointed betwixt him and Sir James, Angus's son, under trust and promise is slain together with his second son and all the principals of his surname ...' He goes on to say that 'James McSorley had directed out of Ireland four hundred men who were the principal executors of this conspiracy ...'

'Pater' was none other than Duncan Campbell of Glenorchy. Nicolson sent his letter straight to Cecil. In his covering letter he writes: 'If Maclean be slain the 'platte' is greater than I dare guess at', and that 'sundry wise men suspect the time now to be very dangerous'.[8] The Scots word 'platte' is a plan for a villainous act. In the sixteenth century however it is probably meant no more than a plan. (I am grateful to Hiram Morgan for this information. He also points out that the murder of Sir Lachlan is reminiscent of the Macdonalds' killing of Sean O Neill in 1567.)

Others thought differently. The king had received a report of what had happened by 15 August, when John Cunningham, the Edinburgh burgess, took a younger son of Lachlan Mor's, who was at school in Edinburgh, to Leith to see James with a petition. The king denied that Maclean had been slain treacherously and said 'it was well fought on both sides'. He would not hear a word about Lachlan Mor being 'slain under tryst and trust', and although he told the boy that he was sorry for him he refused to read the petition, 'saying he would hear no more of it then'.[9] James evidently considered that Sir Lachlan was a casualty in a feud. Neil Mor's murder was probably regarded in the same light. Feud, as we have seen, was still considered to be a legitimate method of obtaining justice.

Yet the timing of James's cavalier attitude to Sir Lachlan's death is curious. In May 1598 it had been observed that there were more feuds in Scotland than there had been for twenty years. The situation was considered to be so bad and royal officials were so frustrated by the king's erratic attention to the problem, that they threatened resignation. As a result the king was sufficiently alarmed to announce that the convention of the estates planned for June 1598 would discuss feuding, and James 'plunged into a bout of work in preparation for it'.[10]

The convention met at Holyrood House on 29 June. Before it met formally the king spent some time in an attempt to mediate between noblemen at feud, who threatened to obstruct the proposed legislation in order to protect their own interests.

After much discussion the opposition forced a vote and it was only by a majority, rather than the unanimous acceptance hoped for by the king, that the 'Act Anent Removing and Extinguishing of Deadlie Feuds' became law.

The act decreed that those at feud appeared before the king and the privy council and that arbitrators were appointed. Feuds were divided into three categories: (1) where there had been no slaughter on either side; (2) slaughter on one side; (3) slaughter on both sides.[11] If the killing of Sir Lachlan was considered the start of a new feud and fell into the second category, it was one in which the crown reserved the right to intervene. Revenge was not left to the offended party, i.e. the Macleans. Yet the crown appears to have done nothing, unless it was referred to the sheriff court of Argyll whose records for this period no longer appear to exist.

By 16 August Nicolson had more damning evidence that there had been a plot to kill Maclean. Apparently Sir James had frequently been writing to his uncle for advice and had invited him to come to Islay to settle 'all questions anent Maclean's lands there'. He had also invited his uncle to appoint the day he should come to Islay and to bring only 200 men with him. Maclean, suspecting nothing, had arrived 'clad in silk without armour and nothing about him but a rapier which Argyll his cousin had given him and a pistol'. He was hardly prepared for war. Nor were 'the best of his kin and his second son', who accompanied him.

According to Nicolson's informant, Lachlan continued to suspect nothing as Sir James appeared to have fewer men with him than he himself had. He did however use third parties to carry out negotiations with Sir James and they spent the day going from one side to the other. At 7 p. m. they had virtually come to an agreement, when Sir James changed his position and sent his uncle a message that 'all was for nought, [and] willing him to do for himself'. At the same time the Macdonalds attacked, leaving Sir Lachlan no time to withdraw. Sir Lachlan and his companies however fought back 'which they did so valiantly' that they put Sir James's men to flight, Lachlan Mor himself killing three of them with his rapier. The Macdonalds however had other men hidden who now charged. Sir Lachlan, seeing his position was desperate, ordered his son to 'begone and save himself and revenge his death'. Maclean himself and his few friends stood their ground and fought to the death. They killed 40 of Sir James's men before Sir Lachlan himself was shot. Then 'Maclean's bowmen seeing Maclean fall, being shot to death, fled, otherways they of Sir James's for all their provision had had more loss ...'[12]

A contemporary source concerning the murder is in Mr David Calderwood's *History*. He notes: 'Upon the 4th of August, Macklaine, with a number of his friends, were slaine treacherouslie by Sir James Mackoneill, his owne sister sonne, being invited to a tryst by the said Sir James, under pretence to setl marches for dividing of their lands'.[13]

Calderwood goes on to say: 'It was constantlie reported, that he [Maclean] was hounded out by the King', i.e. his death was incited by the king, 'for the King never lyked of Macklaine after the 17th day of December'. Calderwood claimed 'the suspicion was confirmed afterwards, in that there was no execution of justice for so villanous a fact'.

That Sir James was never prosecuted for Lachlan Mor's death is certainly apparent from details of his trial in 1609. Sir James was condemned for his treatment of his parents at Askomel and for escaping from prison.[14] Nothing is said about the slaughter on the sands at the head of Loch Gruinart.

The king certainly has a case to answer. Nicolson confirmed that the king disliked Maclean. In his letter to Cecil on 15 August he wrote: 'I hear the King loved not Maclean for three causes: first, for being with the earl of Argyll against Huntly ... 2, because Maclean the 17th December rode post to fetch the earl of Argyll to have assisted the Kirk ... 3, because he heard he was dealing with the Queen to serve her'.[15] The second and third causes of the king's dislike of Maclean are perhaps understandable. Lachlan Mor, despite his flowery rhetoric, had sided with the Kirk against the king.

He had also agreed to serve a 'foreign' monarch in preference to his native king. The first cause is on the face of things inexplicable, for Lachlan Mor had been fighting for the king against his own rebels.

The first reason behind James's dislike of Lachlan Mor goes to the heart of the tortuous politics of late sixteenth-century Scotland, perhaps even shedding some light on James VI's own character. It may also explain why Lachlan Mor was murdered.

King James VI was something of a scholar and was the author of several books. In 1598 he completed his most famous work, *Basilikon Doron*. It was written in Middle Scots. The original manuscript, in the

king's own hand, still survives and is held in the British Library.[16] Seven
copies of an anglicised version were secretly printed in 1599. They were
distributed to James's relatives and close friends, amongst whom were
a group which comprised 'some of my trustiest servants'. Included
amongst them was George earl of Huntly and his fellow Roman Catholic
rebels. The point is that despite their religion these men 'were James's
friends. He knew them well, he dined, hunted and discussed affairs of
state with them. He and they were men of similar interests who shared
the same way of life, not two opposing or hostile parties'.[17] This was
particularly true of Huntly 'to whom James was personally devoted'.

The *Basilikon Doron* purports to be a book of advice written for
James's son and heir apparent, Prince Henry, who was four years old
at the time. It was a literary device of the time to address a book to a
prince, and the king perhaps hoped that his book would be widely read,
particularly in England. It has however recently been convincingly
argued that James in fact did write for himself. Jenny Wormald writes:
'Not the least of the clues is the manuscript of *Basilikon Doron* itself, a
delightful piece of evidence of an author scribbling, scoring out, scribbling again – and the whole lovely mess, which would call down the
wrath of any tutor were a student to present it as an essay, bound in
purple velvet, and stamped in gold leaf with thistles, the Scottish emblem,
and the royal initials, as befitted a King'.[18]

Nowhere in his book does James mention Machiavelli or his notorious
composition *The Prince*. He is also careful to reject Machiavellian teachings, for instance insisting that one king should keep the promises he
makes to another.[19] He was however sufficiently a man of his times 'to
use division and faction to his own ends'.

James was certainly not a closet Catholic. The bulk of his literary
labours was made up of controversial works aimed against Roman Catholicism. He also, latterly, rejected the thinking of Knox and Buchanan
and the *Basilikon Doron* upset Melville by its attack on Presbyterian
thinking which the king believed undermined the authority of a monarch.
By 1598 James was increasingly sympathetic with the church whose
head he would become if and when he inherited from Elizabeth. Until
he did he took a middle way between the threat from Catholic Spain
and the increasing intransigence of his Presbyterian subjects. The king
probably considered the threat to his position from the latter to be the
greater as early as 1592.

James's involvement in the murder plot that eliminated Moray and
Cawdor cannot be proved. It is however clear that he only acted against
the Roman Catholic earls in 1594 when pressure from the Kirk and

Elizabeth made it essential that he did something. His imprisonment of Argyll after Glenlivet and his attitude to Maclean make it seem more than likely that they acted more forcibly than he intended. That the victors of Glenlivet refused to face the king himself is further cause for suspicion.

James's letter to Huntly in 1596 telling him that he must submit and satisfy the Kirk or never 'be a Scotsman again', underlines the political expediency behind [20] the earl's return and helps to explain James's fury with both Argyll and Maclean for siding with the Kirk and almost thwarting the king's carefully laid plans to counter the ministers' position at the height of their 'impertinence'.

Towards the end of August 1598, Nicolson wrote: 'Some suspect Huntly to have been privy to the plot of Maclean's slaughter'.[21] That Huntly, or even James, was behind the events at Loch Gruinart is not impossible. It can hardly be doubted that Lachlan Mor's murder was carefully orchestrated and that he was lured to his death. The fact that he came without armour, with only a rapier to protect him, surely makes this likely. That he left most of his men on Nave Island, where they were unable to launch their galleys and come to his assistance, makes it certain. In his proposals to Cecil over a second front based on Lough Foyle Lachlan is adamant that he must have protection for his galleys. Once the tide went out they were left stranded like whales unable to reach the sea. No Hebridean would have made this mistake unless he came in peace, certain of his nephew's goodwill. What went wrong?

All accounts mention the arrival of a second party who turned the tide in favour of the Macdonalds. The traditional Islay version that they came from Arran is highly unlikely as we have seen that Sir James's grandfather had exchanged all his land in Arran for land in Kintyre. Were they, as Glenorchy suggested, Sir James MacSorley's men from Ireland? Certainly two of his men were in Edinburgh by 15 August.[22] Did they come from Islay?

Sir James MacSorley's brother Randal denied that any of 'MacSorley's bairns' had anything to do with Lachlan Mor's death. He made this statement when he sought Maclean's help in February 1601–2. In the weeks that followed the lord deputy Mountjoy's victory at Kinsale, Randal was desperate for any help he could get. His evidence is not the best but it is evidence.

At the time of Lachlan Mor's death Sir James MacSorley was a great favourite with King James, sending him hawks and cannon retrieved from an Armada wreck.

In a murder enquiry it is said that the investigator should discover who benefited from the victim's death. It is difficult to see what Sir James Macdonald of Knockrinsay had to gain. If, as Nicolson reported, Lachlan Mor had offered to help him regain the Glens, his estate in Ulster, from MacSorley, Sir James had much to lose from his uncle's death. On the other hand MacSorley and his ally Tyrone had everything to gain by Maclean's demise. Lachlan Mor's reputation was formidable. 'Maclean is the man that the Earl most fears', Nicolson wrote to Cecil on 1 July 1598. It is certain since Thornton's visit to Duart that O Neill's spies were aware of his negotiations with Cecil. They probably also would have known of his offer to open up a second front in Ulster at Lough Foyle.

An explanation of what caused the battle of *Tràigh Ghruinneart* perhaps lies in the actions immediately before it of Sir James Macdonald and his illegitimate half-brother Archibald. Sir James was a favourite at court during his time there as a pledge for his father's good behaviour. He was sent by the king to try and persuade his father to keep to his agreement with the commendator of Pittenweem, made in November 1596. He also obtained retrospective permission from the king to apprehend his father. This authority was signed on 8 August 1598, probably before news of the battle of *Tràigh Ghruinneart* reached Edinburgh. Sir James at this time was the king's man and an ally of Huntly.

Archibald, *Gillespick*, on the other hand was his father's man.[23] He was Angus's eldest son by 'Maria Macdonald, daughter of Alexander MacAonghusa of the gentry of Clann Donald'.[24] Archibald was 'a man of age and perfection', when his legitimate half-brothers were 'but young'. He was responsible for recruiting mercenaries for Tyrone and in 1596 was to be 'the General Colonel of all those companies to be brought by him to Ulster'.[25]

When Angus captured Dunyvaig from the king's servants, it was Archibald who actually occupied it with his men.[26] In June 1598 Sir James, who was still acting for the king, wrote to his master 'that his bastard brother that keeps Dunnyveg is gone to McSorley and that McSorley, O Donnell and O Neill agree to assist him'.

It is extraordinary that Archibald should have gone to MacSorley for assistance. His father's experience in the same circumstances was hardly propitious. When Angus had made the same journey in 1596, MacSorley had rightly interpreted Angus's action as a sign of weakness, occupied the Glens, declared that his cousin was illegitimate and claimed his whole estate.

Archibald and MacSorley were however former comrades in arms. Archibald was perhaps emotionally committed to Tyrone and believed that MacSorley would join him in defending Islay from what could be seen as a threat to the Scots Gaeltachd similar to what the confederates were facing in Ulster. Did Archibald return from Ulster determined to turn a peaceful meeting with Sir Lachlan Maclean into an assassination to prevent him from obtaining half of Islay and opening a second front against the confederates? It is the most likely explanation.

The king was furious when he received Sir James's letter. His anger was somewhat mollified when he heard later, about the end of July, that MacSorley 'will not agree with Angus's bastard without the King's mind first be known to him'. What the king's mind was, was revealed on 2 August when Nicolson wrote that he had heard that the king intended 'to send to the rebels (i.e. MacSorley etc.) to forbid them to aid Angus's bastard son'. If such a letter were sent it would have arrived too late.

On 4 August at the latest Archibald probably, and his men certainly, were back in Islay, for Nicolson specifically states that Sir James's Islay men at *Tràigh Gruinneart* consisted of 700 'of his bastard brother's men'. The two brothers were united against the Macleans. Nicolson adds, perhaps significantly, that Sir James had 'men out of Ireland' with him at the battle. These could either be Archibald's men who returned with him, or as Glenorchy reported, those that followed MacSorley. It is however unlikely that MacSorley would have blatantly defied the king at this moment and sent men to assist the Macdonald brothers. He had nothing to gain and a great deal to lose in antagonising James. He also had other things on his mind: the confederates were concentrating their forces to oppose Bagenal's column that set out on 7 August to relieve Armagh, a march that led to the English disaster at the Yellow Ford.

If MacSorley was not involved, it is unlikely that the king was guilty of any involvement in Lachlan Mor's murder. His subsequent actions however explain why he was suspected and there can be little doubt that he welcomed Maclean's demise. Nicolson reported on 15 August that the king was 'glad' at the result of the battle, fearing that Maclean had meant to have killed Sir James. Lachlan Mor's death brought a new situation into being in the Isles. On 26 August Nicolson reported that 'the King was almost never out of Council, devising how to reduce the islanders to his obedience and get his duties'. He goes on to say that James 'had much dealing with Angus and his wife (who cries out of Maclean's slaughter)'.

Angus and his wife were brought to the king from Dumbarton Castle where they had been imprisoned since Sir James delivered them there. Angus agreed that if his life was spared he should 'within 20 days cause his bastard son to deliver Dunnyveg', provided that Archibald was given 'some living to live and be style on'. Angus himself should 'enjoy his own'. Negotiations at Dumbarton between the king and Angus apparently took place whilst they were both on horseback. Nicolson, who was present, writes: 'Angus ... rides up and down with the King guarded with some of the duke of Lennox's men'. During their discussion James received news of the English disaster at the Yellow Ford. It was reported that MacSorley had been killed. Nicolson states: 'I said I was glad and would they were all so. He [the king] said to Angus that I said I would have them all slain. He [Angus] said he "trowed" me but he would all the English had been slain. I replied that then I wished them all indeed slain and though it were with my hands and all false traitors and rebels else. The king laughed and to end the matter said he would wish also, that so MacSorley were living he would that all rebels her Majesty, himself and the King of France had were hanged ...'

It was James's familiarity with Angus and the fact that he was not returned to Dumbarton Castle after this interview with the king but accompanied the lord treasurer to Cardonnell, that encouraged observers to suspect there was some hidden agenda in the king's dealings with the Macdonalds.

Dunyvaig did surrender and Archibald, who I think was the instigator of Sir Lachlan's death, was imprisoned with his father in Edinburgh. It cannot have been too rigorous an imprisonment. On 10 March 1598/9 at Holyrood House, Angus was able to make a grant to his wife for life of sizeable estates in both Kintyre and Islay.[27] Meanwhile when Sir James also arrived in Edinburgh he was seized and held at Falkland. In July 1599 he was sending messages to Huntly 'to come to relieve him'.[28]

It is possible that Lachlan Mor was as much a casualty of Tyrone's rebellion as was the earl's old enemy marshal Bagenal who died at the Battle of the Yellow Ford. Whether Huntly or even King James himself were parties to the murder cannot be proved. If James was involved, he was one of the greatest practitioners of Machiavellian politics in the sixteenth century.

Notes

1. *Clan Gillean*, 157–8.
2. *BCP.*
3. NLS MS 7609, 19–21
4. Gordonstoun, 237.
5. *CSP Scot.* xii, 175–176.

6. *Ibid,* 242
7. Gregory, 284.
8. *CSP Scot.* xiii, 255.
9. *Ibid,* 259.
10. Keith M. Brown, *Bloodfeud in Scotland,* 241–2.
11. *RPC* v (1592–1599), 462.
12. *Ibid,* 261–262.
13. *History of the Kirk of Scotland* (1844), 727.
14. Pitcairn iii, 6–7.
15. *CSP Scot.* xiii, 260.
16. BL Royal MS 18. B. xv.
17. Jennifer M. Brown, 'Scottish Politics 1567–1625', in Alan G. R. Smith (ed), *The Reign of James VI and I* (1973), 28.
18. Jenny Wormald, 'James VI and I, Basilikon Doron ...', in Linda Levy Peck (ed), *The Mental World of the Jacobean Court* (1991), 48.
19. Johann P. Sommerville, *King James VI and I. Political Writings* (Cambridge, 1994), xix.
20. A. I. Cameron (ed), *The Warrender Papers* (Scottish History Society, 1932), ii, 299–301.
21. *CSP Scot.* xiii, 274.
22. *CSP Scot.* xiii, 259.
23. *Ibid,* 267.
24. Kenneth Nicholls, 'Notes on the Genealogy of Clann Eoin Mhoir', *West Highland Notes & Queries* No. 8 (November 1991), 16.
25. *CSP Scot.* xii, 175.
26. *Ibid,* 221.
27. SRO PS1/70, H 232V–233R.
28. *CSP Scot.* xiii, 520.

CHAPTER 22

The Topical *Macbeth*

Macduff. O Banquo, Banquo
Our royal master's murder'd
Lady Macbeth. Woe, alas!
What, in our house?
Banquo. Too cruel, anywhere.

Macbeth Act II, Scene iii

Sir George Mackenzie of Rosehaugh, the seventeenth-century politician and legal historian, believed that Angus's treatment of the Macleans at Mulindry was instrumental in the passing of the statute 'Murder under Trust' in the first Act of the 1587 Parliament[1] which states:

> It is statute and ordaned, that the murther or slauchter of quhatsum ever Our sovereigne Lordis lieges, quhair the partie slaine is under the traist, credite, assurance or power of the slayer: Al sik murther and slauchter to be committed in time cumming, after the daite hereof, the same being lauchfullie tried, and the person delated found guiltie, be an Assise thereof, salbe treason, and the persones found culpable, sall fore fault life, landes and gudes.[2]

More recently it has been argued that Shakespeare had a knowledge of Scots Law and that the murders of both Duncan and Banquo in *Macbeth* are examples of 'Murder under Trust' or *homicidium sub praetextu amicitiae*. It has certainly been recognised for some time that *Macbeth* is different than Shakespeare's other plays. 'No one', Gordon Donaldson wrote, 'would look for information about Danish institutions in *Hamlet* or about the geography of Bohemia in *The Winter's Tale* but *Macbeth* possesses a realism rare in Shakespeare's works. His sources of information presented not only what purported to be history but also facts about the geography, climate and society of Scotland.'[3] Although *Macbeth* is set in the eleventh century the play has numerous characters and incidents in it derived from sixteenth-century Scotland. It has been suggested that Shakespeare wished 'to make his tragedy ... an interpretation of the Scottish ethos ... and wanted to underline the differences between contemporary England and the wilder more turbulent conditions that still prevailed in sixteenth- and seventeenth-century Scotland'. It has also been argued that the Maclean-Macdonald feud has parallels in *Macbeth*. It was just the sort of contemporary event that would have interested Shakespeare and been used to create 'the atmosphere and background of a Scottish tragedy'.[4]

It has never been proved that Shakespeare himself ever visited Scotland. He was however certainly in touch with men who had, including some of his own profession.[5]

Shakespeare's frequent use of legal terms and the knowledge of legal practice shown in his plays and poems have led many to believe that he must at one time have served in an attorney's office. In the Elizabethan age, however, the law, whether civil or criminal, statute or common, had a much greater influence on men's everyday life than it does today. The numerous suits in which his father John Shakespeare and his fellow townsmen were involved either as plaintiffs or defendants would have made the young William Shakespeare familiar with the phraseology of English legal documents.[6] 'Murder under Trust', however, was not an English offence. Shakespeare could only have heard of it in Scotland or from someone who had been there.

The only possible addition that research for this book adds to the debate on Shakespeare's Scottish experiences is the story that Huntly's men at Glenlivet thought they saw a wood moving. Certainly the famous line about Birnam Wood moving to Dunsinane occurs in Holinshed's *Chronicle*, on which we know that Shakespeare based his story of *Macbeth*. But it is just possible that Shakespeare heard the Glenlivet story and it may have persuaded him to use it in his play. It was surely a story that James VI, for whom it is thought the play was written, would have known.

If one accepts that Shakespeare based his play on characters in late sixteenth-century Scotland, it is perhaps possible to obtain an insight into the personalities of the principal characters who took part in the Maclean-Macdonald feud by studying *Macbeth*. Such an exercise is of course speculation. Speculation is historically incorrect. It does however help to ask questions about incidents in Lachlan Mor's career that might not otherwise have occurred to us. For instance, in addition to the killing of the Macleans at Mulindry there are other incidents when either Angus or Lachlan Mor could have been charged with the offence of 'Murder under Trust'. If we ignore Gordonstoun's story of Lachlan Mor imprisoning Angus at Duart, as I think we must, as malicious anti-Maclean propaganda, it is still possible to accuse Sir Lachlan himself of the same crime. He almost murdered Macian of Ardnamurchan at Torloisk and killed his companions. A case could also be made against him for the killing of Neil Mor. Angus or Sir James was thought by many, although not by the king, to have committed the offence at *Tràigh Ghruinneart.* How great a crime did Angus and Lachlan Mor believe they were committing? Was it such a heinous offence or were the islands morally bankrupt? Did Angus, or Lachlan Mor, realise like Macbeth the enormity of the crime he was to commit? Macbeth was in no doubt. In his soliloquy before Duncan's murder he exclaims:

> He's here in double trust:
> First, as I am his kinsman and his subject,
> Strong both against the deed; then, as his host,
> Who should against his murderer shut the door,
> Not bear the knife myself.
>
> Act I, Scene vii

Did Angus plan to murder the Macleans at Mulindry by himself or was he nagged into the act by his mother? Angus was a weak, jealous, unpopular man, who eventually fell out with his allies including Donald Gorm of Sleat and his eldest legitimate son. Agnes on the other hand was as single-minded as Lady Macbeth. All her actions are driven by the desire to look after her children's interest. She was also, as Turlough Luineach found to his cost, quick to take offence. Did Agnes castigate her son's irresolution as Lady Macbeth did her husband's?

> Art thou afeard
> To be the same in thine own act and valour
> As thou art in desire? Would'st thou have that
> Which thou esteem'st the ornament of life,
> And live a coward in thine own esteem,
> Letting 'I dare not' wait upon 'I would',
> Like the poor cat i' th' adage?
>
> Act I, Scene vii

The appearance of witches in *Macbeth*, which has led to a great deal of scholarly comment, helps us to understand the numerous references to witchcraft in Lachlan Mor's story. Witchcraft fascinated Renaissance audiences. In fact it is said that there is not a single play by Shakespeare that does not have some reference to the black arts. Shakespeare is not alone in his fascination with witchcraft. Plays by Marston, Barnes and Dekker, who all had plays running at the same time as *Macbeth,* all feature witches.[7]

There is little doubt that most people in sixteenth-century Scotland believed in witchcraft and there is no reason not to believe that John Campbell of Ardkinglas tried to consult a witch:

> I will to the weird sisters go:
> More shall they speak: for now I am bent to know,
> By the worst means, the worst. For mine own good,
> All causes shall give way: I am in blood
> Stepp'd in so far, that, should I wade no more,
> Returning were as tedious as go o'er:
> Strange things I have in head, that will to hand;
> Which must be acted ere that may be scann'd.
>
> Act III, Scene iv

It is a sentiment that many people who lived in the Hebrides in the sixteenth century would have understood.

The traditional tale about Lachlan Mor consulting a witch before leaving Duart to sail to *Tràigh Ghruinneart* may even be true. The desire to know what was to happen in the future was not uncommon then or now. Few will however have gone to the lengths that two of Lachlan Mor's contemporaries, Alan Og son of *Eachan MacAilean nan Sop* and Lachlan Odhar of Airdchraoishnish, are said to have gone to find out.

Alexander Maclean Sinclair has a story in *Clan Gillean* that they performed the rite known as *Taghairnm nan Cat* or the invocation of the cats.

'They collected a number of cats and took them with them to a barn at Pennygoun in Mull. They began their invocation at the middle of the night between Friday and Saturday and continued it for four days, without tasting any food. Allan was the elder of the two, and acted as high priest. He stood at the door with a drawn sword, and gave the necessary directions. Lachlan's work consisted in putting a live cat on a spit, and roasting him to death before a huge peat fire. In the course of a day or two a black cat appeared before him and said to him, *A Lachainn Uidhir mhic Dhòmhnaill mhic Neill is olc an diol sin air cait*, Lachlan Odhar, son of Donald, son of Neil, that is a bad treatment of cats. Allan at once shouted to Lachlan, *Ge b' e chi no chluinneas tu cùm an cat mu'n cuairt*, Whatever you see or hear keep the cat turning. As Lachlan took the advice given him, he had a large number of black cats before him in a short time. They joined their yells to those of the cat on the spit, and thus tried to frighten him and make him give up his work. They did not enter by the door, which was guarded by Allan. It is evident, then, that they were not real cats; they were demons in the guise of cats. On the fourth day *Cluas Mhòr*, or Big Ear, made his appearance. He was a cat of enormous size, and was black like all the other cats that came in. There was now a cat at the foot of each of the rafters of the barn. *Cluas Mhòr* threatened the performers with the severest punishment, but they paid no attention to him. Indeed they threatened to take hold of *Cluas Mhòr* himself and put him on the spit. When *Cluas Mhòr* saw their determination, he agreed to grant them their petitions. Allan asked for wealth; Lachlan asked for wealth and progeny; each of them received a promise of getting what he desired. It is said that the yells of the cat were at one time so terrific that they were heard distinctly in Morvern.' [8]

The use of cats was only one method said to be used in the Hebrides to summon spirits. Another method was for a party of men to retire to a solitary place, remote from any house. 'There they singled out one of their number, and wrapt him in a big cow's hide, which they folded about him: his whole body was covered with it except his head, and so left in this posture all night, until his invisible friends reliev'd him by giving him a proper answer to the question in hand ...' [9]

Macbeth's visit to the witches' cave and the witches' ritual around the cauldron –

> Double, double toil and trouble;
> Fire burn and cauldron bubble

– would probably have reminded King James, as he watched the play at Whitehall, of stories he must have heard of attempts to summon up the spirits.

James VI had even written a book on *Daemonologie*. He was however gradually to come to the conclusion, perhaps to his embarrassment, that even if witchcraft existed, many of those who had died for it in Scotland had not been witches. [10] In his own lifetime King James travelled from the credulous medieval world to the dawn of scientific scepticism. It is one reason why the last years of the sixteenth century are so fascinating.

Notes

1. NLS Acc 7609, 18; Sir George Mackenzie, *The Laws and Customs of Scotland in matters criminal* (1675).
2. Sir John Skene, *The Lawes and Actes of Parliament, Maid be King James the first, and Successors Kings of Scotland* (1597).
3. Gordon Donaldson, 'Murder under Trust or the Topical Macbeth', *SHR* Vol LXII, I: No. 173: April 1983, 85–6.

4. A. M. Clark, *Murder under Trust or the Topical Macbeth* (1981), 55.

5. Henry N. Paul, *The Royal Play of Macbeth* (New York, 1950), 225.

6. Bernard H. Newdigate, *The Works of William Shakespeare* (1947), vii.

7. Gary Wills, *Witches and Jesuits* (1995), 35.

8. *Clan Gillean*, 349–351. It is evidently based on an anonymous account published in the *London Literary Gazette* (March, 1824), quoted in Lachlan Maclean, *The History of the Celtic Language* (1840), 264–266.

9. Martin Martin, *Western Islands of Scotland* (1716), 110–112.

10. Jenny Wormald, 'James VI and I', in Linda Levy Peck (ed), *The Mental World of the Jacobean Court*, 48.

CHAPTER 23

Loose Ends

Seyton. The queen, my lord is dead.
Macbeth. She should have died hereafter;
There would have been a time for such a word.
Tomorrow, and tomorrow, and tomorrow,
Creeps in this petty pace from day to day,
To the last syllable of recorded time;
And all our yesterdays have lighted fools
The way to dusty death. Out, out, brief candle!
Life's but a walking shadow, a poor player,
That struts and frets his hour upon the stage,
And then is heard no more: it is a tale
Told by an idiot, full of sound and fury,
Signifying nothing.

Macbeth Act V, Scene v

Lachlan Mor was only forty when he died. His plan to invade Ulster in the English interest never took place He disappeared from the scene before the most dramatic events of Tyrone's rebellion occurred. His career is however worth examining if only because for the first time in Hebridean history there is sufficient contemporary evidence to examine a whole man. Lachlan Mor is flesh and blood, a rounded figure. His ancestors have merely been at best one-dimensional cut-outs.

Biographers should explain and not judge. Perhaps they should be counsel for both the prosecution and the defence. They are certainly not judges. The reader must make up his own mind whether or not Lachlan Mor was a hero or a villain. Much of the significance of his career was a matter of timing. He was born at one of the great watersheds in British history. The Reformation in Scotland occurred during his lifetime as did the defeat of the Spanish Armada, the events that led up to the destruction of the last bulwark of Gaelic society in Ireland, and the Union of the Crowns. He also lived when William Shakespeare was writing. Lachlan Mor had probably never heard of Shakespeare, but

Shakespeare had possibly heard of him, and one action at least in which he took part perhaps found its way into *Macbeth*.

What is more surprising is that no Gaelic poetry concerning Lachlan Mor has survived. This is curious. One of the most beautiful examples of bardic poetry is a lament for his contemporary Rory Mor Macleod of Harris, who died in 1626. It was the work of Eóin Óg Ó Muirgheasáin.[1] The Ó Muirgheasáin served the Macleans of Duart as well as the Macleods. Yet if he composed, as surely he or his father must have done, a panegyric to Lachlan Mor, it has not survived. It can be argued that this is chance. It could also be that Lachlan Mor was feared rather than loved and that his death was a relief to everyone. It is surely significant that in almost every story that survives about him he is trying to kill someone: he has his foster-father executed, he is responsible for Neil Mor's murder and that of Macgillivray. He tries to kill Neil Buidh's son. He is only just prevented by his mother's cries from killing her new husband.

It is also worth noting that he was buried in Islay and not brought home to be laid amongst his ancestors in Iona, or if that would have upset his family's Protestant sensitivities, in Inchkenneth where many of his descendants lie. It is perhaps only with the lapse of time that he became venerated by Macleans. A. Maclean Sinclair argues vehemently when he writes of Neil Mor's death that 'The part of the story which states that Lachlan Mor had patched up a false peace with Neil Mor is pure fiction. It can easily be shown that Lachlan Mor committed some high-handed and wrong acts; it cannot be shown however that treachery had a resting place in his nature; it had not'.[2] It is this refusal to acknowledge evidence which gives clan histories their unfortunate reputation.

More recent non-Maclean authors have been less generous than Maclean Sinclair. J. L. Campbell[3] writes that the misfortunes of the Macleans of Duart 'were considered in the Highlands to be the just consequence of their desecration of Iona'. He blames this event on Sir Lachlan Maclean of Duart, who he says 'cannot escape grave suspicion of having been involved'. He also claims that Lachlan, whom he describes as the 'ruffianly megalomaniac "Great McClane" chief of Duart', was born in 1540. Such a date for his birth is quite impossible. Lachlan was at the most only two in 1560 when the Reformation took place and hardly old enough to be involved when – to quote MacFarlane – 'a great many crosses to the number of 360 ... was all destroyed by one provincial assembly holden on the place a little after reformation [and]

the register and records of this Ile ... all written on Parchment [were]
all destroyed by that Assembly that destroyed the crosses'.⁴

Lachlan Mor did not expect to die when he did. He made no provision
for his younger children. Lachlan's second son, who was with his father
at *Tràigh Ghruinneart*, was known as Lachlan *barach*, Lachlan the superior. However 'superior' he was, he received no land from his father.
He was to complain that he was not a chief and had 'nothing bot some
litle steding and roumes in possessioun' and was 'in the qualitie of a
tennent or takisman'.⁵

It is also probable that Sir Lachlan left his financial affairs in disarray.
Not only did Cecil not pay what he had promised him for his services,
but he must have incurred debt in keeping his men together in the hope
that he would use them in Ulster. It would take an unusual combination
of talents to untangle the Macleans of Duart's debts. Many did not surface
for a very long time. For instance in 1635 Maclean of Duart was put to
the horn for a debt that went back to 1596. The original debt was for
850 merks. By 1635, with interest, the sum owing was £2606 Scots.⁶ It
is probable that it was the debts which originated with Lachlan Mor that
ruined the Macleans of Duart rather than any curse for desecrating Iona.

The first attempt on Maclean's estate was made before 1598 was over.
On about 5 December Nicolson wrote that 'There is a purpose for Huntly
to seek Isle of Mull from young Maclean ...'⁷ He thought it 'will not
hold'. On 27 February 1598–9 he wrote again: 'I hear that Huntly has
some intention to get grant of some of Maclean's lands, whereof Maclean's
friends are warned and will see to hinder it this convention ...' Apart
from the Lochaber lands, which as we have seen Huntly did get hold of,
for the present most of the estate remained intact.

*　　　*　　　*　　　*

The earl of Argyll was out of the country when the battle of *Tràigh
Ghruinneart* took place. He was still abroad on 6 February 1599–1600
when Nicolson wrote that he was expected 'to return home this summer'.
He did not however get back to Edinburgh until March 1600–01.

Once he was home the earl made plans to avenge his cousin's death.
On 2 June 1601 Nicolson wrote that the earl 'has his whole country
and their boats and vessels ready for some service, some judge for Her
Majesty, but he is seeking to get Sir James Macdonald to execute him
for Maclean, and he minds to invade his and Angus's lands'. By November
he had carried out his threat and Nicolson reported: 'The earl of Argyll
is gone in arms with 2000 men against Angus Macdonald'.

Something changed Argyll's character when he returned to Scotland from his travels. Instead of sulking at Inveraray, infuriating the king with his lack of activity, the earl did the opposite. It is almost as though the death of the only man he trusted spurred him into action, not just to persecute the Macdonalds, but all his fellow men.

In the years that followed the Campbells extended their territory and influence faster and further than they had done since the aftermath of the Wars of Independence. The methods the seventh earl used earned him the soubriquet *Gillespick Gruamach*, Archibald the Grim. It also brought the Campbells the hatred of most of the Gaeltachd, and the anti-Campbell coalition that turned on the Campbells in the Civil Wars was the earl's legacy to his clan.

*　　　*　　　*　　　*

By the end of October 1599 Sir James Macdonald had bribed his guards and had escaped from prison.[9] Once back in Islay he recaptured Dunyvaig Castle, which he proceeded to fortify with the help of O Donnell, whose daughter he 'had a "platt" for', in which Nicolson writes he was 'disappointed'. He was already married to Cawdor's daughter.

The king was furious at his former favourite's behaviour. He talked of leading an expedition to the Isles. It was, however, as Nicolson expected it would be, nothing but talk. Sir James was denounced as a traitor and the king wrote to both O Donnell and MacSorley to tell them to have nothing to do with him. They appear to have complied and Sir James turned to O Neill 'to seek his daughter'.

Sir James believed that the king had cheated him. He 'intends never to trust the King again to come in his hands', wrote Nicolson on 16 February 1599–1600, 'for that at his last coming he had the King's warrant to come and go free and was nevertheless imprisoned'.

Angus was now released to counter his errant son, leaving only the bastard Gillespick in custody. Sir James, with 400 men, moved to Ireland. By 22 April 1601 he had joined O Neill. Nicolson protested. The king however disclaimed all responsibility for him, stating that Sir James 'stands our declared traitor with whom we have no manner of dealing, his treason being "wyld" and shameful, being in the same case with us as Tyrone with our dearest sister the Queen, so as if he passed to Ireland with a 1000 such his followers being bad and savage thieves, we shall never quarrel if they were all hanged on a day'.

Sir James was as usual incapable of following a consistent course. It was probably Francis Mowbray, Cecil's agent, who wrote to his master in June 1601 that 'Sir James is willing to take the purpose in hand'. He had presumably agreed to assassinate Tyrone. His price was the restoration of his father's lands in the Glens. Instead Sir James was seized by MacSorley and imprisoned in Dunluce Castle. Once again however this extraordinary man turned the tables on his captor and seized the castle. MacSorley was forced to return from Tyrone's service to besiege his own house. By 21 February 1601–2 he had recaptured it. Sir James, however, who seems to have been able to talk his way out of almost any situation, made peace with his cousin. In April 1602 he was back in Kintyre recruiting for the confederates. From there he travelled to Islay. That summer 1500 Maclean invaded the island in a somewhat overdue effort to avenge the murder of Lachlan Mor. Sir James was driven from the island. He was eventually captured, tried for treason and imprisoned in Edinburgh Castle. After his father's eventual death in 1614 he escaped again, led another revolt and fled to the continent. His lands in Kintyre were now firmly in the hands of *Gillespick Gruamach*, whilst those in Islay were taken over by the erstwhile brother-in-law Campbell of Cawdor.[10]

As we have seen, the MacSorleys played a leading role in the ruin of their cousins of Dunyvaig and the Glens. Sir James MacSorley who was reported to have been killed at the Battle of the Yellow Ford in August 1598 had in fact survived. On 14 October 1598 it was reported that 'McSorley has stolen the bastard's wife to Ireland to him'.[11]

James MacSorley was a much 'married' man. His first wife was Mary or Margaret, daughter of Hugh McPhelim O Neill of Clandeboye, to whom he was formally married by the bishop of Derry. He divorced her and she subsequently married Cormac MacBarron, Tyrone's brother. James's second wife is said to have been a Scotswoman and his third was Tyrone's daughter, who was only nine years old at the time of her marriage.[12] He also courted the earl of Gowrie's sister when he visited the Scottish court in 1596. Presumably Gillespick's wife became his concubine.

James MacSorley's marital career illustrates one of the differences by the late 1590s between the Roman Catholics in Ulster and their fellow Gaels in Argyll and the Isles who had become Protestants. For all his sins Lachlan Mor appears to have had only one wife. There is no mention of him having illegitimate children. The same can be said of his cousin Argyll. In Ulster it was very different. In 1601 Tyrone had visitors from Bohemia who wished to discover how successful his rebellion was against Elizabeth. They also visited MacSorley's neighbour O Cahan, at the door of whose house they were surprised to find a group of scantily clad women. Even more startling was the appearance of their host, who joined his guests by an open fire. Casting off his loose clothes and shoes, O Cahan sprawled naked in front of the fire whilst chatting to his guests in Latin. He also invited them to throw off their damp outer garments. They hastily declined out of embarrassment at revealing 'the hitherto well concealed sign of male sexual arousal caused by the nonchalant display of the women'.[13]

Sir James MacSorley died on Easter Monday 1601. He was widely believed to have been poisoned on the instructions of the English authorities.[14] He was succeeded by his brother Randal who was to steer his family successfully through the aftermath of Tyrone's rebellion. In 1602 he was knighted. In 1603, in one of his early acts after succeeding to the English throne, the king made him a grant of both the Route and the Glens in Ulster. In 1618 he was created Viscount Dunluce and on 1620 made earl of Antrim,[15] which makes the point that James's Gaelic-speaking subjects were not always anathema to him. It also shows what might have been if Sir Lachlan Mor had played his cards better.

*   *   *   *

Tyrone's rebellion had dominated much of Lachlan Mor's career. It was to cost the parsimonious Elizabeth £2,000,000, a colossal sum in the late sixteenth century, and the crown was forced to sell large quantities of land to finance the crushing of a full-scale Irish rebellion. The cost was not only in cash. The State Papers record the constant drain of manpower that was necessary to bring Ireland under control. Thousands of recruits marched away to the ports in the West of England. Many found their graves in Ireland.

After the English disaster at Yellow Ford it was essential that a major new initiative took place in Ireland. The earl of Essex, Elizabeth's flamboyant favourite and Sir Robert Cecil's rival, was appointed viceroy.

It so happened that Shakespeare was at work on his play *Henry V* over the winter of 1598–9 when England was mustering troops for Ireland. The play was probably finished about the time the expedition sailed. It was the largest army that England had ever sent to Ireland.

Essex's supporters, the citizens of London, gave him a magnificent send-off in March 1599. As his followers marched out of the City, 'the people pressed exceedingly to behold him for more than four miles space, crying out God save your Lordship. God preserve your Honour'.

Essex's incompetent handling of both the campaign against Tyrone and his failure to read the political runes correctly brought yet another disaster for England. It also brought Essex to the block.

Essex's ruin made Sir Robert Cecil supreme in Whitehall. It also gave him the opportunity to open secret negotiations with King James, and when the old queen finally died in March 1603 it was possible for Cecil to arrange for the peaceful accession of a foreign king. If Ireland had not ruined Essex, the situation might have been very different.

In September 1601 a Spanish army had at long last arrived in Ireland. Instead of landing in Ulster, those elements that were not driven back to Spain by the wind landed at Kinsale. Tyrone was forced to abandon his forests and bogs and his guerrilla tactics to join the Spaniards for more conventional warfare. Outside the walls of Kinsale the Irish were defeated by the clinically efficient Mountjoy.

Tyrone had been right in saying that Elizabeth could afford to lose several battles. He could only lose one. Kinsale was the battle he could not afford to lose. In its aftermath both O Neill and O Donnell left Ireland. The flight of the earls brought the end of Gaelic Ulster. England was determined never to suffer a similar humiliation again. The polity of the Irish Gaeltachd was destroyed and Ulster was settled by English-speaking lowland Scots. Four hundred years later we are still living with the result.

Notes

1. *SGS* viii (i), 27–52.
2. *Clan Gillean*, 156.
3. J. L. Campbell, *Canna: The Story of a Hebridean Island* (1984), 41–42.
4. *Ibid*, 41, quoting MacFarlane's *Geographical Collections* ii, 217.
5. *RPC* xii, 429–430.
6. AT ix, 273.
7. *CSP Scot.* xiii, 351.
8. Edward J. Cowan, 'Clanship and Campbell Expansion in the time of Gillesbuig Gruamach', *TGSI* liv (1987), 271.
9. *CSP Scot.* xiii, 563.
10. Edward J. Cowan, 'Clanship, kinship and the Campbell acquisition of Islay', *SHR* October 1979, 155.
11. *CSP Scot.* xiii, 316.
12. *West Highland Notes & Queries* No. 8 (1991), 15–16.
13. D. B. Quinn, *The Elizabethans and the Irish* (1966), 71–2.
14. *West Highland Notes & Queries* No. 8 (1991), 16.
15. George Hill, *The Macdonnells of Antrim* (1873), 231.

Table 2: The Macleans of Coll, 1528–1631

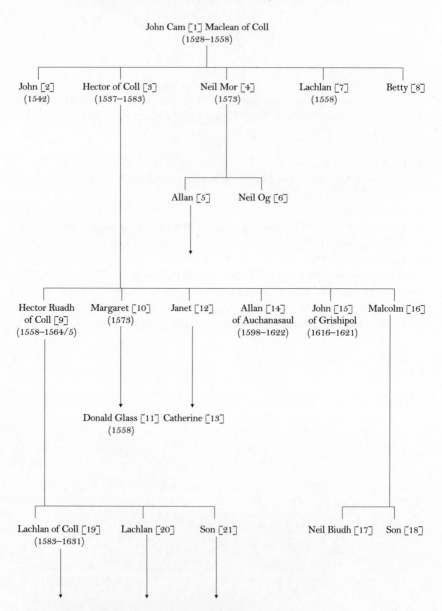

John Cam [1] Maclean of Coll
(1528–1558)

John [2] (1542) — Hector of Coll [3] (1537–1583) — Neil Mor [4] (1573) — Lachlan [7] (1558) — Betty [8]

Allan [5] — Neil Og [6]

Hector Ruadh of Coll [9] (1558–1564/5) — Margaret [10] (1573) — Janet [12] — Allan [14] of Auchanasaul (1598–1622) — John [15] of Grishipol (1616–1621) — Malcolm [16]

Donald Glass [11] (1558) — Catherine [13]

Lachlan of Coll [19] (1583–1631) — Lachlan [20] — Son [21] — Neil Biudh [17] — Son [18]

1. See *Warriors & Priests*, 191–2; *Duanaire Colach*, xx.
2. *Warriors & Priests*, 192.
3. *Warriors & Priests*, 192; *Duanaire Colach*, xxi–xxii.
4. *Warriors & Priests*, 192; *Duanaire Colach*, xxii–xxiii.
5. 'had the six merk lands of Drimnin and Achalinen. He was married to MacPhie of Callacholy's daughter'. Crossapol, 39–40.

6. *Duanaire Colach*, xxiii, 54–87; Crossapol, 39

7. *Warriors & Priests*, 192.

8. *Warriors & Priests*, 193.

9. *Warriors & Priests*, 193.

10. Eldest daughter of An Clèreach Beag and his wife Meve, daughter of Alexander Macdonald of Dunnyveg, 'married to john Dubh predecessor of the family of Kinlochaline' [Crossapol, 36]; 14 May 1573: Contract between Hector Maclean of Duart and 'Iain dow' Maclean, his brother, states: 'Hector also consents to his brother marrying, the laird of Coll's daughter. If he can do so lawfully without slander or offence to the Kirk of God, if he cannot lawfully marry her, he may use her at his pleasure independent of the said Hector till God provide remeid'. [AT,vi]; ND: 'Ane contract of marrage betuix Jon Dow and ye laird of Coilles dochter'; 'Ane acquittance of Johne dow McClanes of two hundryth merks in parte of payment of ye tocher gude giffin with his concubine and appearand spous Margaret Mcclane' [*Celtic Review* 1912, 32–33].

11. Not mentioned in Crossapol; only son of 'John or Eoin duibh... called Donald Glass, who being left hostage by Lachlan Mor, aboard of that ship of the Spanish Armada that was blown up at Tobermory bay in Mull called the Florida, there lost his life in the year 1588' [NLS ACC 7609, 57].

12. Second daughter of An Clèireach Beag and his wife Meve, daughter of Alexander Macdonald of Dunyvaig, 'married to John Garve son of the said John Dubh' [Crossapol, 36].

13. As above issue 'one daughter by him called Catherine, married to Mr Martin MacGilivra of Penigael' [NLS ACC 7609, 59].

14. The eldest son of An Clèireach Beag and his second wife 'the Laird of Loup's daughter sent by his father (sic) to assist Rory More Macleod against the MacDonald of Slate. Macleod happened to have the victory, this was the last contest betwixt these two families (This was presumably the battle of Coire na Creiche which took place on 29 June 1601) [I. F. Grant, *The Macleods* (1959), 196–9, 23–2.] '...commanded a company of his father's (sic) men under Lachlan Mor at Gruinart. Allan was married to Mac iain of Ardnamurchan's daughter by whom he had issue Hector, Ronald and Donald...' [Crossapol, 43]; 13 July 1610: Maclean of Coll 'sall exhibite Allane McClayne, his uncle [RPC 1st Series x, 774]; 23 July 1622: 'The Laird of Coill enterit Allane McClane, his uncle' [ibid, xiii, 20]. He was progenitor of the Macleans of Auchanasaul, in Mull, 'second branch of the family of Coll' [Crossapol, 43].

15. The second son of An Clèireach Beag and his second wife 'the Laird of Loup's daughter' [Crossapol, 43] '...was married to a daughter of the Laird of Mackinnon by whom he had John' [NLS ACC 7609, 41], who was married to a daughter of Rory Maclean Merchant at Glasgow, by whom he had Lachlan, John, Hugh and Charles [Crossapol, 43]; 17 July 1616: Maclean of Coll 'sell exhibite... John McClayne, his uncle' [RPC 1st Series x, 774]; 1619–21: 'John McClayne, his uncle (enterit be Coill)' [ibid xiv, 583].

16. 'There is a grandson of the 4th Laird of Coill Eachin Mac Iain called Neil Bhuidh mac Gille Challum ic Eachin' [Crossapol, 42]. His descendant Lachlan Maclean, 1798–1848, *Lachlan na Caidhlig*, Lachlan of the Gaelic, however, gives his ancestry in his *History of the Celtic Language* (1840), 288, as Maclain mnic Lachin mhic Iain mhic Dhomhnuil mhic Ruari mhic Eachin mhic Neil mhic Challum mhic Lachin mhic Iain – Ghairbh.

17. 'who was a brave man he [was] the best at the bow and arrow in his time, at the time that his friend Niel Mor was taken prisoner a brother of Neil Buidh was also taken by order of Lachlan Mor...' (Crossapol, 42).

18. Neil Budh 'had two sons. Hector from whom descended Hector Buidh that went to America' [Crossapol, 42]. 'Neil Buidh... had likewise a son called John, from whom descends Lachlan Maclain ic dhonid ic ruari that left issue John McLean at Arnpost, Murdoch McLean Tenant at Torestan and Lachlan McLean Tenant at Mibost all have issue' [Crossapol, 42].

19. See index.

20. 'there was a grandson of Hector Roy the 5th laird Lachlan mac lachain, a stout man of whom descended Lachlan Mac Neil ic lachain at Balehough, had a son John Mclean father to Hector McLean at Grimsary and Lachlan McLean at Kilbride' [Crossapol, 42].

21. 'Allan Roy at Feall came out of the family of Coll about that time he was grandfather to the present [c.1830] John McLean miller at Cliad' [Crossapol, 42].

Postscript

This book began as an attempt to understand the society that tolerated the murder of my ancestor Neil Mor Maclean of Quinish. It soon developed into a biography of Sir Lachlan Mor Maclean of Duart, the man behind his murder. Let us end the story where it began. It is pleasing that the victim rather than the victor should have the last word. The winner should not always have the historians on his side.

The traditional version of the story of Neil Mor's career first appears in print in the early nineteenth century. It was told in the pages of the Gaelic periodical, *Teachdaire Gaelach*, 'The Gaelic Messenger' which appeared between 1829 and 1831. Writing under the pseudonym 'P McF', Neil Mor's descendant, the Reverend Neil Maclean, minister of Tiree and Coll, who was known as *Maighstir Niall*, wrote two stories about his forebears.

In 1840 *Maighstir Niall* contributed to the *New Statistical Account*, with an account of his parish. After telling the story of how the Macleans of Coll won the Isle of Coll from the Macneills of Barra, he goes on to say that: 'Afterwards the Isle of Coll was the scene of further bloody contentions.

'The then Chief of M'Lean, who appears to have been of a brave but ambitious and grasping character, formed the design of annexing that property to his own dominions, and thought the young laird of Coll's minority a favourable opportunity for putting his project into execution. In these views he was opposed by Neil Mor, so called from his great strength and stature, who had the management of the property, and acted as guardian to his young nephew during his minority. An armed force having been despatched to subdue and take possession of the island, Neil Mor marched out to encounter them with such followers as he could muster to meet the sudden emergency. The contending parties came to blows at a small rivulet, since that period called *Sruthan nàn Ceann* and, after a bloody battle, the invaders were overthrown with great slaughter. It is supposed the rivulet received its name in consequence of the great number of heads struck off in this engagement.

'Some time afterwards, this brave and disinterested man, who defended the property against all attempts to wrest it from the rightful owner, was treacherously surprised and slain under night at his residence in

Mull, by a party of twenty-four armed men, employed by the chief for this purpose.'

Maighstir Niall nowhere states that he is writing of his own family when he tells his stories of Neil Mor. He does, however, put his name to his article in the *New Statistical Account.* This is more than his uncle, Captain Allan Maclean of Crossapol, did when he wrote his manuscript historical and genealogical account of the Macleans. This manuscript deals at length with Neil Mor and his descendants, 'the first branch of the family of Coll'.[1]

Crossapol explains that Neil was the second lawful son of the third laird of Coll. His mother was a daughter of Fraser of Lovat. Neil received Quinish, the Coll family's estate on Mull. When Neil's elder brother Hector died the heir was a child and Neil took on the management of the estate. During this time Lachlan Mor Maclean of Duart attempted to seize the estate. The first time he tried was on the very day Neil Mor's brother died.

Neil Mor and the cortège were on their way from Breacachadh Castle to the Maclean of Coll's burial ground at Kilunaig. The funeral party had got as far as Clabhach, when a messenger caught up with them to say that Maclean of Duart's men had invaded Coll and were on their way after them.

Neil Mor left his brother's body at Clabhach with a few men to guard it. He hurried back with the rest of his men and defeated the enemy at *Sruthan nàn Ceann.* Crossapol adds an additional story which *Maighstir Niall* was to use in *Teachdaire Gaelach.* Apparently just before the battle began, the Coll men realised that they had left their colours behind and had nothing about which to rally in the forthcoming conflict. Crossapol says that this vexed Neil, but one of his party, a Mackinnon named *Domhnall Mugach,* 'gloomy Donald', who was bald, took off his bonnet and said 'Use this bald head as your rallying point. It will not go backwards in battle'. And with a cheer the Collachs charged their enemy with very satisfactory results. It was not until after nightfall that Neil got his brother interred at Kilunaig.

Crossapol says that sometime later Neil Mor went to Ireland, perhaps in July 1584 when the Macleans landed at Lough Swilly. Here he was taken great notice of by 'Squire Leslie'. Who Squire Leslie was has defeated all my efforts to find out. Evidently he was a man of some importance. His name may have been confused in the telling for neither I nor scholars I have consulted can find any trace of anyone resembling him in the Irish records. However, whoever he was he apparently gave his daughter to Neil Mor in marriage, which made him retire from Ireland sooner than he expected to do.

Neil Mor had a son by Squire Leslie's daughter, called Neil Og. Crossapol describes him as 'a very brave man'. Evidently others thought so too for young Neil is remembered in a lament by his 'sweetheart' *Mòr Nic Phàdein*. She describes him as 'a noble, brave, courageous man, handsome and confident'. She also describes him as *a mhic Nèill bu mhòr gaisgeadh/A fuair a stialladh mun Chlachan*. Colm Ó Baoil has translated these lines as 'Son of Niall of the great valour who suffered a scourging at the Clachan ...'[2] There is little doubt we are talking of the same man as Crossapol's Neil Og.

Crossapol also has a story that is supported by one collected in Mull in 1873 by the folklorist J. F. Campbell. It tells us that Neil Mor's murder was not only the result of his defiance of Lachlan Mor Maclean of Duart over Coll but because when Lachlan Mor ordered him to execute his (Lachlan's) own brother his sword got stuck in such a way that Neil had to put his foot on his victim's head before he could extricate it. Duart was furious, saying that 'Though I ordered the blow I will not bear the disgrace' and ordered that Neil should be killed. Neil fled. He spent the next three years in hiding and only left his hideout when he got word from Duart that he would have safe conduct if he came to make peace with him. Neil and Lachlan Mor met in the north of Mull by a burn called the Allt-Dubhaig which runs into Loch Phrìse.[3] They made their peace and Neil Mor returned home with, as we have seen, disastrous consequences.

Crossapol states that Neil Mor also married the daughter of Hector Maclean, better known as Hector Allansoun or *Eachan MacAilein na sop*. He was Lachlan Maclean of Duart's tutor and had married his charge's widowed mother, Lady Janet Campbell, the eldest daughter of Archibald, fourth earl of Argyll. Neil Mor's son by Hector's daughter carried on the family line (see Table 2).

Yet another account of Neil Mor in popular Gaelic stories was collected by John Dewar in the mid-nineteenth century. Dewar was a woodman employed by the duke of Argyll but spent much of his time gathering tales throughout the Highlands. One such tale tells how the Macgillivrays lost their lands in Mull. Apparently Macgillivray was one day out hunting in the moor when he met an old man. Macgillivray asked him 'What is your news today?' 'I have no news', the old man answered, 'but that Maclean of Aros has killed Niall Mor of Coll. He killed him yesterday.' Macgillivray said, 'That corn will grow as it has been sown, but take you care that you do not tell Maclean what I have said to you.' 'No, no', said the old man. But of course he did and Duart, who also owned Aros, felt he had been insulted and had Macgillivray murdered.[4]

There is a story about Neil Mor's death, which has echoes of William Tell. It only appears in Crossapol's manuscript. Apparently there was a grandson of *an cleireach beag* 'called *Neil Buidh mac gille challum ic Eachain,* who was a brave man. He was the best at the bow and arrow in his time, at the time that his friend Neil Mor was taken prisoner a brother of Neil Buidh was also taken by order of Lachlan Mor Laird of Dowart in order to put him to death with the said Neil Mor – Neil Buidh hearing that there were fifty armed men going with Neil Mor and his brother to be put to death at Clachan Dubh he came upon a precipice above them and cryed out with a loud voice if they would not sett his brother at liberty that he had 25 arrows in his bag or *boly saighead,* and that he was sure of killing one man for every arrow, in hearing this he frightened them so much that his brother was sett free.

'Lachlan Mor after that would put a son of Neil Buidh to death, he took him prisoner, when his father heard of his son's imprisonment, he went to Lachlan Mor and told him that if he would not sett his son at liberty, that he would apply to the laird of Coll and the laird of Loup for assistance and that there would be a great deal of bloodshede before his son would be put to death, Lachlan Mor said "you'll get your son free if you break an egg upon his head with your bow and arrow", which Neil Buidh did, without touching his son'.[5]

Crossapol's manuscript history was not used by any of the three authors who published their histories of the clan in the nineteenth century. It is curious that with so much folklore surviving about him, so little was written of Neil Mor by two of these nineteenth-century authors. 'Seneachie', who published his *Historical and genealogical account of the Clan Maclean* in 1838, does not mention him at all and says only of the Macleans of Crossapol that they were a cadet of the Coll family. He mentions Allan Maclean, late of Crossapol, and his issue but does not mention his predecessors nor any other members of the family.

J. P. Maclean the Cincinnati dentist, who published his *History of the Clan Maclean* in 1889, spent some time in Mull. He does mention Neil Mor and the battle of *Sruthan nàn Ceann* but says that shortly afterwards Duart sent a more numerous force to Coll. They pursued Neil Mor whom they overtook and killed at Clachan Dubh. This compresses the story and places Clachan Dubh in Coll rather than Mull. He does not mention the descent of the Crossapol family from Neil Mor and states only that they were 'among the later cadets of the family of Coll'; otherwise he repeats Seneachie's material.

The final history of the Macleans to be published in the nineteenth century was *Clan Gillean*. It was published in Charlottetown, Nova Scotia in 1899. The author, the Reverend A. Maclean Sinclair, was a Canadian Presbyterian clergyman. He was also a Gaelic scholar. His grandfather John Maclean, known in Scotland as *Bàrd Thighearna Chola*, or the laird of Coll's poet, was born in Tiree in 1787. In 1819 he emigrated to Nova Scotia.[6] Before he left for Canada he was given Dr Hector Maclean's collection of Gaelic poetry by the latter's daughter, Christina Mackenzie. It is now in the Public Archives in Halifax, Nova Scotia.[7] Dr Hector Maclean (1704–1784) is the unacknowledged author of the 'Historical Genealogical Account of the family of Maclean', on which all subsequent accounts of the clan are based. Curiously he does not mention Neil Mor in any of his manuscripts.

Sinclair thus had an additional source of information to his rival J. P. Maclean. He also had a voluminous correspondence with many Maclean tradition bearers both in Scotland and North America. He also had the benefit of the correspondence in the *Oban Times* and other publications which had not been available to J. P. Maclean.

Sinclair does not usually give his references in *Clan Gillean*. When he does he gives them in an unsystematic fashion and does not give the full reference. For instance, when he tells the story of Neil Mor's murder he quotes J. F. Campbell's story, saying only he published it in 1873. As we have seen, it was published in *An Gaidheal*. He translates the story verbatim, adding the comment: 'Ridiculous as the foregoing story is, we have reason to think that there are some persons who regard it as genuine history. They heard it from their fathers, and they believe that their fathers had it word for word as it existed originally. They make no allowance for the changes which a story undergoes in being handed down from one generation to another ...'[8]

Sinclair dates the story to 1596 or the beginning of 1597. He has one story that does not appear elsewhere concerning Neil Mor. Apparently once during his three years in hiding Neil Mor was saved by his wife's wit and strength. Lachlan Mor sent a powerful man named Allan Macdonald to search for the fugitive, arrest and kill him. Allan took fifteen men with him and went to where Neil Mor resided.

When they entered his house they asked his wife if her husband was at home. She went to the other end of the house, where she had Neil concealed, and took out a large bar of iron. She broke a piece of it off with her hands and gave it to the ploughman saying, 'when your master went to the forge he told me to send you after him with a piece of iron; take this with you and tell him that there are men in the house who want to see him'. 'Don't tell him that', said Allan Macdonald, 'we have no business of any importance with him.'

Allan and his men immediately left the house. When they were out of hearing Allan said to the three with him: 'We should be thankful to the Almighty that Neil's wife did not know the business we were on, had she known it, she would have killed us all with that iron bar ...'[9]

It is clear that Neil Mor stories were popular folk tales. How many historical facts are to be found in them is another matter.

When Sinclair deals with Neil Mor in detail, he says it is generally supposed that he was a natural (i.e. illegitimate) son of John, fourth of Coll. He then quotes *Maighstir Niall* in saying that he was a son of Hector, fifth of Coll, presumably quoting the *New Statistical Account*. In fact *Maighstir Niall* never makes the statement, but merely implies that Neil Mor was the uncle of the seventh laird, when in fact he was the great-uncle. I do not know where Sinclair got the information that it was generally supposed that Neil Mor was illegitimate. Allan Crossapol states quite clearly that Neil Mor and his elder brother Hector had the same mother and could therefore not be illegitimate.

Contemporary material that was not available to Sinclair when he published *Clan Gillean* does not support his theory. This new information is an 'old inventory of the Laird of Coll's writs' which was published by the duke of Argyll in 1912.[10] I have not been able to find the original document which the duke says was in sixteenth-century handwriting.

Two items are of particular interest. They are:

24. Ane instrument uppoun Certane Conditions betuix ye said laird of Coll and his brother neill.

27. Ane obligation of hector Mclanes and Jon dowis for ye soume of Vc merks (500) to be payit for Neill brother to ye laird of Coill.

I know nothing more of Neil Mor's life and death. As we have seen, a great deal more can be discovered about the man behind his murder.

Notes

1. Breacachadh Castle Papers (BCP), Red Box Files (RBF): 'A genealogical and historical account of the Clan Maclean'. It is clear from the text that it was written before 1831.
2. *Notes & Queries of the Society of West Highland & Island Historical Research*

(*N & Q*) xxvi, 5; see also Colm Ó Baoill, *Duanaire Colach* 1537–1757 (1997), 4–7. This book appeared after *Murder Under Trust* was completed.

3. *An Gaidheal* (1873), 138,139.
4. John Mackechnie (ed), *The Dewar Manuscripts* (1963), 262.
5. G. A. Hayes-McCoy, *Irish Battles* (1969), 111.
6. *Clan Gillean*, 339, 340.
7. A photocopy (MS 2318) is in Aberdeen University Library. I have to thank its staff for a copy. BCP. RBF: 'Dr Hector Maclean's Poetry Collection'.
8. *Clan Gillean*, 153–155.
9. *Ibid*, 154.
10. *Celtic Review*, viii, October 1912, 97–99.

Index